D0510583

The complete book of
vegetable
gardening

vegetable
gardening

from planting to picking—
the complete guide to creating
a bountiful garden

Fern Marshall Bradley
Jane Courtier

Reader's Digest

The Reader's Digest Association, Inc.
Pleasantville, New York/Montreal

This edition published by The Reader's Digest Association
by arrangement with Toucan Books, Ltd.

Copyright © 2006 Toucan Books Ltd.

First edition copyright © 2006
The Reader's Digest Association Limited
11 Westferry Circus, Canary Wharf
London E14 4HE

We are committed to both the quality of our products and the service we provide
to our customers. We value your comments, so please feel free to contact us on
08705 113366 or via our web site at: www.readersdigest.co.uk
If you have any comments or suggestions about the content of our books, email
us at: gbeditorial@readersdigest.co.uk

All rights reserved. Unauthorized reproduction, in any manner, is prohibited.

Reader's Digest, The Digest and the Pegasus logo are registered trademarks of
The Reader's Digest Association, Inc., of Pleasantville, New York, USA

FOR TOUCAN BOOKS
Design: Bradbury and Williams
Editor: Theresa Bebbington
Managing Editor: Ellen Dupont
Editorial Assistant: Maddy Langford
Index: Michael Dent
Picture Research: Christine Vincent, Maria Bembridge
Proofreader: Marion Dent

Front cover photographs: Photolibrary.com Kathryn Kleinman (top left), Garden Picture
Library Friedrich Strauss (top right), Roy Williams (bottom left and right).
Spine photograph: Krivit Photography/Mike Krivit.

No part of this book may be reproduced, stored in a retrieval system, or transmitted
in any form or by any means, electronic, electrostatic, magnetic tape, mechanical,
photocopying, recording or otherwise, without permission in writing from the publishers.

A CIP data record for this book is available from the British Library

For more Reader's Digest products and information, visit our website:
www.readersdigest.co.uk

Printed in China

10-digit ISBN 0-276-44114-1
13-digit ISBN 978-0-276-44114-1
Book code 410-594

Part 1: YOUR GARDEN

Part 2: THE VEGETABLES

Introduction

There is something satisfying and rewarding about growing your own food. The sense of achievement when you sit before a plate piled high with fresh produce from your own garden is hard to beat. More gardeners are realising that there is nothing difficult about vegetable growing – and that you don't need an enormous garden to do so.

In Part 1 of *The Complete Book of Vegetable Gardening*, Jane Courtier explains the basics of growing vegetables. There's information to follow from the beginning of the season to the end: how to design a garden that's just the right size and style for your needs; how to improve your soil and prepare it for planting; how to raise seedlings and plant your garden; how to water and feed your crops; how to protect crops from pest and weed problems; how to extend the season; and how to harvest and store all the bounty of your garden.

In Part 2 Fern Marshall Bradley gives you the details on growing specific crops. This section organises

FROM A (MOSTLY) ORGANIC GARDENER

Dear Reader,

I prefer to garden without the use of pesticides and manage to do so – most of the time. But sometimes, when caterpillars are on the march against my cabbages or blackflies threaten my beans, I find that a single application of the right pesticide will prevent me from losing the fruits of my labour to pests.

Chemicals aren't all bad. The chemical pesticides that are available to gardeners today bear little relation to those that were common a few decades ago. We no longer use old-style, broad-spectrum, toxic chemicals that persist in the environment for years. They've been replaced by highly regulated, targeted products, often derived from natural sources, which break down quickly and safely after use and leave minimal residues in treated plants.

Ideally, all gardeners would like to grow their food without having to intervene with chemical controls, but it's been my experience that a single, well-timed application of pesticide can prevent a pest or disease problem from ruining a crop. I believe that chemical pesticides should be used only when it's absolutely necessary.

By choosing the right product and following the directions carefully, you can be confident that your garden and your produce will remain safe, healthy and even environmentally friendly.

JANE COURTIER

crops by how they are grown. Thus, you'll find vines such as squash in the *Vine crops* chapter and long-term crops such as rhubarb in the *Permanent plantings* chapter. Each entry will provide all you need to know to grow a crop successfully, including the correct times to plant; whether it's best to start seeds indoors, sow them directly outside or buy in young plants; tips on watering, fertilising and supporting plants; plus important information on how to harvest and store the crop.

Best of the Bunch boxes recommend tried-and-tested varieties, plus some promising newcomers. Varieties come and go, but the descriptions should give you an idea of the qualities to look for and enable you to judge if a new variety is worth a trial.

Problem solver sidebars summarise the symptoms and signs of the most common pest problems, growing disorders that affect a crop and common mistakes, and they offer quick suggestions on how to solve the problem – or how to avoid it the next time you plant the crop.

Each *Planting Guide* is a quick reference to the essential information you'll need before getting started. Watch for the thermometer icon in some entries. It alerts you to crops that are sensitive to heat exposure or chilling during their development. Where possible, the warning alerts you to temperature thresholds that may adversely affect the plants.

In general keep in mind that crops will mature faster in warmer conditions than in cool conditions, and plants may grow more slowly than usual during a drought, even if you provide supplemental water. The time of year you plant has an effect too, because plants grow more quickly during long days than short days.

FROM A COMMITTED ORGANIC GARDENER

Dear Reader,

Right from the start I decided to garden organically. I had a youthful ideal of saving the environment from chemical pollution. Learning how to garden the organic way was fascinating.

I discovered the intricacies of soil biology and the miracle of earthworms. I enjoyed turning raked-up leaves and kitchen waste into sweet-smelling compost. I planted flowers in my vegetable garden to attract beneficial insects. I learned how horticultural fleece can protect plants from adverse weather conditions, as well as from animal and insect pests. I enjoyed the adventure of trying out simple, non-commercial, organic methods: Would slugs really come to a beer-baited slug trap to drink and drown? Could encouraging the right type of wildlife into the garden reduce the amount of pest damage? (Yes, and yes.)

The beauty of tending an organic garden is that each year brings greater success as the natural systems become stronger. For example, I no longer put out slug traps because there is so little slug damage in my garden. I attribute this to healthy populations of slug predators that have grown over the years, especially ground beetles that live under the wood-chip mulch on paths at the border of my garden. I'm now into my third decade as an organic gardener and I am more committed than ever.

Fern Marshall Bradley

FERN MARSHALL BRADLEY

Is organic gardening for you?
In this book you'll find plenty of advice for gardening organically. Eating delicious, freshly picked produce, enjoying the outdoors and feeling connected with nature are the top reasons gardeners give for tending a vegetable garden. Many gardeners prefer organic methods, avoiding chemical pesticides – they love the idea that the food they are growing is pesticide-free. But what happens when things go wrong and organic solutions don't seem to work?

The two authors of this book have different answers to this question. Jane Courtier takes the view that organic methods are the first, best choice, but believes there can be a place for carefully chosen chemical pesticides if a serious insect or disease problem arises. Fern Marshall Bradley writes from the viewpoint of a longtime organic gardener who has chosen not to use chemicals in her garden. Together they've created a book that looks at vegetable gardening from both sides.

As experienced gardeners and gardening writers, Jane and Fern know that there are substantive issues on both sides to consider when deciding whether to be purely organic or not – and in the end, it's an individual choice. Let them help you make up your mind!

Part 1

YOUR GARDEN

1 Planning your garden

Planning a vegetable garden – whether in your own garden or in an allotment – can be almost as exciting as growing the vegetables, and it will ensure that your efforts bring maximum rewards. Think about the type of garden you already have and the type you want. What vegetables would be the best to grow? How can you make the best use of the space you have? What difficulties are there to overcome? The following pages will guide you through all the choices you have to make and provide some new ideas to inspire you.

Your vegetable garden can be decorative and inspiring or functional and plain – the choice is yours. Among the vegetables in this attractive garden are chard, fennel, lettuce and cabbage.

The benefits of planning

Once you have decided to grow your own vegetables, endless possibilities open up before you. Just glancing through a seed catalogue results in a list of exciting varieties you simply have to try – but hold on, the first step is to come up with a plan.

CONSIDERING AN ALLOTMENT?

If your garden is not large enough to grow as many vegetables as you would like, consider an allotment. Contact your local council for details on availability – there is often a waiting list. If you have a choice, pick a site that has an easily accessible water supply and a secure hut where you can leave your tools and equipment safely.

Quick Tip

Out of the shade

When planning your vegetables place tall plantings such as sweet corn or those grown on trellises at the north side of the plot so they don't cast shadows on lower-growing plants.

Unless you have a huge garden and almost limitless time and skills, you probably won't grow half the things you would like to. Therefore, good planning is an important part of vegetable gardening. It enables you to think sensibly about how much space and time you can devote to your garden and what type of vegetables will be most useful to you. It also avoids that embarrassment of riches, the glut – nobody wants to spend lots of effort and time growing more beans than their family and friends can eat.

Whether you are about to start a vegetable plot from scratch or plan to adapt an existing one, spend some time with a notepad and pencil before picking up a spade. Draw up a rough plan of your garden to see how the vegetables will fit in, and how much space you can afford to give them.

There are many different styles of vegetable garden, which are discussed in the following pages. You will probably find that some of them are much more suited to your needs than others. Once you have decided on your garden style, you also need to plan which vegetables you intend to grow (see pages 18–19).

Starting a new plot

Creating your own vegetable garden from scratch is a great opportunity – it means you will be able to avoid some of the common pitfalls. Here are some points to bear in mind when planning a new vegetable plot.

Convenience. If the vegetable garden is close to the house, it will be easy to dash out and pick a few herbs or dig some vegetables for dinner. It will also encourage you to visit the vegetable garden more frequently to take care of the plants. The closer it is, the more often you'll weed, water and check for pests and diseases. Firm pathways around and across the plot will prove a boon for access – and prevent feet from becoming muddy.

Climate. Vegetables will grow best if they are sheltered from strong wind. Fences, walls and hedges can create a favourable, warm, sheltered microclimate within the garden, but be careful that they don't cast too much shade. Vegetables prefer an open, sunny position. Ideally, run rows north to south within the plot to keep shading to a minimum.

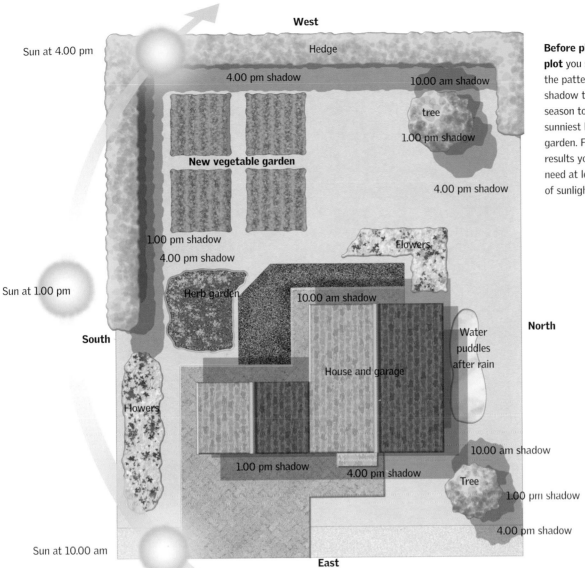

West

Hedge

Sun at 4.00 pm

4.00 pm shadow

10.00 am shadow

tree

1.00 pm shadow

New vegetable garden

4.00 pm shadow

1.00 pm shadow

4.00 pm shadow

Flowers

Sun at 1.00 pm

Herb garden

10.00 am shadow

North

South

Water puddles after rain

House and garage

Flowers

1.00 pm shadow

4.00 pm shadow

10.00 am shadow

Tree

1.00 pm shadow

Sun at 10.00 am

4.00 pm shadow

East

Before planning your plot you should observe the patterns of light and shadow throughout the season to determine the sunniest location in your garden. For the best results your plot will need at least six hours of sunlight a day.

Size. Factors that affect size include your enthusiasm, how many mouths you have to feed, how much time you have available and the size of the garden. Don't be too ambitious: a plot that is too big soon becomes a chore instead of a pleasure. As a guide a standard-sized allotment is 250sq m (300sq yd). However, most people find a half-size plot enough: that's a 9-x-13.7-m (30-x-45-ft) rectangle. Rectangles and squares are more practical than flowing shapes.

Ground preparation. What is currently on the site where you want to position your vegetable plot? Bare soil is ideal, but more likely there is a lawn, which

means stripping the turf. This is not difficult if you use a sharp spade to undercut it. If it's a large area, hire a turf-cutting machine. Trees and shrubs can be difficult to remove, and a site overrun by deep-rooted perennial

weeds can be tough to tame. Consider how much time and effort you are willing to devote to this preparation.

In this typical square plot lettuce, cabbages and peas are grown in rows.

Planning your crops

By taking time to think carefully about the crops you're about to grow you can ensure that you'll get the maximum value from your vegetable garden – no matter its size.

Grow speciality vegetables such as artichokes to enhance your choice of vegetables for your meals.

It's surprising how many times gardeners take a haphazard approach to growing vegetables. Some can't resist the lure of the seed catalogues – and before they know it, they have spent a fortune on at least twice as many packets of seeds as they have room to grow. Others fill half the plot with potatoes and cabbages every year because…well, because vegetable gardens always have potatoes and cabbages. And it's amazing how many gardeners keep on growing Brussels sprouts (or leeks, or spinach, or radishes or whatever) season after season, despite knowing that nobody in the family actually likes to eat them.

Decide what you like. Make a list of the vegetables you'd most like to grow. Unless you have endless space, concentrate on types that are difficult to buy in the shops (such as scorzonera or black salsify), are expensive (such as asparagus), benefit from being eaten freshly picked (such as corn) or are simply tastier than the commercial varieties (such as many tomatoes). Remember to ask the rest of the family for their preferences too.

Check the timing. Make a note of the sowing or planting times of all the crops you've listed, and when they will vacate the soil after harvesting. A spring-sown crop of broad beans, for example, will probably finish cropping by midsummer, which makes way for a quick-growing 'catch crop' such as lettuce, radishes or French beans to be sown in the same piece of ground. Make the plot work hard for its keep.

Look ahead to harvesting. Make a note of what should be cropping, month by month. Where several crops are in peak season at the same time, you should consider whether some of

SUCCESSIONAL PLANTING

You can have a constant supply of fresh vegetables for salads, and avoid waste from growing too much of one thing, by sowing seeds in small batches in the spring and summer.

Instead of filling one row with lettuce, another with onions and a third with radishes, sow only one row – a third of it onions, a third lettuce and a third radishes. Two weeks later, sow another row in the same way, and two weeks after that, a third row. You'll have a steady supply of the vegetables over a longer season.

Quick Tip

At the root

Never grow plants with long tap roots such as carrots and parsnips in freshly manured ground because it causes them to fork and become misshapen.

them can be stored successfully. It's easy to put a surplus of beans in the freezer, but it's far more difficult to cope with a glut of lettuce (see *Successional Planting,* left).

Grow for health and yield. Different vegetable crops tend to take varying quantities of nutrients from the soil. Members of the cabbage family, for example, are particularly greedy when it comes to nitrogen; conversely, peas and beans need only small amounts of soil nitrogen, because of their ability to 'fix' nitrogen from the air. Crop rotation – the practice of moving different types of vegetable crops to a different position in the garden each

By sowing little and often this gardener would have a steady supply of lettuce instead of a glut.

CROP ROTATION PLAN

The most practical rotation for most gardens is a three-year one. For the rotation to work each group must occupy the same amount of space. This makes it difficult to follow crop rotations exactly, so don't worry about achieving perfection. Keep the basic principles in mind and do the best you can. Your need to add lime depends on your soil type and pH.

	YEAR 1	YEAR 2	YEAR 3
BED 1	**Roots** Do not add manure or lime; add a balanced fertiliser in spring.	**Others** Add a balanced fertiliser in spring.	**Brassicas** Dig in manure or compost in autumn; add lime in spring.
BED 2	**Brassicas** Dig in manure or compost in autumn; add lime in spring.	**Roots** Do not add manure or lime; add a balanced fertiliser in spring.	**Others** Add a balanced fertiliser in spring.
BED 3	**Others** Add a balanced fertiliser in spring.	**Brassicas** Dig in manure or compost in autumn; add lime in spring.	**Roots** Do not add manure or lime; add a balanced fertiliser in spring.

1 **Roots** Potatoes, carrots, beetroot, parsnips.

3 **Cabbage family** Brussels sprouts, cabbage, cauliflower, plus swedes and turnips, which are also susceptible to club-root disease.

2 **Others** Beans, lettuce, peas, celery- and parsley-family crops, onions.

year – helps ensure that the soil does not become depleted of nutrients, which it would do if the same crops were taking the same nutrients from the same place year after year.

Different types of crops may be prone to attack by specific pests and diseases. Club-root disease, for example, attacks all members of the cabbage family (brassicas), but it has no effect on carrots, lettuces, tomatoes or other non-cabbage-family plants.

Crop rotation can help to prevent the build-up of some of these specific soil-borne pests and diseases; however, it is not 100 per cent effective. Some diseases such as club root can remain dormant in the soil for as long as 20 years, so a three- or four-year rotation plan is unlikely to starve the disease-causing organisms into submission. However, crop rotation is still effective in preventing other disease problems.

The kitchen garden

It's great to have a garden that's big enough to devote a special area to growing vegetables, as well as fruits and herbs – a traditional kitchen garden. However, large plots require careful planning to ensure they will work well without becoming too time-consuming.

IS A KITCHEN GARDEN FOR YOU?

PROS

• Hedges, fences or walls provide sheltered conditions.

• You can train fruit trees up walls and fences.

• Plenty of room for a variety of vegetables, fruits and herbs.

CONS

• Hedges, fences or walls cause problems with shade.

• Hedges will compete for water and nutrients.

• Soil between rows will become compacted; you'll need to dig the plot over at the end of the season.

• Bare soil between rows can quickly be colonised by weeds.

• The size of a large plot can be daunting, especially when it comes to such tasks as weeding.

• If the plot is large, you may sow too much of a crop.

In the past a large, traditional walled kitchen garden in the grounds of a sizeable house was regarded as useful but dull. It was hidden away at the end of the main garden and screened from view by hedges or walls.

A modern kitchen garden

Today, a kitchen garden refers to a garden with a mixture of vegetables, fruits and herbs. It can be just as decorative and interesting as any flower garden – and there's certainly no need to hide it away from view. In fact, as with any vegetable garden, it is best near the kitchen to make it easier to dig up some leeks or cut a cabbage head in cold weather.

You can provide an old-fashioned traditional touch by including walls, fences or hedges surrounding the garden, or you can leave the plot open to view. Alternatively, you can train a row of cordon or espalier apple and pear trees to make a productive dividing line between the ornamental

Trellises, pergolas and other types of support frames are ideal in the kitchen garden for growing plants that climb such as beans and peas. They also break up the space, creating outdoor garden rooms.

and kitchen areas of the garden. This will add interest by creating an extra garden 'room' without hiding the vegetables, fruits and herbs completely from view.

How does your garden grow?

Vegetables are traditionally grown in straight rows in a single, large, square or rectangular plot. There are usually gaps between the rows to allow the gardener to care for the plants.

Instead of growing vegetables in one large plot, try growing them in a bed system, thereby avoiding the drawbacks of a traditional kitchen garden (see *Is a Kitchen Garden for You?*, left).

Divide the space into a series of beds divided by pathways. Make sure the beds are narrow enough to be reached from the pathways on each side (see *Creating a Bed System,* below right). This will allow you to work in the garden without compacting the

soil by treading on it. (This growing system is also used for no-dig gardens: see pages 42–43.)

Crop rows can be grown more closely together because access is not necessary, so weeds have less of a chance to gain a foothold. The bed system makes it easy to plan rotations and sow in short rows for successional planting (see pages 18–19). Smaller beds also mean work can be divided into small sections at a time.

CREATING A BED SYSTEM

Before marking out the beds, cultivate the whole plot as you would for any vegetable garden, removing all perennial weeds and raking the soil level.

Make the beds 1.2m (4ft) wide so you can reach across half the bed from each side. Because you'll have to walk to the end of the bed to reach the other side, a maximum of 3m (10ft) is a good length. Make the pathways at least 45cm (18in) wide, with a few 60- to 90-cm (2- to 3-ft)-wide pathways, which will be suitable for wheelbarrow access.

Beds can be made level with the surrounding ground, but an edging helps to define them more clearly, and a raised edging allows you to build the beds up by adding organic matter (see pages 22–23).

Surface the pathways in a vegetable garden with bark chips or gravel, preferably on top of a landscape fabric (these are available from garden centres), which will help suppress weed growth.

Raised beds

Raised beds may be low – just a few centimetres above the surrounding ground level – or about waist height, which is especially useful for gardeners with mobility problems.

Many people who grow their vegetables in raised beds follow the no-dig method of cultivation (see pages 42–43). Because no-dig gardeners add large amounts of compost and other organic matter to their beds, the surface of the beds soon becomes higher than the surrounding soil. Although the soil and organic matter can simply be mounded up with sloping sides, using edging to contain the soil is more practical, especially as the layers build up over a few years.

Low beds

The height of a low bed can vary from 10–30cm (4–12in) high, and it may be made from a range of materials, including wood, bricks, blocks and edging tiles. Wood is perhaps the most commonly used

You can stack a few layers of bricks or use them on end for extra height. Don't slope them on an angle – the corners could scrape your knees as you do your gardening.

material, but it should be treated with a safe wood preservative to ensure a reasonably long life.

Old railway sleepers were once commonly used to make raised beds, but because they were treated with creosote, these are unsuitable for garden use. (However, safe, untreated sleepers are sometimes available.) Garden centres and builders' suppliers stock decorative edging materials.

MAKING A LOW BED

You can make a suitable edging from wood planks that are 2.5cm (1in) thick and 15cm (6in) wide. For rigidity sink the planks 5cm (2in) deep into the ground and support them with 2.5-cm (1-in)-square pegs every 1.2m (4ft); nail them to similar pegs that will serve as corner posts.

Alternatively, you can set concrete blocks or bricks into a shallow trench, which will provide stability to these edgings. Make sure you pack the soil tightly around them to hold them in place.

DIMENSIONS FOR RAISED BEDS

	Height	Width (one-sided access)	Width (two-sided access)
Wheelchair gardener	60–75cm (24–30in)	60cm (24in)	90–120cm (36–48in)
Standing gardener	75–90cm (30–36in)	60cm (24in)	120cm (48in)

These can range from inexpensive rolls of plastic to extravagant, beautiful and sometimes expensive antique-style tiles.

High beds

In situations where growing in the ground is impossible – a garden with a solid surface, for example, or where the soil is polluted – high raised beds are ideal. They are also good for gardeners who find bending difficult or impossible, who are wheelchair users or who suffer the annoyances of increasing age such as worsening eyesight, stiffening joints and tiring easily. Raised beds can also be a design statement, adding three-dimensional interest to the garden scene.

If you want to build a raised bed simply for its decorative appeal, you can make it whatever height you like. However, if it is to make gardening easier, the height and width of the bed will depend on who is going to use it, particularly whether it is a gardener who needs to work from a seated position or a wheelchair (see *Dimensions for Raised Beds,* left), or someone who will work standing up.

Gardeners who use a wheelchair will find it much easier to work at a bed designed like a table, where there will be room to roll the wheelchair underneath. Otherwise access will be limited and awkward, involving twisting and stretching. Detailed dimensions and advice are available from many disability groups.

Quick Tip

A super-sized pot
Like pots and containers, raised beds dry out more quickly than the open ground and need frequent watering. Without the proper drainage materials and holes, they can also become waterlogged in wet weather.

CONSTRUCTING A TALL RAISED BED

Tall raised beds are often built from wood, but you can also build them from bricks or stone. If you plan to build the raised bed on soil start with a concrete footing to provide a firm, level surface.

The walls will need to be only one brick thick. To allow for drainage, leave some weep holes at the base of the walls. Finish the walls with suitable coping stones for weather protection; if you choose wide, flat coping it can also double as garden seating.

A mixture of peas and lettuces thrives in this raised bed, which also serves as a frame for nasturtiums.

Because plants grow only in the top 30cm (12in) or so, fill the base with rubble, which will also improve drainage. Finish off with 45cm (18in) of good-quality topsoil, so that it is level with or slightly mounded above the walls to allow for settling.

Wood, metal and other materials are often used for raised beds, too.

Ornamental vegetable gardens

Many vegetables are beautiful – a feast for the eyes as well as the palate. Many varieties are worth growing for their decorative value, whether it's in a carefully planned formal plot known as a potager or mingled with flowers in an ornamental border.

GUIDELINES FOR A FORMAL POTAGER

• Keep the design simple so that weeding and general care of the plants are made easier.

• If you want an edging plant, choose one that doesn't need clipping (such as curly-leaved parsley or golden pot marigolds).

• Choose vegetables that you can sample without spoiling their decorative effect. French and climbing beans, peppers and asparagus peas, for example, can all be picked freely, while taking a few carefully chosen leaves from cut-and-come-again lettuce, kale and Swiss chard won't do any harm.

• Plant late-maturing varieties of vegetables such as leeks, onions, cabbages, carrots and cauliflower to avoid making a hole in the display.

Originally, the French term '*potager*' referred to a kitchen garden that supplied vegetables for the soup pot. However, today it has come to mean a formal vegetable plot where the plants are grown for their ornamental potential, as well as for their crops.

The potager usually consists of a number of beds that are arranged in a neat, geometric pattern – rectangles, squares, diamonds, triangles or circles. The beds are often edged with dwarf hedges, traditionally of box, and are filled with vegetables carefully chosen for their shapes, colours and textures.

While a small-scale potager for the home garden can look splendid, don't underestimate the amount of work involved. A formal potager must be kept neat if it is to look attractive, and that means frequent weeding and careful attention to pest and disease control.

Dwarf hedges look lovely, but remember that they will need lots of clipping (and that 'dwarf' usually means crawling along on your hands and knees with the secateurs). In addition, unless you're prepared to ruin your carefully planned display, you won't be able to harvest many of the vegetables.

The large cabbage leaves make an impact planted next to flowers in this garden.

Vegetables in flower borders

An easier way to grow vegetables for their decorative qualities is to mix them with flowers and shrubs in an ornamental border. Use plants such as climbing beans on a tepee of canes or stately globe artichokes to provide tall focal points at the back of the border, and fill the front of the beds with low-growing edgers such as frilly-leaved lettuce or parsley, or culinary thyme.

Groups of bold, textured Swiss chard, colourful bush tomatoes, hummocks of French beans and lacy-leaved carrots can fill in the middle ground alongside flowering perennials or shrubs.

The dark red leaves of chard are the perfect foil for these bright cosmos.

Quick Tip

New favourites

When growing vegetables for their decorative qualities, you should always check the latest seed catalogues. New, ornamental varieties of old favourites are introduced every year, reflecting their growing popularity.

ORNAMENTAL VEGETABLES

Here are just a few suggestions for vegetables that have decorative qualities. These will look stunning in most flower borders. You can also try experimenting with other vegetable varieties, including bush tomatoes.

Artichokes With their tall, stately habit and architectural, jagged-edged, silver leaves, globe artichokes make a bold and brilliant statement in any garden.

Asparagus peas An open-growing bush with attractive trifoliate leaves and lovely cinnamon-red, pealike flowers. These are followed by unusual and delicious winged pods.

Bean (runner) These have a climbing habit with attractive, scarlet flowers all summer. 'Hestia' is an unusual non-climbing dwarf variety that has red and white flowers.

Peppers Small-fruited chilli peppers are eye-catching; try 'Etna', with brilliant red fruits in upright clusters, or 'Fiesta' with yellow, purple or red peppers.

Herbs Try varieties in unusual colours such as purple-leaved or variegated sage, purple basil, golden thyme and golden marjoram. Fennel has a delicate ferny foliage, and the bronze variety is particularly striking.

Swiss chard 'Bright Lights' is one of the best mixtures, with red, gold, pink, white, orange and violet stems topped with deeply quilted, rich green leaf blades.

Lettuce Any good seed catalogue will feature many handsome lettuces: 'Lollo Rossa' and 'Lollo Bionda' are old favourites with crisply crimped, frilly leaves, and there are some excellent oak-leaved types such as deep red 'Flamenco' or 'Delicata'.

Salad onion Try red-shanked 'Rossa Lunga de Firenze' or 'North Holland Blood Red'.

Summer squash There is no end of varieties here: 'Sunburst' and 'Nova' both have golden, scalloped patty-pan fruits; 'Nova' also has contrasting green tips. Slender, bottle-shaped 'Zephyr' has yellow fruits that look as though the tips have been dipped into pale green paint.

The interesting fruits and large architectural leaves of squash make an unusual, attractive addition to an ornamental garden.

Vegetables in small spaces

No garden is too small to grow a few vegetables – you can grow reasonably sized crops in the smallest of spaces, even on balconies and patios.

KEEP IT SAFE

If you are growing vegetables on a roof terrace or balcony, make sure it can bear the load – soil-filled containers are heavy, especially just after being watered. Consult a structural engineer if you have any doubts.

Always ensure window boxes and hanging baskets are safely secured, particularly if they are several stories up. Don't be tempted to balance a box on the window ledge without any restraints, and make sure the fixture for a hanging basket is completely secure.

Few gardeners are lucky enough to have a huge garden with limitless space for vegetables. Even in large gardens, vegetables often compete for space with decorative flowers and shrubs. Modern gardens are becoming smaller and smaller, and in some cases only a tiny patio garden or compact balcony is available.

With such limitations, it is easy to think that home-grown vegetables are out of the question – however, that's not the case. First of all, vegetables and flowers can co-exist happily in an ornamental garden (see pages 24–25), and if soil beds are not available many vegetables grow well in containers (see pages 44–45), which are ideal for patios and balconies. Even a kitchen window sill can be pressed into use for growing herbs and perhaps a chilli pepper or a compact variety of tomato.

What to grow

The choice of vegetables is important where space is limited. Consider the following points when choosing them:

Colourful red and yellow peppers brighten up a small patio vegetable garden.

High yielding. A container that has been planted with one courgette will supply you with up to 15 fruits over the summer – enough for several meals. However, the same container planted with spinach might give you enough leaves for only a single serving – if you are lucky. When choosing plants, look for ones that give the maximum return for the space they occupy. Good choices include climbing beans, tomatoes, courgettes and lettuce.

High value. Main-crop potatoes are easy to find and inexpensive when bought from the shops, so don't consider growing them if you're short of space. However, early or out-of-season potatoes are a different matter; get the timing right and you could be enjoying home-grown new potatoes at a time when they cost a fortune at the shops – or when they are completely unobtainable. Likewise, instead of growing common lettuce, seek out seeds of frilly-leaved or coloured varieties that fetch a premium in the shops; grow red salad onions instead of the normal white ones or globe-rooted carrots instead of the usual long varieties.

Easy to grow. The smaller the space for growing, the smaller your margin for error. If one lettuce in a row of 20 bolts to seed, it's not a disaster; however, if it's one lettuce out of only three, it assumes much greater significance. Of course, your success rate will depend on your garden conditions and your experience, and these will affect your choices.

Vegetables and herbs such as asparagus, cabbage, sage, thyme and marjoram can be added to a flower border.

In this hanging basket French marigolds add a splash of colour, while sage and lettuce provide a leafy backdrop.

CHOOSING THE VEGETABLES

GOOD TO GROW

• **Lettuce** Choose cut-and-come-again varieties to provide a steady supply of leaves; also select varieties that are difficult to find or expensive to buy.

• **Green beans** Look for dwarf varieties that can be grown in a hanging basket; you can also grow climbing varieties in containers.

• **Tomatoes** Look for varieties specially bred for trailing over a hanging basket such as 'Balconi' or 'Gartenperle'.

• **Courgette** Golden-fruited types such as 'Gold Rush' provide a bright splash of colour in a container.

AVOID

• **Cauliflower** It is prone to several pests and diseases and will not form good heads unless the soil conditions are perfect.

• **Globe artichokes** These large plants take up lots of space, yet they only provide a small yield.

• **Chicory** It needs forcing and careful blanching.

• **Spinach** It shoots to seed quickly in warm, dry weather and needs lots of space for a reasonable crop.

• **Cucumber** (Greenhouse types) Do not allow the flowers to be fertilised, or bitter and misshapen fruits may result.

Problem gardens

Not every garden is perfect for growing vegetables – however, there are often simple solutions for most common problems. You can enjoy growing your own produce in even the most unpromising situations.

VEGETABLES FOR A PARTIALLY SHADY PLOT

On a partially shady plot, there's little point in growing sun-loving vegetables such as tomatoes and peppers. However, if your plot receives a minimum of two to three hours of sun a day, you can successfully grow the following moderately shade-tolerant vegetables and herbs:

beetroot	kohlrabi	rhubarb
broccoli	lettuce	salsify
chives	mint	spinach
garlic	parsley	turnips
kale	radishes	

Quick Tip

Whitewash

Shade cast by buildings can be difficult to handle, but you can maximise the amount of available light by painting all the surrounding surfaces white.

Most vegetables need plenty of direct sunlight to grow and crop well: six hours of summer sun each day is considered ideal. Good light will encourage sturdy growth and good leaf formation, which will enable the plant to carry out efficient food production through photosynthesis. This, in turn, will lead to heavier and better-quality crops.

Shady situations

Excessive shade will result in spindly plants that are more vulnerable to pest and disease attack. They often fail to reach their full cropping potential.

If the shade is cast by tree and shrub branches, this is usually easy to deal with by pruning or removing the plants involved. (However, if the problem plants are on a neighbour's property, preserve good relations by first discussing your pruning plans with your neighbour.) Consider lowering tall hedges to reduce the amount of shadow they cast – you will still retain the benefit of their protection. Walls and fences also offer valuable protection for vegetables, but they can cast a deep shadow if they are too tall. Consider replacing part of the wall or fence with a lower barrier on the side that causes the most shade problems.

Temperature extremes

Vegetables are either warm-season lovers or cool-season types. Warm-season crops are sensitive to any frost and need a long, hot growing season to do well. Temperatures must be above 15.5°C (60°F) – a temperature of 21°C (70°F) is preferable. Cool-season vegetables that are moderately hardy to frost hardy will do best in growing temperatures of 15.5–26.5°C (60–80°F). Sustained periods of higher temperatures will reduce both yields and crop quality.

In most temperate regions both warm-season and cool-season crops can be grown successfully as long as the timing is right. In cool areas use cloches and horticultural fleece to provide extra protection from low temperatures, and start plants indoors to gain an early start to the growing season (see pages 74–81).

Low-lying areas of the garden may become frost pockets. Because cool air sinks, it rolls down to the base of a hill and settles there in a chilly pool.

Terracing will create flat beds for growing vegetables. The walls help support the soil.

A solid barrier such as a wall or fence can cause a frost pocket to form by preventing the cold air from flowing down the hill, so bear this in mind when putting up barriers around the vegetable garden.

In hot climates time the sowing of cool-season vegetables so that they crop in spring or autumn, and avoid the hottest months. Provide shade and overhead irrigation to lower temperatures and avoid drought stress.

Slopes

A gently sloping garden is not too much of a problem for vegetable growing, particularly if you are lucky enough for the slope to face the right direction and allow the plants to bask in extra sunshine. However, a steep slope can be a real problem, and it can easily provide you with a demonstration of how soil erosion

occurs — it takes little time for rain to wash soil down to the base of the slope. In this situation terracing is the only answer. Use the 'cut and fill' method by cutting partially into the slope and partially building it out to make one or more flat beds for growing vegetables.

Soil problems

The majority of poor soils can be improved (see pages 32–39). However, if your garden soil is unsuitable for vegetable growing — it is shallow or stony or it has been polluted by industrial waste — you can grow vegetables in containers or raised beds filled with imported, good-quality topsoil. If the natural soil is polluted, line the base of a raised bed with a landscaping (geotextile) fabric that will prevent the vegetables' roots from penetrating into the polluted area.

Poor drainage is another problem. You can improve heavy clay soil that does not drain freely by applying organic matter, but some sites have a more serious problem where water simply cannot get away because of the underlying ground structure. In this case it may be necessary to install a drainage system consisting of plastic perforated pipes or tile drains.

Wind

In exposed windy areas protect vegetable plots by erecting windbreaks. Avoid putting up a solid barrier such as a wall or

close-boarded fence — this deflects the wind over the top only for it to be pulled down and cause turbulence just beyond the barrier. Windbreaks should be around 50 per cent permeable to be effective. Hedges, open-style fences or plastic windbreak netting are all good solutions for reducing the strength of the gusts to less damaging levels as they pass through them.

Raised beds and containers are a solution for gardens with poor soil conditions.

VEGETABLES FOR THE RIGHT SEASON

Cool-season vegetables:
beetroot, broccoli, broad beans, Brussels sprouts, chives, cabbage, carrot, cauliflower, celeriac, celery, chicory, Chinese cabbage, cress, endive, fennel, garlic, kale, kohlrabi, leeks, lettuce, onions, parsley, parsnips, peas, potatoes, radicchio, radishes, rocket, salad onions, salsify, shallots, spinach, swedes, Swiss chard, turnips.

Warm-season vegetables:
aubergines, beans, cucumbers, melons, okra, peas, peppers, sweet potatoes, courgettes and squash, sweet corn, tomatoes.

2 Preparing the ground

Before you start sowing seeds, buying plants, and getting your vegetable garden under way, you need to ensure that the soil – the plants' home – is in good condition. For your vegetables to thrive, they need a well-prepared plot that will provide them with all the necessary food, water and support from the beginning.

Understanding how soil provides for plants will enable you to decide what you need to do: whether or not you need to dig; what you can add to your soil to improve it; and whether it needs lime or additional fertilizers. Get these right, and you'll have a successful harvest.

A well-prepared vegetable plot will provide ample rewards at harvest time.

All about soil

Soil is a wonderful material. It takes thousands of years to form – broken down from rocks by wind, rain and frost – and it is teeming with life we cannot see. Understanding soil and knowing how to look after it are vital for the production of strong, healthy plants.

Plants miraculously make food out of light and air, but to make that miracle happen, they have a few requirements. They need water and a variety of mineral nutrients, and they usually need somewhere to anchor themselves while they grow. For most plants, this is where soil comes in.

Soil may have started its life as rock, but in the process of its breakdown into tiny particles, it has acquired a few other constituents. Variations in the proportions of these constituents mean there are different types of soil, some of which are better for plant growth than others.

When soil is mixed with water and shaken up, the sediment settles in layers, allowing you to determine the proportions of silt, clay, and organic matter in the soil.

VEGETABLE PH PREFERENCES

Most vegetables prefer soil between pH 6.5 and 7.0, but the following types will tolerate soil with higher levels of acid (below 6.0) or alkaline (above 7.0).

Acid-tolerant plants (below pH 6.0)	Alkaline-tolerant plants (above pH 7.0)	Alkaline and acid-tolerant plants
Aubergine 5.5–6.8	Asparagus 6.5–7.5	Celery
Carrot 5.5–6.8	Beetroot 6.5–7.5	Garlic
Celery 5.5–7.5	Brussels sprouts 6.0–7.5	
Endive 5.5–7.0	Cauliflower 6.0–7.5	
Garlic 5.5–7.5	Celery 5.5–7.5	
Potato 5.8–6.5	Cucumber 6.0–7.5	
Radish 5.5–6.5	Garlic 5.5–7.5	
Rhubarb 5.0–6.8	Leek 6.0–7.5	
Sweet potato 5.5–6.5	Melon 6.0–7.5	
Watermelon 5.5–7.0	Okra 6.8–7.5	
	Onion 6.0–7.5	
	Shallot 6.5–7.5	

The main constituents are:

Soil particles. The size of broken-down rock particles in soil varies: the largest are sand; smaller particles are silt; and the smallest are clay. Most soil has a mixture of sand, silt and clay. An even mixture is a loam, but one type often predominates. The soil is then known as a sandy loam, a clay loam and so on.

Organic matter. This is any living thing that has died. Plants grow in the soil, die, rot down and are absorbed back into the soil as humus. Plants are also eaten by grazing animals, who return them to the soil as manure; the animals also die and are broken down and incorporated into the soil, too.

Living organisms. In addition to the larger soil-dwelling creatures that we can easily see such as earthworms and insects, soil is full of microscopic life forms. These micro-organisms are various fungi and bacteria – many of which have an important role in breaking down plant and animal matter into humus. Not all of the soil's living population are helpful; many insects, eelworms and mites are plant pests, and some types of fungi and bacteria cause devastating diseases.

Air and water. These are essential constituents of soil. The fragile root hairs that grow from a plant's roots seek out the moisture and dissolved minerals that are vital for growth. They also need air to function, as do soil micro-organisms. The amounts of water and air within the soil depends upon its structure (see pages 34–35).

Nutrients

While plants make their own food using energy from sunlight, they need mineral nutrients to do so. When dissolved in soil moisture, these nutrients are taken up by the roots.

The major nutrients required are nitrogen, phosphorus and potassium – often abbreviated to their chemical symbols of N, P and K. Nitrogen stimulates leafy growth, phosphorus helps root development, and potassium encourages flowers and fruit.

Other mineral nutrients needed in smaller quantities are calcium, sulphur and magnesium, plus trace elements, which include iron, boron, copper, manganese, molybdenum and zinc.

Different soils vary in the quantity and quality of these nutrients. If sufficient nutrients are not present in the soil, they can be added in the form of manure, compost or various manufactured fertilisers. Soil-test kits for checking your soil's nutrient status are available from garden centres.

SOIL ACIDITY

Soil may be acid, alkaline or neutral. Most vegetables grow best in soil that is just on the acid side of neutral. However, if the soil becomes too acid, club-root disease, which affects members of the cabbage family, can become a real problem. Conversely, soil that is too alkaline can 'lock up' various nutrients and make them unavailable to plants.

Soil acidity is measured on a pH scale: a pH between 1.0 and 7.0 is acid; pH 7.0 to 14.0 is alkaline and pH 7.0 is neutral. Simple soil-testing kits, available from garden centres, reveal your soil's acidity, but do several tests in different parts of the garden for the best results. For a more detailed analysis, you can send samples to a commerical laboratory for testing.

Most vegetables grow best at about pH 6.5. If the soil is more acid than this apply ground limestone to reduce the acidity:

this is especially helpful to prevent club root in cabbage-family plants. Depending on the soil, the amount of lime to apply varies. As a guide, adding 270g per sq m to sandy soil, 540g per sq m to a mixed loam, and 800g per sq m to clay will raise the pH by one unit – for example, from pH 5.5 to pH 6.5.

Lowering the pH of an alkaline soil is not practical, but knowing your soil is alkaline will warn you that you may need to apply a fertiliser that contains trace elements.

Dip a test strip into soil mixed with water and compare its colour with those on the chart.

pH Test 1

pH 8.0 — pH 7.0 to 14.0 is alkaline
pH 7.0 — pH 7.0 is neutral
— pH 6.5 is best for most vegetables
pH 6.0
pH 5.0
pH 4.0 — pH 1.0 to 7.0 is acid

Quick Tip

Telltale blooms

If you have a hydrangea (*Hydrangea macrophylla*), you can use the colour of its blooms to determine the soil pH where it is planted. If the flowers are pink, the soil is generally above pH 7; blue, pH 6.5 or lower.

Improving your soil

Few gardens are blessed with perfect soil, but fortunately there's plenty that can be done to improve it. Building up soil fertility will pay dividends in heavier, tastier crops.

Imagine a glass jar filled with golf balls. Because the balls are relatively big, there are large air spaces between them. Now imagine the same jar filled with dried peas – the air spaces between the peas are much smaller. If the jar is filled with sugar crystals the spaces between the crystals are comparatively minute.

This is a little like soil. Sandy soil has large particles with plenty of air surrounding them. Soil that is mainly silt has smaller air spaces and slow water drainage, while clay particles have tiny air spaces between them, and water is often trapped by surface tension around the particles.

Identifying your soil

The best garden soil is loam, made up of a mixture of sand, silt and clay. Moisten a pinch of soil and rub it between your thumb and forefinger. Sandy soil feels gritty, silty soil feels slippery and clay soil feels sticky. Try moulding a handful of moist soil into a ball. If it falls apart it's sandy; if it moulds easily into a ball it contains lots of clay. If you can give the ball of soil a polish with your thumb, there's an even higher proportion of clay.

Sandy soil has large particles and drains rapidly. It dries quickly in hot weather.

Loam consists of a friable (crumbly) mixture of sand, silt and clay.

Sandy soil is quick to warm up in spring, is light and easy to manage and is rarely waterlogged. However, it is a hungry, thirsty soil, because water and dissolved nutrients drain through it before plants can use them.

A heavy, clay soil remains cold for longer in spring, and it is difficult to dig. It soon becomes waterlogged and

To test for clay squeeze a ball of moist soil in your hand. If it forms a firm ball it's clay.

Clay soil has tiny particles that trap water and can make the soil waterlogged.

airless in wet weather, yet it can bake rock hard in droughts. However, clay soil usually contains good quantities of vital plant nutrients.

Improving soil structure

The structure of both very heavy and very light soil can be greatly improved by adding organic matter.

Fibrous organic matter helps to break up clay soil, making it easier to dig, and it encourages soil particles to stick together so that drainage is improved. In free-draining soils it acts like a sponge, soaking up moisture and holding on to it so that it remains available to plants. (For more about organic matter see pages 36–39.)

Cultivation

Digging and forking are cultivation techniques that involve turning over and mixing layers of soil. This helps to break up the hard surface soil cap to let in air and moisture. It allows heavy, sticky soil to be broken down by exposing it to the weather, it incorporates organic matter and it breaks up any hard layers of soil that have formed below the surface.

However, cultivation does have its drawbacks. Carelessly done, it can damage soil structure and cause compaction on heavy soils; it can also bring buried weed seeds up to the surface where they can germinate.

Quick Tip

Walking a plank

Clay soil is easily compacted when wet. Avoid walking on wet clay soil and taking heavy equipment such as wheelbarrows across it. Where you cannot avoid it, put a plank down to walk or push a wheelbarrow on – it will help to spread the load and limit the damage.

EARTHWORMS

The presence of earthworms will greatly improve the structure of your soil. They make burrows, which help to bring air into the soil and allow water to drain away. These burrows may extend as far as 2m (6ft) below the surface of the soil.

Earthworms eat organic matter such as dead leaves, rising up to the surface and dragging the leaves down into their burrows. They also ingest soil as they burrow through it, depositing the sifted remains as casts either on the soil surface or within the burrow. These habits incorporate large amounts of surface organic matter into the soil and begin the process of breaking it down. They also mix up the layers of soil.

Earthworms can be encouraged by spreading large amounts of organic matter such as compost and leaf mould (see pages 36–37) on the soil surface. They are usually particularly abundant in no-dig plots (see pages 42–43) because of the amount of organic matter used. In fact, they will do the soil mixing and 'digging' for you.

Worms sold as bait in fishing shops are brandling worms. Don't be tempted to buy these worms to add to garden soil; they don't do the same job as earthworms.

CULTIVATING YOUR SOIL

You will find these tools essential for soil cultivation.

Tool	Use
Spade	For digging: keep the blade clean and sharp so that it slices down into the soil with minimum effort. Stainless steel spades are easier to use because the soil doesn't stick to them. However, they are more expensive to buy.
Fork	Useful for turning the soil in spring after frost has done the hard work of breaking it down over winter.
Rake	Breaks the soil surface down into really fine crumbs and levels it for sowing seeds and planting; also removes surface stones and weed debris.
Trowel	For digging individual planting holes or removing deep-rooted weeds.

Enriching your soil

Organic matter is a valuable addition to almost any soil; however, you'll need a lot of it for even an average-sized vegetable garden. A compost heap is one way to ensure a good supply – for free – but there are other ways of obtaining useful organic matter too.

OTHER SOURCES OF ORGANIC MATTER

Depending on where you live, you may be able to obtain other useful organic products.

• Mushroom compost is rotted horse manure previously used for growing a crop of mushrooms. Lime is used in the mushroom-growing process, so it is not suitable for alkaline, chalky soils.

• Spent hops are available cheaply or free from breweries. They are difficult to handle because they are wet, and they will give your garden a distinctly interesting aroma when fresh.

• If you live near the coast you can collect seaweed, which is rich in nutrients. It is wet and bulky, and it can attract flies unless covered, so add it to the compost heap in small quantities.

By its nature, organic matter is bulky, often making it difficult to transport. However, if you can overcome that problem, there are useful sources that can be valuable for improving your garden soil.

Compost. Home-made compost is the primary source of organic matter for most gardens. It helps dispose of waste plant material, and it is on site, ready to use. (For making compost see pages 38–39.)

Leaf mould. Because they take longer to break down, you should compost autumn leaves on their own instead of adding them to the compost heap. You can make a standard compost heap for them (see page 39), but a simple way to compost leaves is to place them in plastic sacks along with a few layers of garden soil. Tie the neck of the sack when it is full, puncture the sides of the bag several times with a garden fork to provide air holes, then leave the bags in an out-of-the-way corner for six months to a year until the mixture is dark brown and crumbly.

Autumn leaves are composted in a separate pile on their own and will eventually turn into leaf mould.

Manure. Animal manures are excellent soil additives, providing useful quantities of plant nutrients as well as having a beneficial effect on soil structure. Allow manure to rot down before you use it in the garden. Fresh manure can scorch plant roots if it comes into contact with them. It also uses nitrogen as it starts to decompose and will take that nitrogen from the soil, stealing it from the plants. Stack manure into a pile and allow it to rot down, or add it to the garden compost heap.

Horse manure is probably one of the most available types, and it tends to rot down more quickly than farmyard manures from cows and pigs.

Poultry manure is lightweight but caustic and will need to be well rotted before you can use it, so add it to the compost heap. It can be extremely smelly, and because it usually comes from animals raised in crowded, unpleasant conditions, you may also have moral objections to using it.

Manures are often mixed with the animals' bedding. Straw is much better than wood shavings, which will take a long time to decompose.

Using organic matter

It is usually best to compost organic matter before using it. However, you can use fresh organic matter by spreading it on a cleared vegetable plot in the autumn, because it will have time to rot down before sowing and planting in the spring.

You can add organic matter to the soil in three ways: place it in the base of a trench and cover with soil; mix it into the soil with a fork or spade; or apply it as a surface layer (called a mulch), which will be taken down into the soil gradually by earthworms. Placing it in the bottom of a trench is a good method for thirsty plants with deep roots such as scarlet runner

Green manure plants have been chopped down and left to wilt. They will be dug into the soil where they will add nutrients, which will enrich it.

beans, where it will form a spongy moisture reservoir. Mix the organic matter with the soil if you want to get it to the area quickly where plants can take advantage of it. If you spread organic matter as a mulch, earthworms will do the same job but they take more time. Mulching also suppresses weed growth, retains soil moisture (if the soil is already moist) and prevents an impenetrable crust or cap from forming on the soil surface.

Green manure

Plants that are grown specifically to be dug into the soil are known as green manure. They are useful as a cover crop where an area of the vegetable plot is left bare for several weeks, because they help prevent weeds from taking over and, when dug in, they enrich the soil for the next crop.

Sow green manures in late summer and early autumn and cut them down in spring; or sow in early spring and cut down as the space is needed. Dig the plants in while they are young, before they flower, or the stems become tough and difficult to incorporate.

PLANTS FOR GREEN MANURE

You can grow one of a number of plants for making green manure. Here are the most popular choices:

- Legumes (members of the pea and bean family) because they have the unique ability to take nitrogen from the air and convert it into a form that is usable to plants. Suitable plants include alfalfa (lucerne), clover, agricultural lupin and vetch.

- Buckwheat, rye and mustard.

Quick Tip

Buying manure

Because most animal manures are so bulky, several proprietary, pre-rotted, bagged manures are available from garden centres. They are more expensive but easier to transport.

Making your own compost

Compost adds organic matter to your soil. This matter will supply essential nutrients, regulate moisture, improve soil texture and encourage beneficial micro-organisms. Making your own compost is easy – and it also helps to dispose of garden waste.

Compost is simply partially rotted plant and animal matter. When exposed to the right conditions, the original constituents will decompose until they become unrecognisable, forming a dark, moist, crumbly material with a pleasant earthy smell. If left alone the matter will eventually turn to compost over several years. However, if it is encouraged to break down in the correct way, it is possible to have compost suitable for enriching your soil after only a few months.

The process of decomposition is carried out by micro-organisms (see pages 32–33), and it requires air, moisture and warmth. Air helps to break down the material – a process known as aerobic decomposition. Airless, or anaerobic, decomposition means slimy, evil-smelling compost, at least in the short term. To allow air to circulate, mix dense materials that will form a solid mass such as grass with open material such as prunings and plant stems or chopped straw.

The plant material added to the heap usually supplies enough moisture. However, in dry weather you may need to water the heap; use a watering can or hose fitted with a rose.

As they work micro-organisms will usually create the warmth that is necessary for the decomposition process. However, if a new pile is slow to build up heat, you should add a compost accelerator such as sulphate of ammonia (available in garden centres) or a layer of fresh

Creating compost

You can make your own compost in a few easy steps. Turning the compost isn't essential, but it speeds up the process by adding air and spreading the heat more evenly (the heat often concentrates in the centre of the heap).

In rainy climates keep excess water out of the heap – too much moisture lowers the temperature and excludes air. A protective cover will keep out excess moisture as well as hold in heat.

1 Build up the first layer of garden waste. Keep adding to the heap until the layer is 30–45cm (12–18in) deep.

2 Cover the waste with a layer of garden soil about 3in (7.5cm) deep. Continue the layers as you build up the heap.

farmyard manure. Both of these supply the nitrogen that is necessary for the micro-organisms to thrive.

The compost heap

At its simplest, a compost heap is just that – waste material piled up in one place. By banging four sturdy corner posts into the ground and securing chicken wire around them, you can help to keep the heap tidy and manageable; however, wooden planks nailed to the posts instead of chicken wire will look better and encourage faster decomposition by holding in warmth. Enterprising gardeners can use bricks, concrete blocks, old pallets or various other odd materials they might have to hand. For the average garden, a compost heap of 1cu m (3cu ft) is generally a suitable size.

Proprietary compost containers are available in a range of sizes and styles, but make sure they are large enough to be practical. You can make one from a large rubbish bin. It needs holes in the sides to allow air to reach the decomposing material. Remove the bottom to allow worms to enter the heap to help the decomposing process.

COMPOST MATERIALS

All organic matter – material that was once alive – can, in theory, be composted. However, some waste is better left out of a compost heap. A mixture of different materials will help air to circulate and provide both carbon and nitrogen.

ADD

• In the autumn, plant debris from borders and the vegetable garden.

• Grass clippings not treated with selective weed killer (but mix them with bulky waste first).

• Damaged fruits and vegetables.

• Fruit and vegetable trimmings from the kitchen.

Add with care

• Tough prunings and woody stems; shred these before adding to the heap – or they'll rot slowly.

• Annual weeds before they go to seed – the seeds do not decompose.

• Fallen leaves: these take time to rot and are best composted as leaf mould (see pages 36–37).

AVOID

• Perennial weeds or invasive plants: adding a few parts of a plant such as root from bindweed can cause a garden infestation when the compost is spread.

• Diseased plants: some parts of a heap may not reach a temperature that kills all disease spores. Diseases such as club root on brassicas, halo blight on beans, potato blight and white rot on onions can spread in compost. Burn affected plants.

• The first two or three grass clippings from lawns treated with selective weedkiller. Some plants such as tomatoes are affected by even a trace of weedkiller.

• Cooked food and meat products: these attract vermin such as rats.

3 Turn the compost heap – sides to middle and top to bottom – when it is half full and again when it is almost full, or about every three months.

4 When the heap is full, cover it with a piece of old carpet or a sheet of strong black plastic, but check occasionally to ensure the heap does not become too dry.

5 Once the heap is full and rotting down, start another one – this will allow time for the first heap to mature.

Digging: when and how

Few things are more satisfying than the sight of a freshly dug vegetable plot – and digging provides a whole range of benefits for your vegetable plants.

IS DIGGING FOR YOU?

PROS

• Breaks up compacted soil layers and improves aeration and drainage.

• Removes roots of old crops and weeds, which makes sowing and planting possible.

• Kills annual weed growth by burying the weeds.

• Mixes organic matter into the root zone of the plants.

CONS

• Hard work.

• Can damage the soil structure, especially on heavy clay soils.

• Digging can bring annual weed seeds buried deep in the soil up near the surface, where they can germinate.

One way to look at digging is to think about it as healthy exercise rather than hard work. Why pay to go to the gym when you can achieve the same result in your own garden for free? The best way to tackle the job is to do a little at a time instead of trying to do it all at once – and use a well-balanced, comfortable spade.

When to dig

Start digging as soon as you clear any crops in the autumn. Dig the area over in small sections, as space

Single digging

The simplest and most common method of preparing a plot is single digging. Start by marking the centre of your plot with string tied to stakes. It will be a guide for your first trench. As you dig the soil, turn over each spadeful as you toss it into the previously dug trench, thereby burying any surface weeds.

1 Dig the first trench 30cm (1ft) wide and a spit deep – the depth of the spade's blade – and store the soil in a wheelbarrow.

2 Scatter a layer of compost over the bottom of the trench to help improve the quality of the soil.

becomes vacant. Leave the soil in rough, sizable clods. This exposes the maximum surface area to the weather, particularly to the effects of repeated freezing and thawing, which will break the clods down into small particles, thereby doing much of the hard work for you. The earlier you complete the digging in the autumn or early winter, the more time the weather will have to do its work.

In spring, just before sowing and planting, you may need to turn the soil over again with a fork to break it down further. Any remaining clods will usually shatter easily if struck sharply with the back of the fork. On light soil, you may need to only rake the soil to give it the fine, friable (crumbly) texture needed for sowing.

How to dig

A spade is the normal tool used for digging, but some people find a fork easier to use, especially on heavy soil. Stainless-steel spades are expensive, but they have a long life and often make work easier because the soil slides off the blade cleanly.

When turning a spadeful of soil over, keep one hand low on the shaft,

near the blade, to provide you with the maximum leverage. You should avoid overloading the spade with too much soil, which will make digging more difficult. Tools with extra-long handles are available from garden centres; these can be gentler on the back.

Before you begin to dig, warm up with stretching exercises to avoid injury. As you dig, straighten up and stretch the spine backwards frequently. You can also avoid injury by starting off gently, digging 20–30 minutes at a time, then building up to about an hour.

DOUBLE DIGGING

Double digging, also known as trenching, is harder work than single digging but it can provide worthwhile results – in trials, yields have been improved by 30 per cent or more.

The benefits of double digging last for several years. It is worth doing the first time a new plot is dug, then every four or five years.

Take the soil from a trench as you would with single digging (see below), but make it 60cm (2ft) wide. Fork over the base of the trench another spit deep and incorporate compost before soil from the next trench is thrown into it, thereby breaking up the consolidated area (the pan) that forms below the normal digging level. This will allow the plant roots to penetrate more deeply and improves the plants' water uptake, which increases yields.

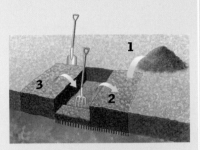

When double digging be careful not to mix the lower infertile soil with the topsoil in which the plants grow.

---

3 Dig another trench next to the first one, turning the soil over into the neighbouring trench. Continue to the end of the plot.

4 Finish off the last trench with the soil stored in the wheelbarrow.

Quick Tip

Too wet?

Don't attempt to dig when the soil is wet because this will damage the structure of heavy soil by compacting it further. You should be able to walk on the soil comfortably, with only a little of it clinging to the soles of your boots.

No-dig gardening

Anyone who has laboured to dig over a large vegetable plot will be attracted to the ease of the no-dig system. Many enthusiasts feel it is a growing system that is closer to nature – where regular digging is unknown.

IS THE NO-DIG SYSTEM FOR YOU?

PROS

• Avoids the hard labour of wielding a spade.

• Does not upset the natural balance of soil organisms that can be caused by digging.

• The soil structure is not compacted because the soil is not trampled on.

CONS

• May not be suitable for heavy soil such as clay.

• Weeds may be a problem in the first few years.

• Large quantities of good-quality compost will need to be transported and spread.

Instead of the soil of a bare plot being turned over in the autumn, in the no-dig system a 2.5–5cm (1–2in)-thick layer of rotted organic matter such as compost or manure is spread over the surface. Earthworms gradually pull this compost layer down and mix it up with the topsoil, which improves the fertility of the soil.

This layer of mulch will protect the soil surface from sun and wind, thereby keeping it moist and helping to even out temperature fluctuations. This helps micro-organisms in the soil (see pages 32–33) to flourish. The mulch will also help to protect the soil from beating rain, which can spoil the structure of the soil and form a hard, impenetrable cap on the surface.

In the spring you can sow seeds directly onto the mulched surface and, ideally, cover them with another layer of organic matter.

Before you get started

Plan and prepare ahead. Start by obtaining enough good-quality organic matter for the size of your plot. Few gardens are able to supply a sufficient quantity of compost, so you'll need to find a bulk supplier of manure or other organic matter – preferably one who can deliver to your garden. Remember that materials

Sturdy black plastic covers an area of weeds. Without sunlight, they will die in a few months, and you can start a no-dig plot.

Steps to no-dig gardening

Although not essential, most plots will benefit from a low border of planks or bricks set around the edge to keep the deep mulch in place, particularly because it builds up over several years. A system of pathways or planks on the beds is necessary to avoid walking on the soil and compacting it.

1 In the autumn clear the plot of weeds, using a fork to lift out any perennials. If there are many weeds, cover the plot with sturdy black plastic from early spring to late autumn. Remove the plastic; rake off and dig up the dead weeds and roots. Or use a weedkiller such as glyphosate.

2 You can use naturally rot-resistant wooden planks or planks treated with a preservative to hold the compost in place. Nail them to stakes driven into the ground. Leave pathways between the beds to avoid stepping on the soil.

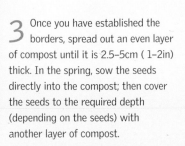

3 Once you have established the borders, spread out an even layer of compost until it is 2.5–5cm (1–2in) thick. In the spring, sow the seeds directly into the compost; then cover the seeds to the required depth (depending on the seeds) with another layer of compost.

that are not rotted such as fresh straw will take nutrients out of the soil, so they are not recommended.

A small-plot alternative

This is not a true no-dig method, but it is handy for a plot less than 1.5 by 4.5 m (5 x 15 ft). After clearing the weeds in the autumn (see box, left), spread layers of wet newspaper over the area; then build up layers of organic matter, alternating compost and grass clippings with shredded newspaper or chopped leaves until the layers are 15cm (6in) deep. Let the bed decompose over the winter. It should be ready for planting in spring. After the growing season, fork over the bed, incorporating some underlying soil into the organic matter on top.

Does it work?

No-dig gardening is most successful on soil with a good structure, where plenty of organic matter is available, and many gardeners have obtained good results. If weeds are a problem you'll need to persevere in the first few years. Once the original weed seeds have sprouted, new ones are not brought up with digging, so the problem will lessen with time.

One of the benefits of digging is that it introduces air into the soil, and heavy soil can begin to suffer from lack of aeration after a few years of no digging. If you have heavy soil, this system might not be right for you.

Quick Tip

Pathways

When you plan the borders, make sure the pathways are large enough to fit a wheelbarrow – you'll need it to transport the compost.

Vegetables in containers

There's a surprising number of vegetables that can be grown successfully in containers. If you don't have a large garden, containers are a great way to maximise your use of space.

Ask most gardeners what type of vegetables can be grown in containers and they will usually come up with tomatoes and, after a little thought, perhaps peppers and aubergines. After that, they normally run out of ideas. However, there are plenty more crops that can be grown successfully in pots, growing bags and even window boxes and hanging baskets – these are ideal for people who have patio gardens.

Types of container

Plastic and clay pots. The larger the pot, the less frequently it will need to be watered. The minimum practical size container for most vegetables is 20cm (8in) deep, but 30cm (12in) deep is better. Make sure there are adequate drainage holes.

Window boxes. Many seed catalogues have a section for baby or mini vegetable varieties, several of which are good for window boxes. Carrots (especially round-rooted varieties), radishes and greens are all worth trying, as well as some compact herbs such as thyme, basil, marjoram, chives and parsley.

Hanging baskets. Special basket varieties of tomatoes make a colourful feature, particularly with a few thyme or rosemary plants tucked in among them. You could even try a dwarf runner bean such as 'Hestia' in a basket. If you are growing vegetables in hanging baskets, remember that you will need to water them frequently.

Growing bags. There is a limited depth of compost in growing bags, so these also need frequent watering; otherwise, they are convenient to use.

Planting vegetables in a window box

Choose compact cultivars to grow in window boxes. If planting perennial herbs ensure that there is proper drainage to avoid waterlogged plants in winter.

1 Carefully remove transplants from the tray or pots; make sure you avoid damaging their roots.

2 Leave enough space between plants to allow room to grow – the spacing will depend on the vegetable type.

Quick Tip

Feeding time

Plants in containers need feeding as they develop because there is a limited nutrient supply in the compost. Apply a liquid feed every 7 to 14 days, or use granular, powder or slow-release fertilisers (see pages 88–89).

Supporting container-grown vegetables

Some vegetables need a large container and require some type of support for climbing such as peas and climbing beans.

1 Place a layer of stones or broken pottery over the drainage holes, then add a suitable compost to the container. Use a dibber to make seed holes for peas or beans.

2 Thin seedlings so there is an outer ring of plants, along with several plants in the centre.

3 Before the seedlings begin to climb, add supports by pushing bamboo canes into the soil (avoid disturbing the plants) and securing the top ends together with twine, forming a wigwam shape. Encourage the plants to climb around the canes while they are young.

Staking can be a problem for taller crops, but special growing bag supports are availabe from garden centres. Most of the crops in *What Vegetables Can I Grow?* (right) are suitable for growing in a growing bag – even potatoes can be grown in one, although the yield may be small.

Preparing the containers

Good drainage is important for all container-grown plants, so check that there are plenty of drainage holes. (It is easy to add more holes to plastic pots by drilling them with an electric drill.) Raise containers off the ground on pot feet or bricks to allow water to flow through the holes freely. Cover the base of the container with pieces from broken clay pots or large stones in a layer 2.5–5cm (1–2in) deep.

Fill the container with either a soil-based or a soilless potting compost. Soil-based composts hold moisture well and have a higher level of nutrients than soilless types – they also make the container more stable and are less likely to blow over. However, they are heavy, making the bags of compost awkward to transport and large containers difficult to move once they are filled. Both compost types provide good results, so the choice is a matter of personal preference.

When using soilless compost, especially in small containers such as hanging baskets, growing bags and window boxes mix in some moisture-retaining granules (available from garden centres), because these will cut down the amount of watering needed and protect plants from drying out.

After planting, cover the surface of the compost with gravel or shredded bark mulch to help cut down moisture loss. Keep the compost just moist at all times. In sunny or windy weather the containers may need watering twice a day.

WHAT VEGETABLES CAN I GROW?

You should avoid growing some vegetables in containers, either because they need lots of space and a long growing season for a good yield such as Brussels sprouts and asparagus, or they have long, deep roots such as parsnips and salsify. However, you should get good results with some of these vegetables:

- Aubergine
- Baby beetroot
- Carrots (short-rooted types)
- Courgette
- Cucumbers
- Pole beans
- Herbs
- Kohlrabi
- Lettuce and other greens
- Melons
- Peppers
- Potatoes (new)
- Radishes
- Tomatoes

3 Sowing and planting

The really exciting part of vegetable growing is witnessing the conversion of a packet of dry, shrivelled-looking seeds into rows of vigorous, healthy plants. It is important to remember that vegetable plants are at their most vulnerable stage when they are young and need special care. The following pages contain advice to help you give your seedlings and young plants the best possible start, whether you are sowing them directly in the vegetable plot or in containers for transplanting – or if you are bypassing the sowing stage altogether and buying young plants.

Some young plants will benefit from a protective cover, whether provided by cloches, a cold frame or a greenhouse.

A planting strategy

Careful planning is the best way to get the most from your vegetable garden. Many gardeners don't have the space – or time – to grow everything they would like, so it's a matter of establishing your priorities before you start buying tempting packets of seeds!

The following questions will help you get a better idea of your requirements and limitations so that you can plan your crops effectively:

What do you want from your vegetable garden? You should think about the reasons you want to grow vegetables. You may be determined to grow all the vegetables necessary to supply your household needs so you can be sure of enjoying fresh, healthy, organically grown produce at all times. Or perhaps it's the fun and challenge of actually growing the crops that appeal to you most – and the harvest is a welcome bonus. Some gardeners are content to continue buying reasonably inexpensive staples such as potatoes at the shops and concentrate on growing the more unusual and exotic vegetables that are expensive or difficult to find.

How much space do you have? This is a limiting factor for many gardeners. If you want to get the most out of a small area concentrate on the crops that produce the biggest potential harvest per m (ft) of row. In the *Guide to Vegetable Yields* (left), these weights are only approximate. The actual yields vary considerably, according to your soil type, climate and expertise. However, the chart will enable you to compare the different crops. If space is limited, for example, runner

GUIDE TO VEGETABLE YIELDS

The following yields are for planting a row 1m (3ft) long.

Vegetable	Yield	Vegetable	Yield
Bean, runner	6kg (13lb)	Salad onion	340g (12oz)
Bean, French	1.5kg (3lb)	Squash	4kg (9lb)
Beetroot	2.5kg (5lb)	Spinach	1kg (2lb)
Broccoli, sprouting	1kg (2lb)	Swede	2kg (4½lb)
Brussels sprout	2kg (4½lb)	Sweet corn	2lb (1kg)
Cabbage	3.2kg (7lb)	Tomato	7lb (3.2kg)
Carrot	3.2kg (7lb)	Turnip	2kg (4½lb)
Cauliflower	2kg (4½lb)		
Celery	1.5kg (3lb)		
Chinese cabbage	1.5kg (3lb)		
Courgette	3kg (6½lb)		
Leek	3.2kg (7lb)		
Lettuce	1kg (2lb)		
Onion, bulb	2.5kg (5lb)		
Parsnip	3.2kg (7lb)		
Pea	2kg (4½lb)		
Potato	4kg (9lb)		

Runner beans will produce a much greater yield than dwarf beans.

beans will be a better option in your garden than spinach.

It's also useful to know how long a crop will occupy the ground (see *Sowing to Harvest Times,* below); you can grow a whole series of short-term crops such as lettuce and radishes in the time it takes Brussels sprouts or winter cabbage to mature.

How much time do you have? If you are trying to grow vegetables as part of a busy working and family life, you will need a different approach from someone with plenty of time on his or her hands, who sees vegetable gardening as a serious hobby. You should be sensible about the hours you can put in and if time is short, choose crops that are easy to care for instead of labour-intensive ones.

Be realistic about your capabilities. If you are new to vegetable growing, you can build your confidence with easy crops such as lettuce, carrots and beans before trying the challenge of aubergines or cauliflower.

What about the family? Consider how many people you are growing for – there's no point in producing dozens of courgettes, tomatoes or lettuce if there are just two of you to eat them. And don't forget people's likes and dislikes, too. It is surprising how many gardeners grow Brussels sprouts or parsnips, although no one in the family enjoys them.

SOWING TO HARVEST TIMES

The chart below provides the average length of time you will need to wait between sowing seeds and harvesting your vegetables.

Short-term crop	Time	Medium-term crop	Time	Long-term crop	Time
Asparagus pea	8 to 10 weeks	Aubergine	20 weeks	Artichoke, globe	8 months
Bean, French	8 to 12 weeks	Bean, broad	14 to 26 weeks	Artichoke, Jerusalem	40 to 50 weeks
Bean, runner	12 to 14 weeks	Carrot	16 to 20 weeks	Asparagus	12 months
Beetroot	12 to 16 weeks	Cabbage (summer and autumn)	20 to 26 weeks	Broccoli, sprouting	40 weeks
Broccoli	12 to 16 weeks	Cauliflower (summer)	20 to 26 weeks	Brussels sprout	28 to 36 weeks
Cabbage, Chinese (and Asian greens)	10 to 14 weeks	Celery	18 to 30 weeks	Cabbage (spring)	30 to 36 weeks
Carrot (early)	12 to 16 weeks	Herbs	12 to 18 weeks	Cauliflower (spring)	40 to 46 weeks
Corn salad	16 weeks	Pea	12 to 32 weeks	Celeriac	30 to 35 weeks
Courgette and marrow	10 to 14 weeks	Peppers	18 weeks	Garlic	24 to 30 weeks
Cucumber	12 to 14 weeks	Potato	20 to 22 weeks	Horseradish	28 to 30 weeks
Fennel	10 to 14 weeks	Potato, sweet	18 to 24 weeks	Kale	30 to 35 weeks
Kohlrabi	8 to 12 weeks	Pumpkin and winter squash	10 to 19 weeks	Leek	30 to 45 weeks
Lettuce	6 to 14 weeks	Salsify and scorzonera	25 weeks	Onion, bulb	22 to 46 weeks
Mesclun	3 to 8 weeks	Shallot	18 to 26 weeks	Parsnip	34 weeks
Okra	16 weeks	Swede	20 to 24 weeks	Rhubarb	15 months
Potato (early)	13 to 16 weeks	Tomatillo	18 weeks		
Radish	3 to 12 weeks				
Salad onion	10 weeks				
Spinach	8 to 14 weeks				
Sweet corn	14 weeks				
Swiss chard	12 weeks				
Tomato	16 weeks				
Turnip	6 to 12 weeks				

Asparagus needs to grow a considerable length of time before you can harvest the spears.

All about seeds

Seeds are plants in waiting. All they need are the right triggers such as moisture and warmth to start growing.

A seed contains an embryonic plant in a dormant state, plus a reserve of energy to tide the new seedling over until it has developed sufficiently to fend for itself. The seed will remain dormant, protected by its outer casing, until the germination process is triggered by both moisture and warmth.

Importance of size

Once you open half a dozen packets of vegetable seeds, you will appreciate how widely they vary in size and appearance, and this will dictate how you sow them. Big, chunky runner bean seeds, for example, are easy to place individually at the correct spacing. However, tiny carrot seeds must be sown in a thin stream, and the resulting seedlings need to be thinned out to the right spacing later.

Seed size also affects sowing depth. Food reserves in the seed keep the seedling going from the moment of germination until the seedling breaks through the soil surface into the light. The larger the seed, the more reserves it contains. If a tiny seed is sown too deeply, its meagre food supply will run out before it manages to fight its way up through the soil.

Buying seeds

Seeds are available from every garden centre in the spring, but a much bigger selection is available from mail-order catalogues and Internet sites that specialise in selling seeds. The seed catalogues usually appear in late autumn or early winter, and they are nearly always free and contain a wealth of information. Look for advertisements in gardening magazines; once you're on the mailing list, the catalogue will usually keep coming every year.

What's on the packet?

Many seed packets have a colour picture on the front of the variety they contain – these pictures are always useful guides. However, you shouldn't reject packets from seed companies that don't produce colour pictures. These companies often stock less common varieties, and they may also provide more seeds in a packet, so you'll get more for your money.

Along with the type of vegetable, the seed packet should also provide a variety name such as bean 'Romano', lettuce 'Buttercrunch' or beet 'Boltardy'. There are international standards for plant names to ensure that the same variety is not available

CHECKING SEEDS FOR VIABILITY

If you have seeds that are a few years old and you're not sure if they are worth sowing, you can try this test:

Place a folded paper towel in the base of a wide-mouth cup or dish and moisten it. Place 10 seeds on the moist paper towel, put the dish in a plastic bag and seal it. Place the dish in a warm, dark place: a 21°C (70°F) temperature is ideal.

Check every other day that the paper towel is still moist, and after 10 days, count the number of seeds that have germinated. If the number is five or less, throw the seeds away. If it is six or seven, sow the seeds only if they are expensive or difficult to replace. If 8 to 10 seeds germinate, they are fine.

A GUIDE TO SEEDS

As a rough guide, you can divide seeds into large, medium and small types. Remember, the sowing measurements are only a guide – no one expects you to get the depth exactly right.

Size	Small	Medium	Large	Extra large
Description	Seeds that are difficult to handle individually such as carrot, leek, lettuce and onion.	Most vegetables such as the cabbage family, tomatoes and parsnip.	Those that can be handled individually such as beans, peas, sweet corn and courgette.	The largest seeds such as runner and broad beans.
Sowing instructions	Sow small seeds 6mm (¼in) deep.	Sow medium seeds 12.5mm (½in) deep.	Sow 2.5–3.75cm (1–1½in) deep.	Plant 5cm (2in) deep in light soil.

under several different names. The accepted way of writing a variety name is to enclose it between single quotation marks; however, this is not always practised on seed packets or in catalogues.

Many varieties are labelled as 'F1 hybrids'. This means that they are the first generation of seeds from a deliberate cross between two different named varieties. F1 hybrids are often more vigorous and produce heavier, more uniform crops. These seeds are usually also more expensive than 'open-pollinated' varieties – plants whose flowers have been fertilised by those of the same variety while growing in the field.

Seed packets will usually inform you of the year the seeds were packed. There may also be instructions for sowing the seeds and growing the plants. However, these are often generalised, and you will probably need to adapt them for your particular garden, although some seed companies do provide detailed information on their packets.

The packet may sometimes say that it contains 'treated' seeds. This means that the seeds are particularly prone to pest or disease attack, so they have been pretreated with a fungicide or pesticide for improved germination. The seeds are dyed to make this treatment obvious, and you should wear gloves whenever you handle them. If you want to use only organic gardening methods you may prefer to avoid these seeds.

Storing seeds

If vegetable seeds are kept cool and dry, they can remain dormant but viable (capable of germination) for a number of years. However, for most vegetables, the fresher the seeds, the better the result. Old seeds germinate more slowly and patchily, and they may completely fail.

Store seeds in a cool, dark place, preferably in a sealed container with a sachet of silica gel to absorb any moisture. Also take note of the 'best before' date, which should be stamped on the packet. As a guide, five years is the maximum storage time for most vegetable seeds: onion, parsnip and sweet corn have much shorter lives and will remain viable for only a year or two.

Quick Tip

Shallow truth

Lettuce is unusual in that the seeds need light to be able to germinate, so it is particularly important to avoid burying lettuce seeds too deeply.

Preparing your plot for sowing

Many vegetable crops are sown outside, directly in the positions where they will mature, so it's worthwhile spending some time getting the vegetable plot into the ideal condition for the seeds.

STONY SOIL

Stony soil can be a nuisance because stones can make it difficult to draw a drill and sow evenly. However, if you rake away stones too energetically, you may bring more stones from below the surface up to the top.

Lightly rake the uppermost stones from the soil surface, gathering them with short strokes. Pick the stones off the soil and save them for another use such as making a path.

Most vegetables are sown in spring (although there are some vegetables sown outdoors in summer and autumn). For these spring-time sowings, prepare the soil in your vegetable plot in the autumn (see pages 30–43), so that winter frosts can help loosen the soil before sowing time arrives. However, you'll still have to add some final touches.

Reasons for a fine tilth

The object of working the soil for spring sowings is to break it down to a fine tilth – that means reducing the texture to small, even crumbs. If you sow seeds into rough soil full of clods, the seeds will end up at varying depths and not always with good access to soil moisture. This will lead to uneven germination – not to mention the practical difficulties of trying to draw a straight drill in lumpy soil.

Seeds are much easier to sow in a fine, crumbly soil where they can be covered to a consistent depth. The seeds will germinate much

Quick Tip

Frosty surprise

Don't be tempted to start work too early in the year. An early warm break in the weather that makes you think spring is here can be followed by a return to winter conditions. Be guided by the average dates of the last frost in your particular region.

Preparing the surface

If you dug over your plot in the autumn (see pages 40–41), you may need only a rake to prepare the surface of your soil for sowing. Alternatively, you may need to turn the plot over with a garden fork and break up large clods into a suitable size for raking. If the soil is wet wait until it has dried. When you can walk over the soil without it clinging to your boots, you know it's ready for you to start work.

1. If necessary turn over the soil and break up any large clods using a fork or a hoe; then begin levelling the soil with a rake.

more rapidly and consistently, and the seedlings will be able to push straight up through the soil crumbs instead of having to find their way round the clods.

When to prepare

If the soil is wet don't try to prepare it for sowing – it won't break down properly. You should wait until there are several fine, dry days, preferably with a brisk wind, which will help dry out the surface.

If you have a heavy soil such as clay that is always wet and difficult to work in spring, you can use cloches from late winter onwards to cover an area where you want to sow early crops. This will keep the soil dry and allow you to rake it down for sowing earlier than normal in the spring.

Assessing the soil

The amount of work needed to get soil in the right condition for sowing varies from garden to garden and from year to year. If you finish all your autumn digging on time, have a reasonably light soil and have a winter with lots of freezing and thawing to help break up the soil, you may need

only a rake to prepare the surface for sowing. If you're not so lucky you may need to turn the plot over with a garden fork to break up large clods into a suitable size for raking, but even this should be fairly light, quick work.

Creating a fine tilth

Once all the clods are broken down to pieces no bigger than the size of a fist, it's time to start raking. Raking removes stones and the remains of weeds, reduces the soil to fine crumbs and levels the surface of the plot. It is something of an art, but it's an art that's easily achieved with practise.

After levelling, it's a good idea to firm the bed, particularly if the soil is light in texture. You can do this simply by treading across the soil, using a rapid, shuffling gait that may bring a few strange looks from the neighbours but that is efficient at firming the entire soil surface evenly.

Once the plot is levelled and firmed, it's time to use a metal rake to achieve the final fine tilth. Work the rake lightly, with long, sweeping strokes. Break up any stubborn remaining clods with a sharp blow from the back of the rake.

USING RAKES

Ideally you should have two rakes: a wide, wooden one for levelling (but these are hard to find) and a smaller, metal one for creating a tilth and covering seeds. The secret of raking soil to a level is to handle the rake lightly. Let the rake almost float over the soil as you pull and push it in sweeping strokes while holding it at a low angle to the soil surface. Don't be tempted to dig the rake in or push down on it while raking – you'll only make troughs and hills that will be difficult to level out. Rake in several different directions for a good finish.

2 As you level the soil, you can break up any large clods of soil into tiny pieces with the back of your rake, using a good sharp wallop.

3 After levelling the soil, firm it by treading across the plot. However, for heavy soil firm lightly with the palm of your hands instead.

4 Create the final fine tilth with a rake, using long, sweeping strokes and applying light pressure until all the soil is ready for sowing.

Sowing seeds outdoors

Many vegetables are sown directly outdoors, where they will grow and can be harvested. Sowing in rows is the most common method, but there are other ways that can sometimes work better.

The usual way to sow seeds is in parallel rows across the vegetable garden. Mark out the position of the first row with a garden line – a piece of twine stretched taut between two sticks. For a shorter row you can use a length of wood as a guide.

Making a drill

Use the corner of a draw hoe to pull out a drill. To make sure the row is straight, place one foot on the line to hold it in the correct position as you make the drill. (For the correct depth of the drill see pages 50–51.)

Using the corner of a draw hoe, pull out a shallow drill in the soil along a taut garden line. Try to keep the drill an even depth.

If the soil is dry water the base of the drill before sowing. Take care to use a gentle stream of water. You can use a light dribble from a hose or create a gentle stream by putting your thumb partially over the spout of a watering can.

Sowing seeds in a drill

Try to space the seeds evenly as you sow them along the drill. You can tip some seeds out into the palm of one hand and take pinches of them to sprinkle along the row, or you might prefer to tap them carefully straight

Sow the seeds evenly along the length of the drill, whether you tap them straight out of the packet or use another method.

out of the packet. (Creasing the edge of the packet to form a funnel will give you more control over the flow of seeds.) Some people prefer handheld seed sowers, which can be bought inexpensively from garden centres or mail-order catalogues.

Use whatever method you feel most comfortable with, as long as you're able to sow the seeds thinly and evenly. Small seeds such as carrots and lettuce are usually sown along the whole length of the row – and the seedlings are then thinned out to the correct spacing later.

Larger seeds are easier to handle, so you can sow them at their final spacing from the beginning – this is known as sowing at stations, and it uses fewer seeds. You can use this technique for crops such as French beans, parsnips and beets. To allow for germination failures sow three seeds at each station – weed out the surplus seedlings later.

Another method is to sow seeds at half their final spacing – for example, if you are growing beans 15cm (6in) apart, you can sow the seeds 8cm (3in) apart, then remove the surplus seedlings later. These extra seedlings are often useful for

To make a double row, use the full width of the blade of a draw hoe to make a wide drill in the soil. Alternatively, you can use a spade to lift out the soil.

Sow the seeds in two rows along each side of the drill. Alternatively, you can broadcast, or scatter, the seeds over the base of the drill.

To make a shallow drill for small seeds, lay a rake along the soil where you want your row to grow. The handle of the rake will leave a depression that you can use as a drill.

transplanting to fill up any gaps in the rest of the row.

Once the seeds are sown, cover them with soil as soon as each row is completed. Use a metal rake to pull the soil back to fill the drill evenly, being careful not to disturb the seeds. Finally, firm the soil, either by walking along the drill or tamping it down with the back of the rake. Label the row with the variety and the date of sowing, and move the garden line into position for the next row.

Other ways of sowing

Sowing in drills across the vegetable garden is convenient, but there are other methods that can work better.

Short rows. It is often impractical to harvest and use a whole, long row of a single crop such as lettuce before it goes to seed: in these cases, it can be more sensible to sow short rows. You should consider splitting a row into three sections and sowing them with different vegetables – for example, one-third with lettuce, one-third with radish and one-third with spring onions.

Wide rows. Peas are usually sown in drills about 15–20cm (6–8in) wide. Use a garden line or length of wood to guide a draw hoe or spade to make the drill. You can broadcast the peas over the base of the drill or sow them in two rows (see above). You can also use these wide rows for patches of lettuce and mesclun crops.

Broadcast. Instead of sowing seeds in drills, you can broadcast them by scattering the seeds over an area of soil in the same way you would sow a lawn. Some crops such as lettuce are sown with this technique in little square beds, but it makes controlling weeds difficult. As an alternative to broadcasting, sow seeds in closely spaced, short rows within the beds. It is then easy to distinguish between crop seedlings and weed seedlings when they emerge, and you can use the hoe or hand weed until the crop plants grow large enough to cover the whole bed.

Individual spacing. You can sow large seeds – runner beans, for example – by simply pushing them into the soil instead of drawing a drill, which can save time. You can use a dibber to make the hole for the seeds, but first mark the depth on the dibber so that you can ensure you sow the seeds at the correct depth.

Mounds. Squashes do well when they are sown on a little hill of soil. The necks of the plants are prone to rot if they are surrounded by moisture, and sowing on a hill ensures the water can drain away from the stems. Draw the soil up into a mound, and sow three seeds into the top. Make a moatlike channel circling around the base of the mound, which will divert water to the roots, where it will be needed.

When mounding seeds, draw the soil up into a mound about 10cm (4in) high and 20cm (8in) across; then sow three seeds into the top of the mound.

Special sowing techniques

Seeds usually germinate easily, but there are times when a little extra help is required. There are several ways of making sure you get the best results from your sowings.

For seeds that are slow or difficult to germinate try a technique known as fluid sowing. It is also a good technique if you are sowing early in the spring, when weather and soil conditions are unpredictable.

The technique involves first pre-germinating the seeds in a warm place indoors and then mixing them with a carrier gel before 'sowing' them in the garden. Because germination has already taken place, the seeds grow quickly, even if in cold soil. Fluid sowing is useful for slow-germinating seeds such as parsley, parsnips and celery and in short-season areas for carrots and other root crops, lettuce and cabbages.

Steps to fluid sowing

To prepare the seeds first line the inside of a plastic sandwich container with paper towel. Moisten the paper towel thoroughly before scattering the seeds thinly over it. Cover the container and keep it at 21°C (70°F). Check the container every couple of days; as soon as most of the seeds show signs of germination, it is time to sow them. The emerging roots should be only just visible (you will need a magnifying glass for small seeds); if they are allowed to develop too far the process will fail.

Make a gel to carry the seeds. Use a wallpaper paste (choose a fungicide-free one) diluted 50 per cent with water, or mix 30–45ml (2–3tbsp) of cornflour with 575ml (1pt) of boiling water and allow it to cool. Make the gel thick enough so the seeds remain suspended and don't sink.

Wash the pre-germinated seeds off the paper towel into a sieve with a gentle stream of water and then stir them into the gel with your fingers until they are well distributed. Put the gel into a plastic bag, snip off one corner and squeeze the gel into an already prepared, moistened drill. Cover the seeds as usual.

Pelleted seeds

Seeds that are individually coated with a clay compound that sets hard are

Stale seedbed

This technique helps to prevent annual weeds from swamping your seedlings. Allow weed seeds buried in the top of the soil to germinate, then destroy them before planting vegetable seeds. When you destroy the weeds, be careful to do so in a way that does not disturb the soil any further.

1 Prepare the seedbed about two to three weeks before you want to sow your vegetables, then wait.

2 Within a short time there will be a flush of weeds from the seeds that have been brought close to the surface by your cultivation.

To use a seed tape cut it to the appropriate length, place it at the bottom of a drill and cover it with soil.

known as pelleted seeds. The hard coating makes the seeds larger and evenly rounded, so they are easier to handle and space accurately. Some seed coatings include nutrients or fungicides. Pelleted seeds do not necessarily germinate more quickly – in fact, they may germinate more slowly. Keep the soil moist after sowing to allow the clay coat to break down.

Seed tapes

Small seeds are sometimes glued onto long, thin strips of paper at the correct spacing – these are called seed tapes. Simply lay a length of tape along the base of a drill and cover it with soil. The paper will rot away, and the seedlings will emerge perfectly spaced and in nice straight rows.

You can make your own seed tape using strips of 2.5cm (1in)-wide plain paper such as photocopy paper or newspaper. Make a glue by mixing together flour and water until the mixture is the consistency of gravy. Use a small artist's paintbrush to dab a dot of glue at regular intervals along the paper at the appropriate spacing for the seeds: gently place the seeds on the glue. Allow the glue to dry.

Catch crops

Some crops are slow to germinate and develop. To make maximum use of space in your vegetable garden you can plant quick-growing 'catch crops' in between them. You'll harvest the quicker-growing crop before it starts to compete with the slower one.

A classic combination is parsnips and radishes. Parsnips can take 28 days to germinate, whereas radishes need less than a week. Sow the parsnips at appropriately spaced stations (see pages 54–55) and sprinkle radish seeds in a drill in between each station. Cover the seeds as usual. You will be able to start eating the radishes before they interfere with the parsnip seedlings. The radishes will also help prevent a cap, or crust, from forming on the soil, which allows the germinating parsnips to push through more easily.

Other slow-germinating crops include beets, Swiss chard, endive, leeks, onions and parsley. For catch crops try spinach and lettuce. You can also try successional cropping (see page 18).

HOT WEATHER TIPS

Most seeds need warmth to germinate. However, for many vegetables, germination will be hampered if temperatures reach above 30°C (86°F). Lettuce seeds are especially vulnerable. They become dormant at soil temperatures above 25°C (78°F).

The timing of sowing is essential; for example, sow lettuce seeds in the early afternoon during hot spells, so that the critical germination process is most likely to take place during the coolness of night time. You should water the bottom of the seed drills immediately before sowing to keep the temperature down.

In countries with consistently high temperatures the problem is often resolved by pre-germinating the seeds under controlled, cooler conditions indoors and then using the fluid-sowing technique or transplanting the seedlings (see pages 68–69).

3 Careful hoeing, using a sharp blade that slices off the weeds at the soil surface, will kill the weeds, or use a flame gun or herbicides.

4 As soon as the weeds are gone, you can sow the vegetable seeds with as little soil disturbance as possible.

Quick Tip

Marker crops

The catch-crop technique is useful as a marker to show where a slow-germinating row has been sown. You'll appreciate this marker when you need to weed between the rows before the slow-growing seedlings appear.

57

Care after sowing

A newly emerged seedling is very vulnerable, but a little special care will ensure that it soon develops into a strong and healthy young plant.

During the first stage of the germination process, the seed absorbs water from the surrounding soil, which softens the seed coat so that the young root can emerge. Part of the reason for breaking the soil down into fine crumbs is to ensure that the seed will be in contact with sufficient soil moisture for this process to happen. The process can take from one or two days to several weeks, depending on the type of seed.

The emerging seed

Once the seed absorbs enough water, and if the soil temperature is suitable, an embryonic root known as the radicle will grow. No matter which way the seed is positioned, the radicle will grow downwards, guided by a positive response to gravity. Fine root hairs develop on the rapidly growng root, and these absorb water and minerals from the soil. The root helps to anchor the plant in the ground.

Shortly after root growth begins, the seed's shoot starts to develop. The tip of the shoot – the plumule – is held between two bulky seed leaves, or cotyledons, which help to protect the plumule as it pushes through the soil. The shoot responds to gravity, but

with a negative response, growing in the opposite direction to gravity.

While the seedling is growing up through the soil, it relies on the food stored in the seed leaves. The leaves start to photosynthesise to make energy from sunlight only when the seedling breaks through the soil surface. Bury a seed too deeply, and its food supply may run out before the seedling reaches the surface.

Seedlings can push past small obstacles in the soil. However, if they hit a larger obstacle such as a stone, they have to find a way round it before they can continue towards the surface. A fine, light, crumbly soil, free from stones and other debris, makes life easier for the seedlings, helping them to reach daylight quickly.

Providing the right conditions

Make sure you keep the soil moist, but not flooded, at all times after sowing. Watering the drill before sowing is the best way to supply moisture, but if conditions are extremely dry in the following days, additional watering may be necessary before the seedlings emerge.

Be sure to water using a watering can with a rose or a sprinkler to give a fine spray; a jet of water is likely to wash the seeds out of the soil. Heavy droplets can also cause the surface layer of soil to form a hard cap, or crust, as

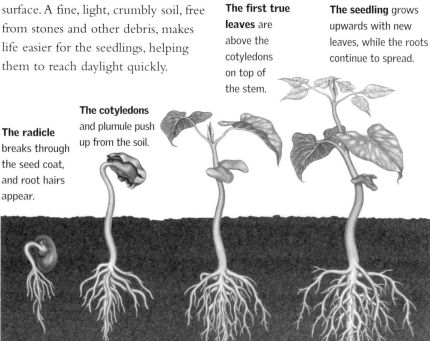

The first true leaves are above the cotyledons on top of the stem.

The seedling grows upwards with new leaves, while the roots continue to spread.

The cotyledons and plumule push up from the soil.

The radicle breaks through the seed coat, and root hairs appear.

Thinning

Seedlings will need thinning once they are large enough to handle easily but before they start to crowd one another. Select the strongest seedlings to leave in place at the appropriate spacing, and carefully remove all the others.

1 If your plants are not growing closely together, you can slice off the extra seedlings with a sharp hoe blade.

2 To remove nearby seedlings hold the remaining plant with a finger at each side; push down as you tug away the others.

3 You can use the extra thinnings by carefully planting them in a less crowded area in the plot. You should hold them by their leaves.

4 After thinning, water the seedlings using a watering can with a fine rose or a fine spray from a hose.

it dries, which the seedlings might not be able to penetrate. Capping is a particular problem on fine, silty or clay soil. Covering moist soil with finely shredded bark, a single sheet of wet newspaper or horticultural fleece will help keep the moisture in and prevent

a cap from forming. Make sure you remove the paper or fleece once the seedlings emerge, before it restricts their growth.

Soil temperature is more difficult to control than moisture, so getting the timing of sowing right is the

most important factor. If a sudden, unexpected cold spell arrives after sowing, you can use horticular fleece, cloches or plastic tunnels to protect the seedbed from the worst of the weather.

After germination, continue to keep the soil moist, but make sure you still use the fine spray to avoid damaging the young plants.

Thinning

Seeds are sown relatively thickly to allow for inevitable germination failures. Once the seedlings are through the soil, they will grow quickly and you will soon find them competing for space. At this point, the young plants usually require thinning to the recommended spacing.

It is often a good idea to carry out thinning in two stages. If the final spacing required is 15cm (6in), thin the seedlings first to 8cm (3in) apart, then to their final spacing a few weeks later. This helps to avoid gaps in the row where selected seedlings have died.

PEST CONTROL

Some pests are attracted to plants by the scent produced by their bruised foliage – this is how the carrot fly, for example, finds its targets. Thinning out seedlings will release a strong scent, so you should do your thinning shortly before dusk, giving the adult flies minimal time to track down the source.

You can help disguise the scent by growing a strong-smelling herb such as rue or chamomile near your plants. However, don't grow parsley, which is related to carrots and is also attractive to carrot flies.

A guide to sowing seeds

This chart is a quick at-a-glance guide to basic sowing information. For detailed information see the full entries for each vegetable.

Vegetable	When to sow	Spacing (between rows)	Spacing (within rows)	Comments
Beetroot pages 194–95	Early to late spring; again in midsummer	45cm (18in)	10–15cm (4–6in)	Intensive spacing: sow thinly over a 30–45cm (15–18in)-wide bed.
Broccoli rabe page 175	Early to mid-spring	45cm (18in)	15cm (6in)	Can broadcast seeds in wide rows; thin to 7.5cm (3in) for intensive spacing.
Broad beans pages 148–49	After all danger of frost is past	45–75cm (18–30in)	15cm (6in)	Intensive spacing: 15cm (6in) apart on centre.
Carrots pages 192–93	Early spring to late summer	15–30cm (6–12in)	5–10cm (2–4in)	Sow seeds every 3 weeks if you want a succession crop.
Celeriac page 201	Early spring	60cm (24in)	20–25cm (8–10in)	Intensive spacing: 30cm (12in) apart on centre.
Chicory page 134	Early to mid-spring; again in midsummer	45–60cm (18–24in); for grumolo 30cm (12in)	25–30cm (10–12in); for grumolo 15–20cm (6–8in)	In hot-summer areas sow to avoid leaves maturing in peak heat.

Vegetable	When to sow	Spacing (between rows)	Spacing (within rows)	Comments
Climbing beans pages 150–53	After all danger of frost is past	Double rows: 60cm (2ft) apart, 1.5m (5ft) between rows	15–23cm (6–9in)	Or sow seeds at the base of stakes or tepee poles; thin plants.
Courgettes and marrows pages 226–27	Early summer, after all danger of frost is past	60–90cm (24–36in)	60–90cm (24–36in)	In cold areas raise seeds under cover.
Kohlrabi page 179	Mid-spring to late summer	30–90cm (12–36in)	15cm (6in)	Sow seeds every 2 weeks for a succession crop.
Lettuce pages 128–31	Early spring until autumn	45–60cm (18–24in)	15–30cm (6–12in)	Try to time the sowing to avoid the hottest periods of the summer.
Melons pages 234–37	After all danger of frost is past	1.2–1.8m (4–6ft); for watermelon, 1.5–2.1m (5–7ft)	1.2–1.8m (4–6ft); for watermelon, 1.5–2.1m (5–7ft)	Raise seeds in a heated greenhouse or propagator.
Mesclun pages 136–37	Early spring until autumn	7.5–15cm (3–6in)	Sow lightly	Alternatively, you can broadcast seeds lightly over a wide row.
Okra pages 220–21	Early to mid-spring	45–90cm (18–36in)	30–60cm (12–24in)	Raise seeds in a heated greenhouse or propagator.
Onions pages 158–61	Early to mid-spring or autumn	30–45cm (12–18in)	10–15cm (4–6in)	For salad onions sow thinly and harvest without thinning.
Parsnips page 197	Early spring	45–60cm (18–24in)	10–15cm (4–6in)	Seeds are slow to germinate.

(Continued)

Vegetable	When to sow	Spacing (between rows)	Spacing (within rows)	Comments
Peas pages 144–47	Early spring to mid-summer	60cm (24in)	10–15cm (4–6in)	Choose different varieties to harvest over a longer period.
Pumpkins and winter squash pages 228–33	Early summer, after all danger of frost is past	1.50–1.8m (5–6ft)	1.8m (6ft); compact varieties, 0.6–1.2m (2–4ft)	Raise seeds under cover.
Radishes page 196	Early spring through to mid-summer	15cm (6in)	5–10cm (2–4in)	You can sow seeds in succession throughout the season.
Rocket page 132	Early to mid-spring; again in late summer	15cm (6in)	2.5–15cm (1–6in)	Close spacing provides baby leaves for harvesting.
Salsify and scorzonera page 202	Early spring	38–45cm (15–18in)	10–15cm (4–6in)	Keep the grassy seedlings weed-free.
Spinach pages 138–39	Early spring; again in mid- to late summer	45cm (18in)	10–15cm (4–6in)	You can sow seeds later to overwinter for a spring harvest.
Sweet corn pages 240–43	After danger of last spring frost is past	90cm (36in)	7.5–10cm (3–4in)	Plant in blocks of at least 4 rows to ensure pollination.
Swiss chard pages 140–41	Early spring and again in mid- to late summer	30–60cm (12–24in)	15–30cm (6–12in)	Less likely to bolt than spinach during hot weather.
Turnips pages 198–99	Early spring and again in mid-summer to autumn	45cm (18in)	2.5–15cm (1–6in)	Space close to harvest greens; use wider spacings for roots.

Starting transplants

While many vegetable crops are left to mature where they are sown, others are moved to new positions as young plants. There are several reasons why this may be a good idea – and there are some occasions when it is a bad one.

PROPAGATORS

Heated propagators are special units for raising seeds and cuttings; they supply a gentle warmth to the sowing compost, which helps ensure quick, even germination and rooting. An electric cable runs through the base of the propagator and can be thermostatically controlled to achieve the ideal level of heat. Seed trays filled with compost and sown in the traditional way are placed on top of the heated base.

Some propagators are supplied with their own covers to keep humidity levels high; if not you should fit each tray with its own individual plastic propagator top.

Starting plants off in one spot and moving them to another saves wasting space in the vegetable garden. Brussels sprouts, for example, need plenty of space as they mature, but as seedlings and young plants, they are happy growing close together. Starting them in a separate seedbed allows the area earmarked for their final positions to be used for a fast-growing crop while the sprouts are still in their early stages. (For more information about sowing in seedbeds see pages 66–67.)

Starting under cover

Sometimes seeds are sown indoors, in a heated propagator or greenhouse, or under cover outdoors earlier than they can be sown outside, and then transplanted to their final growing position. This gives the plants a good start, and in cooler areas it enables

You can sow large seeds in individual compartments in a seed tray filled with a sterile sowing compost.

Growing seedlings don't need such a humid atmosphere – too much humidity encourages fungus diseases such as damping-off.

When pricking out, handle the seedlings by their seed leaves (the first, expendable pair of leaves that open). Never touch the stems.

earlier harvesting than would otherwise be possible. Starting seeds under cover is also good for seeds that are difficult to germinate such as celery and for types that are difficult to find or are expensive. When sown in containers under cover, it is easier to provide them with the best conditions for germination than when sown outside.

Sowing in containers

You can sow seeds for transplanting in trays or pots, according to the type of plant and the size of seeds. Use a sterile sowing compost to avoid problems with weeds and soil-borne pests and diseases often found in garden soil. Fill the seed tray or pot evenly, pushing the compost out to the corners of the tray, and level it off and firm it with a presser. Water the compost, using a fine rose on the watering can; then allow it to drain for an hour or so before sowing.

Space large seeds by hand: shake out smaller seeds thinly and evenly over the surface of the compost. Cover the seeds with more sowing compost to the recommended depth; you can shake the compost through a small garden sieve for an even distribution. Cover the containers with plastic propagator tops, a sheet of glass or an upturned seed tray to keep in the moisture and warmth. Add a sheet of newspaper on top of a transparent cover.

Keep the seeds in an even warmth (check the packets for the suggested germination temperature) and keep the compost just moist. Once the first seedlings appear, remove the newspaper or upturned tray to allow light to reach the plants; when the first seedlings reach the glass cover remove that too. Propagator tops have extra headroom, so they can be left on the trays or pots for longer, but when all the seedlings appear open the ventilators or prop the cover up for good air circulation. When watering is necessary use a fine rose to avoid damage and keep the compost moist, never wet.

Pricking out

If the seeds were well spaced or individually sown, the young plants may be able to remain in the same containers until it is time to plant them in their final positions. However, most seedlings will need replanting to give them more room to develop, and this is known as pricking out. They can be spaced farther apart in another tray or moved to individual pots.

Prick out seedlings as soon as they are large enough to handle. Use a dibber to lever the roots carefully out of the compost: you may need to lever up a small clump of seedlings and gently untangle the roots. Make a hole with the dibber in the new container of sowing compost; then lower the seedling into it, making sure the roots make contact with the base of the hole and are not dangling in midair. Firm the seedling in gently.

When the container is planted, water it, using a fine rose, and put it in a well-shaded place. The seedlings often droop after pricking out, but after a few hours they should recover and you can bring them into the light.

TRANSPLANTING PROBLEMS

Transplanting often involves damage to the roots and gives the plants a slight 'check' to their growth. For this reason it is not a good idea to transplant root crops such as parsnips, salsify, scorzonera and carrots, because any damage to the young root will cause it to be misshapen at maturity.

Root disturbance can also cause susceptible crops to bolt, or run to seed, prematurely – Florence fennel, spinach, lettuce and Chinese cabbage are often affected in this way.

However, it is still possible to transplant these difficult plants. You can sow individual seeds in soil blocks or in fibre pots, which can be planted in their entirety to avoid root disturbance.

Starting transplants in seedbeds

You can sow vegetables that don't need the extra protection of a greenhouse in an outdoor seedbed, then transplant them to their final positions at a later date.

BEATING THE COLD

In cold areas cover the seedbed with cloches or similar devices in late winter. This will keep off the rain and snow and allow the soil to dry out and warm up more quickly, so it can be prepared for sowing earlier in the following spring. It is also possible to make a seedbed within a frame, sowing directly into the soil. This will give the seedlings maximum protection in the early stages of growth, when they are at their most vulnerable. You should harden off seedlings raised in a frame before transplanting them (see pages 68–69).

There are two main vegetable candidates for sowing in a seedbed: the members of the brassica, or cabbage, family – particularly those that mature in the winter and spring – and leeks. Sowing them in seedbeds avoids wasting space in the garden. (For vegetables that shouldn't be transplanted see page 65.)

Determining the size of the bed

The size of your seedbed will depend on the number of plants you intend to grow. As a rough guide, most cabbage-family plants will require a final spacing of about 60cm (24in) apart. You can thin seedlings in the seedbed to 5cm (2in) apart and grow them in rows 15cm (6in) apart. This means that a seedbed row 60cm (24in) long should provide enough young plants for a crop row that is 7m (24ft) long.

Preparing the soil

You should prepare the soil as you would for sowing into the vegetable garden (see pages 52–53). An advantage of a seedbed is that it

Making a seedbed

Ideally, choose a site where the seedbed will be in a sheltered position. The soil should be fertile and easily worked so that you can prepare a fine tilth.

1 To mark out the area for your seedbed, you can use twine held in place by stakes at each corner.

is a small area, which is much easier to get into an ideal condition for raising seedlings. Add plenty of well-rotted compost or similar organic material in the autumn, and rake the soil to a fine tilth in early spring. Cabbage-family plants prefer a firm soil, so remember to tamp the seedbed area thoroughly.

Sowing the seeds

Because the seedbed is usually small, it is not normally necessary to use a line for sowing. Instead, press the handle of a hoe or rake into the soil to make a drill. On heavy soil, this may compress the soil too much; instead, lay a tool handle on the ground as the guide and pull out the drill with a hoe in the usual way.

Sow the seeds thinly along the drills. Because the seedlings will be transplanted, some root damage is bound to occur, but thin sowing will help prevent a tangle of roots and keep the damage to a minimum.

When sowing several different types of cabbage-family plants, you should label each drill as soon as it is sown. Otherwise you'll find that trying to distinguish between rows of almost identical-looking cabbage, cauliflower and Brussels sprout seedlings is not easy.

Caring for the seedlings

Cabbage-family plants will usually germinate within 7 to 14 days; leeks take a little longer at 21 to 25 days. Once the seedlings emerge, keep the soil moist by watering through a fine rose. The object is to keep the young plants growing without any interruption to their growth.

When cabbage-family seedlings are large enough to handle, thin them to 3–5cm (1–2in) apart. Slender leek seedlings do not usually need thinning as long as they have been sown reasonably thinly.

Cabbage-family plants will be ready for transplanting after five to seven weeks, when the plants are about 10–15cm (4–6in) high. Try not to delay any longer; the larger the plants, the more of a growth check they will receive. You can transplant leeks when they grow to about 15–20cm (6–8in) tall – usually about 8 to 10 weeks after sowing – when their stems are about half the thickness of a pencil.

BUYING TRANSPLANTS

If you don't have the space or time to raise your own plants from seeds, you can buy young plants for transplanting from garden centres and mail-order suppliers. They are available either as bare-root plants that have been lifted from the open soil or plug plants, or (more expensively) as plants growing in containers of various sizes.

Make sure that bare-root plants look fresh and healthy, and that their roots have been carefully wrapped to protect them from drying out while you bring them home. As soon as you get home dunk them in a bucket of water and plant them without delay.

When buying cabbage-family seedlings, be aware that you can import incurable club-root disease into your garden. If possible always raise your own seedlings. If you buy transplants ask your supplier if they have been raised in sterile compost. If not you shouldn't buy them.

2 After preparing the soil, lay the handle of a garden rake or fork on the ground and step on it to form the drills.

3 Sow the seeds thinly along each drill. Remember to label each drill so you can identify the young seedlings.

4 Cover the seedlings with a thin layer of soil: without pushing it down, use a rake to move the soil at right angles to the drill.

Planting out transplants

It's important to plant out young vegetables as soon as they are ready – a delay could reduce both the quality and quantity of the harvest. You also need to take steps to reduce the stress on transplants as much as possible.

If you delay the transplant of cabbage-family plants for only two or three weeks, you will reduce both the yield and the quality of the crop, because of the greater stress suffered by larger transplants. (To determine when they are ready for transplanting, see pages 66–67.) This is also true for other vegetables that have been grown under cover, although some vegetables such as leeks are less sensitive to transplanting.

Hardening off

If young plants have been raised under cover indoors, in a greenhouse or in a frame, they must be hardened off – gradually acclimatised to the cooler temperatures in the open garden – before they will be ready for planting

in their final positions. Moving them straight from a warm environment to one that is several degrees colder will seriously affect their growth, sometimes to such an extent that you will lose any advantage of an early start.

Hardening off should take about two weeks. First increase the amount of ventilation the vegetables receive under cover; then move them to a sheltered position outside during the day, bringing them under cover again in the evening. After a few days, you can leave the plants in a sheltered spot outside all day and night; finally, move the plants from the shelter to an open position just before planting.

A frame is a useful adjunct to a heated greenhouse. Young plants can

start their hardening-off process in the closed frame, with more ventilation given day by day until the frame lights are left open entirely.

Choosing the day

The ideal weather for transplanting is overcast and still; a hot, sunny, breezy day will make it difficult for plants to recover from the inevitable wilting when they are newly planted. Wait a few days for better conditions, if possible, or tackle the job in the evening when it is cooler.

Preparation for planting

You should thoroughly prepare the designated area for planting. Although the soil does not have to be as fine as the tilth needed for sowing seeds, it should be raked down well and the soil should be crumbly to allow the plants to grow quickly.

A few days before transplanting, water the young plants thoroughly, ensuring the water penetrates to the plants' full rooting depth. This will help to reduce root damage when lifting the plants.

Before lifting the plants or knocking them out of their pots, make sure you have everything ready for planting –

Planting out

Before starting dig a hole the appropriate size for each vegetable plant with a trowel. Once a row has been completely planted, water the row, providing enough water to penetrate the whole rooting area.

1 Loosen the soil in the pot or tray by tapping the container. Tip up the container to help ease the plant out, and gently handle the plant by the soil ball – avoid holding it by the stem.

2 Carefully lower the plant into the hole. Make sure the roots are touching the base of the hole.

3 Fill in the hole with good-quality soil, and firm in the soil with the heel of your hand or by treading. Test that the plants are firm enough by tugging gently at a leaf – there should be no movement of the plant in the soil.

slide out with minimum disturbance to the roots.

If young plants have been raised in trays, loosen the compost by shaking the tray firmly from side to side and tapping the base on a hard surface. Then prise up a section of the compost and carefully separate the plants, teasing the roots apart.

Preparing seedbed transplants

Try to minimise the time the seedlings are out of the soil. If you are lifting young plants from a seedbed, don't lift all the seedlings at once. Take only as many as you can plant and water within 20 minutes or so, then return for another batch.

To lift the plants push a fork deeply under the row of transplants and lever them up carefully. When transplanting cabbage-family plants you should handle them by their leaves to separate the individual plants, teasing the roots apart while trying to retain as much of the soil clinging to the roots as you can. Lay the plants in a tray and cover them with damp sacking or newspaper until you can plant them in their new positions.

> **CARING FOR TRANSPLANTS**
>
> The transplants will flag at first, but they will soon recover if they receive enough water. If the transplanting day is sunny lay a horticultural fleece or single sheets of newspaper over the top of the plants to shade them until the evening. To get the plants off to the best possible start, give them an application of a balanced liquid fertiliser immediately after planting. Continue to water as necessary over the following days.

for example, put a straight line in position ready for the first row.

Preparing potted transplants

If a vegetable plant has been raised in an individual pot you should remove it from its container by turning the pot upside down, then, with the plant stem between your fore and second fingers, rap the top edge of the pot firmly on a hard surface. This should enable the root ball of the plant to

69

A guide to transplanting

The following pages provide a quick reference on information for transplanting. For more detailed information see the full entries for each vegetable.

Vegetable	When to sow	When to transplant	Spacing (between rows)	Spacing (within rows)	Comments
Aubergines pages 218–19	Early to mid-spring under cover	Early to mid-summer, after all danger of frost is past	45–60cm (18–24in)	45–60cm (18–24in)	Aubergines do best grown to maturity in a greenhouse.
Broccoli page 174	Early spring through to mid-summer	Mid-spring and late summer	60cm (24in)	45cm (18in)	The sowing and cropping time will vary according to the varieties you choose.
Brussels sprouts pages 172–73	Early to mid-summer	Mid- to late summer	45cm (18in); for tall varieties, 60cm (24in)	45cm (18in); for tall varieties, 60cm (24in)	You can sow a range of varieties to harvest Brussels sprouts over a longer period.
Broad beans pages 148–49	Mid- to late spring under cover	Early summer, after all danger of frost is past	45–75cm (18–30in)	15cm (6in)	You can also sow broad beans in autumn if you live in a mild area.
Cabbage pages 170–71	Early spring to mid-summer	Mid-spring to late summer	45cm (18in); for small heads, 30cm (12in)	45cm (18in); for small heads, 30cm (12in)	With the right varieties, you can grow cabbages all year round.
Cauliflower pages 176–77	Early spring to early summer	Mid-spring to midsummer	60–90cm (24–36in); intensive spacing, 45cm (18in)	38–60cm (15–24in); intensive spacing, 45cm (18in)	Sowing and cropping times vary according to variety.

Vegetable	When to sow	When to transplant	Spacing (between rows)	Spacing (within rows)	Comments
Celeriac page 201	Early spring	Mid- to late spring	60cm (24in)	20–25cm (8–10in)	You can also plant celeriac 30cm (12in) apart on centre.
Celery page 200	Late winter to early spring	Mid- to late spring	60cm (24in)	23–30cm (9–12in)	You can also consider planting celery about 30cm (12in) apart on centre.
Climbing beans pages 150–53	Mid- to late spring under cover	Late spring to early summer, when all danger of frost is past	Double rows: 0.6m (2ft) apart, with 1.5m (5ft) between rows	15–23cm (6–9in)	Sowing climbing beans under cover will give you a longer cropping season.
Courgettes and marrow pages 226–27	Mid-spring under cover	After all danger of frost is past	60–90cm (24–36in)	60–90cm (24–36in)	To establish transplants cover with a tunnel or fleece.
Cucumbers pages 224–25	Early to mid-spring under cover	After danger of frost is past; in greenhouse, mid- to late spring	30cm (12in)	30cm (12in)	Or sow outdoors in mounds 90–120cm (3–4ft) apart.
Florence fennel page 203	In early spring under cover	Mid-spring	25–30cm (10–12in)	25–30cm (10–12in)	Sow varieties that are bolt resistant in modules or peat pots to minimise root disturbance.

(Continued)

Vegetable	When to sow	When to transplant	Spacing (between rows)	Spacing (within rows)	Comments
Kale page 178	Mid-spring to midsummer	Early to late summer	45cm (18in)	30–45cm (12–18in)	Firm the soil thoroughly on transplanting and water until established.
Kohlrabi page 179	Early to mid-spring	Mid- to late spring	30–90cm (12–36in)	15cm (6in)	Sow in modules to protect roots; transplant eary to avoid bolting.
Leeks pages 164–65	Late winter to early spring	Late spring to early summer	30–45 cm (12–18in)	10–15cm (4–6in)	Can sow indoors 10–12 weeks before outdoor planting date.
Lettuce pages 128–31	Late winter to early spring under cover	Mid-spring	45–60cm (18–24in)	15–30cm (6–12in)	When transplanting, handle the plants carefully to minimise root disturbance.
Melons pages 234–37	Mid-spring under cover	Late spring to early summer, after all danger of frost is past	1.2–1.8m (4–6ft)	1.2–1.8m (4–6ft)	Choose varieties suitable for cool climates.
Okra pages 220–21	Early to mid-spring under cover	Early to mid-summer, after all risk of frost is past	45–90cm (18–36in)	30–60cm (12–24in)	Use a black plastic mulch to warm the soil planting; handle transplants carefully to protect roots.

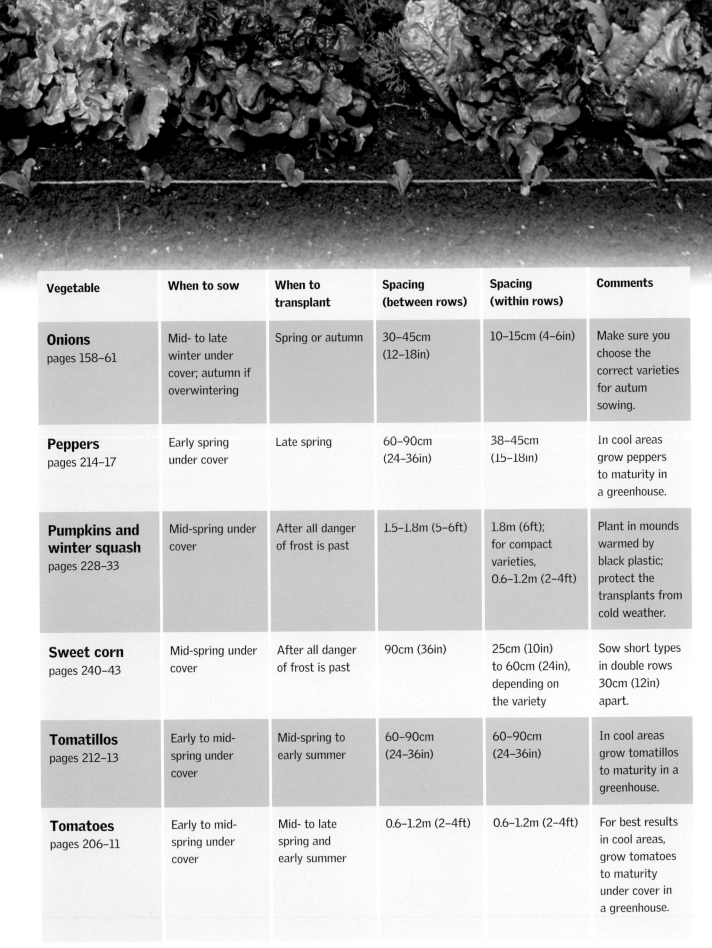

Vegetable	When to sow	When to transplant	Spacing (between rows)	Spacing (within rows)	Comments
Onions pages 158–61	Mid- to late winter under cover; autumn if overwintering	Spring or autumn	30–45cm (12–18in)	10–15cm (4–6in)	Make sure you choose the correct varieties for autum sowing.
Peppers pages 214–17	Early spring under cover	Late spring	60–90cm (24–36in)	38–45cm (15–18in)	In cool areas grow peppers to maturity in a greenhouse.
Pumpkins and winter squash pages 228–33	Mid-spring under cover	After all danger of frost is past	1.5–1.8m (5–6ft)	1.8m (6ft); for compact varieties, 0.6–1.2m (2–4ft)	Plant in mounds warmed by black plastic; protect the transplants from cold weather.
Sweet corn pages 240–43	Mid-spring under cover	After all danger of frost is past	90cm (36in)	25cm (10in) to 60cm (24in), depending on the variety	Sow short types in double rows 30cm (12in) apart.
Tomatillos pages 212–13	Early to mid-spring under cover	Mid-spring to early summer	60–90cm (24–36in)	60–90cm (24–36in)	In cool areas grow tomatillos to maturity in a greenhouse.
Tomatoes pages 206–11	Early to mid-spring under cover	Mid- to late spring and early summer	0.6–1.2m (2–4ft)	0.6–1.2m (2–4ft)	For best results in cool areas, grow tomatoes to maturity under cover in a greenhouse.

Extending the growing season

If the growing season is too short for all the crops you would like to grow, there are methods you can use to lengthen it, from simply mounding soil over potato shoots to protect them from late spring frosts to creating an indoor space to start seedlings.

HORTICULTURAL FLEECE AND FILM

These protective materials are made either from a lightweight, woven fabric or from a clear, perforated plastic film. You can lay them on top of growing crops without damaging them. Both types allow moisture and air through to the plants while providing a degree of protection from cold weather, as well as from insects and animals.

You should anchor horticultural fleece or film securely around the edges by digging them into the soil or weighing them down with stones. Although they stretch to an extent to accommodate growing crops, you will need to adjust them occasionally to prevent damage to the plants.

In cool and temperate regions you can extend the season by sowing seeds and growing seedlings early in the year, before spring arrives. However, warm-season vegetables such as tomatoes and peppers will not survive even a slight frost, and in many places frosts occur into mid-spring. Yet, if sowing seeds is delayed until all risk of frost has passed, the remaining season may be too short to allow the plants to reach maturity.

The answer is to provide protection to allow the seedlings to thrive. Even crops that are not frost-tender can benefit from being started under protection; the warmer conditions allow faster growth, giving plants under cover a head start over those sown outside, leading to earlier crops.

Areas where spring comes late often have to suffer the double blow of autumn and winter arriving early, too. However, plants that have not finished producing their crop by the time the autumn weather arrives can often be safeguarded against early frosts, wind and rain by using movable forms of protection, such as cloches and horticultural fleece. The extra days gained can make all the difference to your final harvest.

Simple forms of protection

If the forecast of a late, sharp spring frost takes you by surprise when potato shoots are thrusting through their ridges, or tender seedlings are beginning to show in their drills, don't panic. You can protect early potatoes by earthing them up every two or three weeks once the shoots appear. Carefully pull the soil over the top of the shoots with a draw hoe. This will protect them from frost damage and the shoots will soon push their way through the soil. Or you could use single sheets of newspaper or horticultural fleece laid over the

Piles of loose dry straw, leaves or compost can provide some insulation against cold weather in the autumn.

Horticultural fleece can be stretched over vegetable plants such as these carrots to provide protection from cold weather.

the type of vegetable you are growing – and you need to keep the soil moist.

Light is vitally important. If you don't have enough room on a sunny window sill, position a table near the window. Alternatively, clear a space elsewhere in the house and provide light for the plants by suspending a fluorescent workshop light over the plants. By using linked chains to support the light, you can adjust the height of the light so that it remains 5–10cm (2–4in) above the seedlings.

Avoid starting the seeds too soon, or you could find the seedlings will become too leggy and rootbound to transplant to a bed outdoors. For more about sowing seeds indoors see pages 64–65; for growing plants in a greenhouse see pages 78–81.

top of the shoots. This method also works well with newly germinated seedlings. Weight down the edges of the paper or fleece with soil to prevent it from being blown away.

The shoulders of root crops such as swedes, parsnips and carrots can be damaged by exposure to hard frost at the soil surface. Heaping dry leaves, straw or compost over the rows before cold weather sets in will give them protection, and it will make it easier to dig the crops up in freezing spells.

Heavy clay soil takes a long time to dry out and become fit to break down for sowing seeds. You can speed up the process of preparing the soil by covering it with cloches or sheets of sturdy black plastic from mid-winter onwards. This will keep off the rain and snow, allowing the soil to dry out and warm up. Black plastic is particularly good at retaining warmth.

Cloches

Early cloches were bell-shaped and made from heavy glass to fit over individual plants. Nowadays, cloches are available in many different types and styles. They are normally shaped so that they can be placed end to end to form a continuous cover over a row of plants.

Glass cloches provide excellent shelter from cold and wet weather, and they can raise the temperature of the air considerably, as long as the ends of the rows are blocked. They are also stable. However, glass has a number of drawbacks; it is fragile, dangerous when broken (a point to keep in mind if there are young children in the garden), expensive and heavy to move around. Cloches made from corrugated or sheet plastic are much cheaper and easier to move, but not quite as effective at trapping warmth. Remember that they need to be firmly anchored in place.

Cloches may be barn-shaped, tent-shaped or semi-circular. Check how much headroom the different types provide and whether it is sufficient for your plants.

Setting up an indoor space

Gardeners living in a region with a short growing season can still grow plants with a long growing season by starting them indoors, as long as they are provided with the correct conditions. The soil temperature needs to be warm enough for the seedlings to germinate – this will depend on

PLANTS TO START INDOORS

The following plants are among the best ones that you can start off indoors:

Broccoli	Cucumbers
Brussels sprouts	Leeks
Cabbage	Lettuce
Cauliflower	Onions
Chive	Tomatoes

Quick Tip

Light fantastic

If your row of cloches are within reach of an electrical socket, you can add extra warmth by running two lines of outdoor Christmas lights inside the row of cloches, one along each side. The heat from the bulbs lifts the temperature a few degrees.

Tunnels and frames

Structures in the vegetable garden such as tunnels and frames provide more facilities for raising tranplants – or even for growing crops until they reach maturity.

COLD-FRAME VEGETABLES

You can grow the following vegetables to maturity in a frame:

early carrots   cucumbers
winter lettuce   some melons
spring lettuce

Sometimes plants growing in their permanent planting positions will need protection to help them survive a late frost in the spring or an early one in the autumn. The same methods for providing this type of protection can also be used to harden off transplants (see pages 68–69).

Tunnels

You can easily obtain tunnels made from polythene sheeting, which are versatile products for the garden. They are lightweight and simple to work with. Although they do not have a long life (two or three years), they are inexpensive to replace.

Polythene sheeting is often used to form long, low tunnels that are about 30–60cm (12–24in) high, and these can be used as a type of cloche (see page 75). You can easily construct a low tunnel yourself by driving a series of metal hoops into the ground, stretching the polythene over them and securing it in place with either twine or more metal hoops. Form the ends of a cloche by gathering together the polythene and tying it to a stake. To ventilate the tunnel simply push the polythene up along the sides.

You can create a tunnel for any size that is required, whether it is to cover a single row of seedlings or a whole patch of early lettuce crops – you can even construct it as a walk-in tunnel

Quick Tip

Make a frame

You can build a frame using an old window from a reclamation centre. (If you're not sure if it has lead paint, apply a coat of an exterior paint.) Make the base from wood the size of the window, with a height of about 60cm (24in) at the back, sloping to 45cm (18in) at the front.

that is large enough to work in. Walk-in polytunnels are available as self-assembly kits of steel hoops and heavy-gauge polythene that has been stabilised against ultraviolet light to improve the length of its life.

Walk-in tunnels are less expensive and easier to put up than a glass greenhouse, but they have their drawbacks. They are not suitable for exposed windy sites because strong winds can distort the framework. While they can be heated, they are not as efficient at keeping the heat in as a greenhouse, and condensation can be a problem because ventilation is limited to the ends of the tunnel.

The frame

A 'cold' frame is often used unheated – it is a little like a large cloche built in a permanent position – but it can also be heated. A traditional frame has a base of bricks or wood. The base is slightly higher at the back than the front, and it is covered by a sloping glass top, known as a light. The slope ensures the frame receives the maximum sunlight, and it also sheds rainwater effectively. Modern frames may be made from either metal or plastic, and they often have two sloping roof sides rising to an apex, similar to the roof of a miniature greenhouse.

Frames are ideal for vegetable plants that do not need the full protection of a heated greenhouse, and they are perfect as a halfway stage for vegetables being hardened off before being transplanted. They can be heated, either with small electric or paraffin heaters or with soil-warming cables (see box, right).

SOIL-WARMING CABLES

During the plant-growing process germination requires higher temperatures, and this heat can be supplied effectively by soil-warming cables (available at garden centres), a convenient and economical way of providing 'bottom heat'.

Fill a frame or box with about 5cm (2in) of sharp sand and lay the cable on top, running it back and forth in loops about 8cm (3in) apart. Cover it with another 5cm (2in) of sharp sand, and place the trays and pots on top for sowing. You should use a thermostat, which will keep the heat set at a pre-determined temperature.

Plant-heating mats, also available at garden centres in a range of sizes, are easier to use. All you'll need to do is simply place your pots and trays directly on top of the mat.

To provide ventilation in the frame you can prop open or remove all or some of the lights. When purchasing a frame, look for one with lights that are hinged and fitted with a stay to hold them open – the lights can be heavy and unwieldy to move around.

You should position your frame in a sunny but sheltered site, so that the sloping side receives the maximum sunlight. On cold nights you can place a layer of old carpet, sacking or a similar material over the lights for extra insulation.

The polythene sheeting on this tunnel is stretched over a tentlike frame. Push back the plastic to allow ventilation or if the plants become too hot.

Starting plants in a greenhouse

A greenhouse is perfect for raising plants that benefit from an early start. While the weather outside is still too chilly for sowing, strong seedlings can develop in the warmth of a greenhouse.

is convenient to the house and that preferably has access to the water and electricity supply.

The greenhouse effect

A greenhouse is always a few degrees warmer than the outside temperature, even if it is unheated. This is partially because it is an enclosed space that is sheltered from wind and weather. It is also due to the 'greenhouse effect', where light, as short-wave radiation, passes through the glass panes and is converted into infrared waves, or heat, within the greenhouse. Glass is far less permeable to the longer-wave infrared, so the heat is trapped within the greenhouse, steadily building up as more light waves continue to come through the glass.

MOVING AIR

Ventilating a greenhouse is important because plants thrive in a 'buoyant atmosphere' – an area with good air movement. An automatic vent opener, which is controlled by the greenhouse temperature, will help to achieve the correct balance between warmth and ventilation. In windy weather when you shouldn't open the vents, use an electric fan (with the heater off) to keep the air circulating.

A greenhouse can be an expensive purchase, but it enables you to achieve more from your vegetable garden. Apart from early seed sowing to raise your own transplants, you will be able to grow out-of-season crops, such as winter lettuce, spring carrots and early summer French beans. In cool or unpredictable climates, you can use a greenhouse to successfully grow heat-loving crops such as tomatoes, aubergines and melons.

There is a choice of greenhouse shapes and styles. Buy as large a model as your budget can afford – while keeping heating costs in mind – and position it in an open, sunny site that

Quick Tip

Playing safe

Use a qualified electrician to set up the electricity supply to a greenhouse. The damp atmosphere and frequent use of water in a greenhouse make it vital that the electricity is installed correctly to prevent the danger of electric shock.

CHOOSING A GREENHOUSE

Framework	Pros	Cons
Timber	Some gardeners prefer its traditional appearance. Western red cedar has a natural resistance to rot and insect attack.	Needs regular maintenance to ensure a long life. Cedar is expensive; softwoods do not last many years.
Aluminium	Strong, durable and maintenance free. Those with a powder coating come in a range of colours.	Plain, uncoated ones are not attractive.
Plastic (PVC)	Maintenance free and retains heat well.	Does not have the strength of aluminium or timber.
Cladding	**Pros**	**Cons**
Glass	Looks attractive and provides the best light transmission. Strengthened tempered glass is the most durable type.	Breakable; dangerous if you have small children. Tempered glass is less dangerous but is the most expensive cladding material.
Rigid plastic sheets (acrylic or polycarbonate)	Inexpensive. Much lighter in weight than glass, so the greenhouse frame does not have to be as sturdy, which will reduce costs further.	Not as attractive as glass.

The temperature in an unheated greenhouse will still fall to low levels on cold nights or on dull winter days when there is no sun to warm it. Fortunately, many vegetable plants don't need frost-free conditions. Young cabbage-family plants, lettuce, peas, carrots and leeks, for example, benefit from the warmer conditions in the greenhouse on sunny days, but will not be harmed if the temperature drops to freezing occasionally.

If starting tender plants – such as aubergines, beans, peppers, squashes, cucumbers, melons, courgettes, sweet corn and tomatoes – in an unheated greenhouse, don't sow them too early; just one frost could kill the seedlings.

You don't need to sow early to gain an advantage. Greenhouse-raised plants will still be more advanced than those grown outside, even if they are both sown at the same time.

Heating the greenhouse

Providing heat in the greenhouse will allow you to grow a wider range of vegetables and to start them earlier. Electricity is the most convenient form of greenhouse heating. Electric heaters have thermostats that save wasting fuel and protect against an unexpected frost. The heat is clean and dry, providing a good growing atmosphere, especially if you use a fan to circulate the heat.

If there is no electricity supply to the greenhouse, choose between gas and paraffin. Gas heaters are best. Less expensive paraffin heaters are basic. They need to be lit and inspected daily, are rarely controlled by a thermostat and produce water vapour, which can encourage fungus diseases. If not maintained, they can also release damaging fumes.

Care of young plants

Keep seedlings growing without a check until they are ready for planting in their permanent positions (for sowing and pricking out, see pages 64–65). Make sure they have plenty of space and light: overcrowded plants are pale, spindly and weak, and they will take longer to become established after transplanting. Crowded plants are also more prone to attack by fungal diseases, because when overcrowded they create a humid atmosphere.

REDUCING HEAT COSTS

Heating can be expensive, but there are several ways to keep the cost down:

• You can line the interior of the greenhouse with bubble polythene to insulate it. Take the lining down as soon as it is no longer needed, because it cuts down the amount of light entering the greenhouse.

• Heat only a small area of the greenhouse, sectioning it off with polythene sheeting. Alternatively, a large, enclosed heated propagator may be sufficient for your needs.

• To avoid wasting fuel, use a form of heating that can be thermostatically controlled.

Maturing plants in a greenhouse

Some regions are just not warm enough to enable you to grow reliable crops of heat-loving vegetables outside. However, if you give these plants the shelter of a greenhouse it will be a different story.

LIGHTEN THE DARKNESS

A greenhouse may provide the warmth that is missing from our gardens in winter, but there is another vital ingredient for good plant growth – light. Out-of-season vegetables will rarely be as good as those grown in the main growing season, because the lack of light in short winter days limits their development.

In the greenhouse natural daylight can be supplemented with artificial light to improve the development of vegetables. Ordinary light bulbs are not suitable, and special plant-growing lamps provide just the right type of light for growth but are relatively expensive. Compact fluorescent bulbs are a useful alternative. Suspend the bulbs above the plants, about 10cm (4in) over the top of the crop. Use the artificial light to supplement daylight, providing plants with a total of 8 to 10 hours of light per day.

Although a greenhouse is useful for starting crops early, when conditions outside are far too cold for sowing seeds, the benefit of a greenhouse is probably most truly appreciated in the cool-weather areas. There are several vegetables that won't thrive in cool conditions, and in these regions they will provide a good, reliable harvest only if they are grown under cover for the whole of their lives.

Native heat lovers

The heat-loving vegetables originally from hot-weather regions such as South America and Africa will generally thrive in a greenhouse. While many varieties will provide a reasonable harvest outside in a good summer, you can obtain the largest and best-quality crops by growing these plants in a greenhouse.

The favourite vegetable for growing in a greenhouse has to be the tomato. Tomato plants are reasonably compact, not too difficult to grow and provide a rewarding harvest. Cucumbers and peppers are probably next in order of popularity, followed by aubergines and melons. The more exotic vegetables such as tomatillos and okra are the province of the more adventurous gardener.

Out-of-season crops

Greenhouses can also provide the home gardener with the luxury of out-of-season crops. Even a humble lettuce becomes a treat when it is freshly harvested in the middle of winter, and a picking of French beans in early spring is a delightful foretaste of the summer crop to come. These out-of-season crops make good use of the greenhouse at a slack time of year.

Greenhouse borders

You can grow plants in containers in the greenhouse or grow them in a soil border if there is one. Plants grown in the border will have a free root run and are less likely to suffer from water shortages. This is particularly important for tomato plants, because water stress when the fruit is forming can result in blossom end rot. Growing plants in the border also saves spending money on compost and containers.

However, border soil will need replenishing with organic matter such as well-rotted compost or manure every year, plus an application of a general fertiliser before planting in spring. If the same crop is grown in the border for several years, there could be a build-up of specific pests and diseases, which means it will be necessary to replace the soil.

Greenhouse containers

Containers such as tubs or large clay or plastic pots filled with potting compost can be used for greenhouse vegetables. However, growing bags have become increasingly popular because they are inexpensive and easy to transport and plant.

Because containers and growing bags have a relatively small volume of compost that soon becomes filled with roots, plants grown in them are prone to drying out. All container-grown vegetables will need careful watering, as often as twice as day in hot weather.

Providing support

Virtually all greenhouse vegetables will need some form of support as they grow, to prevent them from flopping over and to keep the crop accessible and free from damage. Provide bushy plants such as peppers, tomatoes and aubergines with a tall cane and gently secure them with soft twine as they grow.

Another method is to tie a length of twine to either a piece of bent wire pegged firmly in the soil or around the base of the stem, just below the bottom leaf. Attach the other end to a metal eye or hook on the greenhouse roof immediately above the plant – make sure the twine is not quite taut. As the plant grows, gently twist the main stem round the twine. This is a good method for plants in growing bags on a firm floor, where there is nowhere to secure a stake in the ground.

VEGETABLES FOR THE GREENHOUSE

The following crops can be grown in the greenhouse – sowing them directy in the border or in containers.

	Directions	Varieties
French bean	Sow in containers with bottom heat in mid-winter and transplant to the border or growing bag when approximately 10cm (4in) tall.	'The Prince' is a good compact variety.
Carrot	Sow in early autumn for a winter crop, or from mid-winter to spring for harvesting in early summer.	Choose short-rooted varieties such as 'Amsterdam Forcing' or round-rooted types such as 'Parmex'.
Lettuce	Sow from autumn to early winter for harvesting in winter and spring. Sow seeds in soil blocks or fibre pots to prevent root disturbance when transplanting.	Choose a variety specifically bred for winter greenhouse harvesting, such as 'Kellys'. Plants won't form a firm heart.
Potato	Plant two tubers in a growing bag or one in a 30cm (12in) pot of compost in late summer for a winter harvest or mid-winter for a late spring crop.	Choose an early (fast-maturing) variety such as 'Swift', 'Dunluce' or 'Rocket'. Don't expect a big yield.
Salad onion	Sow thinly in early autumn for a spring crop.	'White Lisbon' is one of the most popular and reliable varieties.
Radish	Sow in early autumn or from late winter to mid-spring; they should be ready in 4 to 8 weeks.	Any variety can be used, but 'Wintella' and 'Marabelle' are specially bred for early crops.

You can also grow vining plants such as melon up twine or wires secured to the roof, using two or three horizontal wires about 25cm (10in) apart, along which you can train the fruit-bearing side shoots.

81

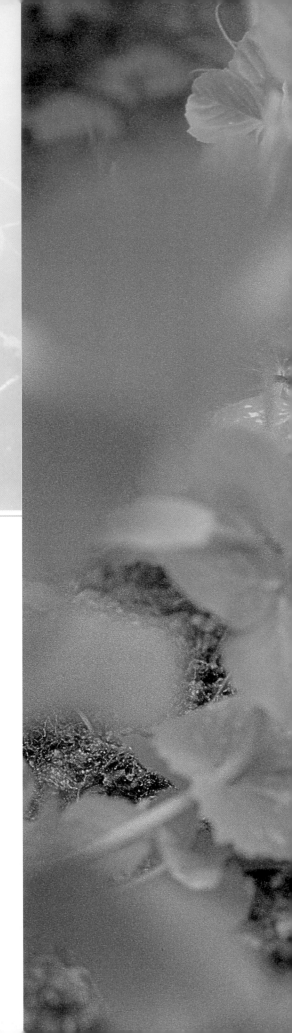

4 Making your vegetables grow

You've planned, dug, sown and planted, and now you can feel a great satisfaction as you survey your vegetable garden filled with healthy young plants. It's a great achievement, but now is not the time to let your guard down. It's up to you to keep those plants growing well until harvest time.

Your vegetables will need watering, feeding and supporting as they grow; they will also need your help to battle against weeds, pests and diseases. Make sure you spend a few minutes each day walking around your plot to see what needs to be done.

Make it a daily routine to inspect your garden and perform any necessary tasks. By taking early action you'll keep work to a minimum.

82

Watering vegetables

All plants need water to grow, and sometimes natural rainfall just isn't enough. Watering your crops can make all the difference to the eventual harvest, but it's important to know when and how to water to get the best results.

Without a water supply, many of a plant's natural processes are impossible. Germination, the beginning of a plant's life cycle, is triggered when the dormant seed absorbs moisture from the soil. As the plant grows it will need water for photosynthesis, for respiration and to dissolve and transport nutrients. Without water, plant cells become limp. The plant can no longer stand up or hold out its leaves to capture sunlight's energy or keep itself cool in hot temperatures.

How plants get water

A plant absorbs water from the soil, where it is held in gaps between the soil particles (see pages 34–35). The water is absorbed by tiny, delicate root hairs that fringe the roots, and it is continually pulled up through the plant by the power of transpiration (where water vapours pass through the stomata, or pores, of the leaves).

Because moisture is lost to the air through the leaves, plants with large surface areas of leaf lose water faster than those with narrow, needle-like leaves. Most water is lost when the weather is hot and sunny, and also when it is windy – moving air whips moisture away from the leaves quickly.

As long as there is sufficient water in the soil to replace the moisture that is lost, no harm is done. But sometimes plants can't keep up with the demand. This is usually because there has been no rain to replenish the soil water. However, it can also be because the delicate root hairs have been damaged and they are not able to do their job properly. This is why, when it comes to watering transplants, they need careful attention until the roots have had time to re-establish themselves.

Water conservation

Much of the water in the soil goes to waste, either draining away before

To determine if your plants need watering, you can carefully dig a hole a few inches deep – be careful not to disturb the plant's roots – then check the soil.

plants can tap into it or evaporating from the soil surface. Whatever you can do to prevent this waste will save you time and energy, as well as conserve the water supply. There are several methods that you can use:

Improve the soil. You can dig in bulky organic matter such as garden compost or manure to improve the soil structure and its capacity to hold water (see pages 36–39).

Quick Tip

Sweet tomatoes

Watering tomato plants frequently will increase the total yield, but the flavour of the fruits will suffer. Once plants are flowering, water only as necessary to keep the soil just moist – then you will be able to enjoy the sweetest fruits with the richest flavour.

BEST TIMES TO WATER CROPS

Root vegetables

Beetroot, carrot, parsnip, potato, radish, salsify, scorzonera, swede, turnip

Extra water promotes leafy growth on root crops but not root growth. Water as needed while plants are young to help them grow steadily. After a prolonged dry spell, heavy rain or watering can cause roots to split, so water occasionally during a drought to prevent this damage. Potatoes respond well to watering when the tubers are forming (when flowering starts); you can increase both the size of tubers and overall yield. For the best response from early crops, wait until the tubers are marble size before watering.

Leaves and shoots

Asian greens, cabbage-family plants, celery, chicory, endive, lettuce, radicchio, spinach, Swiss chard

For the best-quality harvest do not allow this group to suffer a water shortage at any stage of growth. The best response to watering comes about 10 to 20 days before the crop will be ready for harvest, so if water is in short supply, this is the time to apply it. Give only enough water to moisten the top 30cm (12in) of soil; too much water can cause maturing lettuce and cabbage heads to split. Widely spaced winter cabbage-family plants such as Brussels sprouts are unlikely to need watering.

Fruits, pods and seeds

Aubergine, beans, peppers, squash, peas, sweet corn, tomato, courgette

A bountiful harvest will rely on watering at the right time. Water after transplanting, but unless conditions are so dry that the plants begin to wilt, do not water again until flowering begins. Watering too early will encourage leaf and shoot growth at the expense of flowers, which reduces yields. Once flowering starts and while fruits are developing, watering increases the numbers of flowers, the percentage of flowers setting fruit, the number of seeds per pod and the overall yield (but see *Sweet Tomatoes*, opposite).

Mulch. When the soil is moist – in the spring or after a thorough watering – you can mulch the surface to block evaporation by using compost, commercial mulches or black plastic sheeting. Straw and grass clippings are sometimes recommended, but unrotted materials such as these are best applied where there are no growing vegetables, because they take nitrogen from the soil as they rot down. You can sprinkle a nitrogen-rich fertiliser such as bone meal on the soil before you apply the mulch.

Control weeds. Weeds steal water from vegetables. Deal with them often and while they are still small, using a sharp hoe to slice the weeds off at the soil surface. Avoid disturbing the soil to prevent turning up new weed seeds.

Plant at the correct spacing. If you leave the recommended amount of room between neighbouring plants, they won't compete for water.

Provide a free root run. Cultivate the soil deeply, breaking it down to a fine crumbly texture, which will allow the roots to extend freely in their search for moisture. Because many gardeners dig to just one spade's depth year after year, a hard, impenetrable layer (known as a pan) can form just below this depth. Double digging (see pages 40–41) every four to five years will overcome this problem.

Do I need to water?

Most gardeners water crops on a haphazard basis – the soil looks a bit dusty on the surface, and it hasn't rained for a few days, so it's probably time to get the hose out. However, it is best to be a bit more scientific about it. The truth is that water is a limited resource and it's important that we don't waste it – or waste our time applying it. And water applied at the wrong time can actually harm the crops we are trying to help.

If you think your plants may need watering, dig a hole a few inches deep with a trowel to see what conditions are like in the plants' root zone. If the soil below is dry it might be time to water. Check with the chart (above) for the most efficient times to water different types of vegetables.

Plants need moist soil to germinate and must be watered after transplanting (about 300ml/10oz of water per transplant). Or water only when the soil is dry, applying 9–18 litres per sq m (2–4gal per sq yd).

The exception is plants growing in containers such as tomatoes and peppers, which have restricted root space. They will need more frequent watering than those grown in open ground or soil borders.

Watering systems

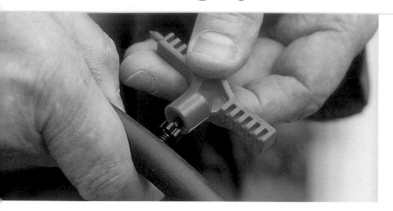

Watering plants can seem like a lot of work, but there are plenty of methods to make it quicker, easier and more efficient. The one that is right for you will depend on the size of your garden, your climate and your budget.

CHOOSING A WATERING METHOD

Before deciding which method of watering is right for you, ask yourself these questions:

- How large is your vegetable garden? A watering can will suffice for a small garden; a hose or automatic watering system is preferable for a large garden.

- How much time do you have? Watering the garden with either a watering can or hose will be time-consuming; an automated system won't.

- What is the climate like in your area? If there's plenty of rain you won't need to water nearly as much as if you live in a warmer, drier region.

- How much money are you prepared to spend? A hose will cost only a fraction of the price of an automated system.

Using a watering can may be an acceptable choice if you have a small garden; however, it will soon become a trial in a large garden, especially in a dry summer, when watering becomes a regular chore. For effortless watering you can install a fully automatic system that will look after the garden's water needs even when you are away – but it will be comparatively expensive.

The watering can

For small vegetable gardens and containers, a watering can is sufficient. Choose a watering can that is nicely balanced, easy to carry and has a long spout for a good reach. It may be made of metal or plastic: although plastic is lighter and cheaper than metal, it has a shorter life. The most popular sizes are 4.5 litres (1gal), 7 litres (1½gal), and 9 litres (2gal). Although large cans will cut down the number of trips you need to make to the tap and back, they can be heavy when full, so you may need to compromise.

To break up the water into a shower of droplets, which will be more gentle on your plants, all spouts should be able to be fitted with a rose.

Like the cans, the roses may have a metal (brass) or plastic face. Use the rose face-up for the gentlest shower; turn it face-down for a soaking.

Hose

A hose will enable you to apply large quantities of water with less effort than carrying a heavy watering can back and forth. To prevent water from siphoning back into the water supply, you may have to attach a special valve to the tap to prevent backflow. In a drought there may be restrictions on watering your garden. You may have to apply for a licence for a hose or fit a water meter.

There are many types of hose, so shop around to see what best meets your needs. There are anti-kink hoses, hoses that flatten for easy storage, through-flow hoses that can be used even when they are partly stored on a reel and coiled hoses that take up less space. The diameter of the hose also varies; the larger the diameter, the more water the hose delivers, and the further from the tap you can use it without losing pressure.

You should fit a hose with a device to break up the water into droplets. Spray guns come in a range of styles and patterns, allowing water flow to be adjusted from a strong, far-reaching jet to a gentle shower. Among the most useful are those that have a water-stop connector to enable you to turn the hose off at the delivery end, without trailing back to the tap. Make sure that the hose and all the connectors are of good quality and correctly fitted, otherwise the hose may burst apart at the connectors when the water-stop valve is used.

Sprinklers can also be useful for watering vegetable gardens, and they come in a number of patterns to suit different plots. However, because they throw water droplets into the air, they lose much of their water by evaporation before they reach the soil, especially in dry, sunny weather. Sprinklers are the least efficient method of watering.

Automatic watering systems

Systems that automatically water your garden can be an efficient way of watering – not only efficient in time,

but also in the amount of water used. You can buy a complete kit from a garden centre. It contains a pressure regulator, a length of supply hose that connects to the tap, micro-tubing to take the water from the supply hose to the plants and drippers, sprinklers or a seep hose for the final delivery of water to the plants.

A basic system can be set up and operated by turning the tap on and off, or it can be fully automated by adding an automatic timer. This is programmed to switch on and off at set hours, and will continue to water the garden while you are away from home. You can also set it to turn on at night, so that water is not wasted through evaporation.

Before buying your watering system, contact your water supply company to see which regulations and requirements may apply to its use.

A rose breaks up the stream of water into droplets. Use it face down to give plants a soaking.

THE SEEP HOSE

A different type of 'sprinkler' is the seep hose or drip tubing. One type is a porous hose that leaks water gently along its length and can be laid along rows of vegetables or buried just beneath the soil surface.

Another type is a soft hose perforated at intervals on one side. It lays flat on the soil surface (or under a light mulch) when not in use; it becomes rounded and emits water once the tap is turned on. It is available in single or double tubes; set it hole-side down.

A seep hose is an efficient way of applying water because little water is lost through evaporation into the atmosphere.

Quick Tip

Getting connected
You should invest in good-quality connectors for your garden hose. Simple brass or plastic push–click connectors are much quicker and easier to use than connectors that screw together.

Feeding your plants

Vegetables need a range of nutrients to grow and develop. These nutrients are available in the soil, but sometimes not in the right quantities for the best growth. Fertilisers can help to make up for any shortfall. Nutrients are absorbed through the plants' roots and, to a much lesser extent, through their leaves.

Nutrients in the soil are often in short supply where greedy vegetables are grown. Different soils contain varying amounts of nutrients, and different crops also vary in their individual nutrient requirements. You can test the nutrient level of your soil (see pages 32–33) or rely on your plants to indicate a deficiency (see *Nutrient Deficiencies,* right).

Fertilisers

You can apply fertilisers to increase nutrient levels. Organic fertilisers come from something that once lived such as bone meal or composted manure. Some gardeners also count naturally occurring fertilisers such as rock phosphate or rock potash as organic. Some organic gardeners have ethical concerns about using by-products of animal slaughter such as bone meal or blood, fish and bone.

Artificial fertilisers are manufactured from non-organic sources. As far as plants are concerned, all fertilisers, organic or artifical, are broken down to identical chemicals.

Formulations

Fertilisers may contain a single plant nutrient (straight fertilisers) or a combination of nutrients (compound fertilisers). Straight fertilisers include sulphate of ammonia (a nitrogen source) and superphosphate (a phosphorus source). Compound fertilisers usually consist of nitrogen, phosphorus and potassium (N, P and K) in varying proportions. These proportions are given on the package – NPK 7-7-7 is a balanced fertiliser, while NPK 5-5-10 has a greater amount of potash. Some compound fertilisers also contain trace elements such as iron and boron, which are needed in only tiny amounts.

Quick Tip

Hand protection

Wear gloves when you apply powder or granular fertilisers because they can irritate the skin. It is important to make sure that cuts and scratches on your hands are covered up.

NITROGEN REQUIREMENTS

Some vegetables are more likely to need fertiliser applications.

High	Medium	Low
Beetroot	Asparagus	Broad beans
Brussels sprouts	Aubergine	Carrot
Cabbage	Lettuce	Cucumber
Cauliflower	Onion	Parsnip
Celery	Peppers	Peas
Leek	French beans	Radish
Potato	Squash	Swede
Spinach	Sweet corn	
Swiss chard	Tomatoes	

Compost tea

Adding compost to your soil will improve its nutrient content. Watering plants with compost tea will supply nutrients more quickly. To make this tea place well-rotted compost in a bucket of water and leave it to soak for several days; then strain it through cheesecloth. Use one part compost to between five and eight parts of water. You can put the compost inside sacking and suspend it in the water to avoid having to strain the liquid.

Applying fertilisers

You must apply fertilisers carefully. A dry non-organic fertiliser can damage or kill plants if it coats the foliage and buds, or granules lodge in the growing points. Too much fertiliser will harm the plants. Fertilisers come in three forms: powders, granules and liquids.

Powder and granular fertilisers. Some powder fertilisers dissolve in water, but others, especially organic versions, are spread on the soil, as are granular fertilisers. You can apply a side-dressing of fertiliser by spreading it in a band around the plant or alongside it, but not too close to the stem. Work it into the top few inches of soil, using a rake or hoe. Choose a still day so that the fertiliser is not blown away.

Follow the package instructions for application rates. If rates are given as grams per square meter (or ounces per square foot), measure out a square meter on a patch of soil, weigh out the quantity of fertiliser and spread it as evenly as possible. This will give you a visual idea of the correct application rate. If rain does not follow within two or three days, water it in enough to moisten the soil – don't flood it.

Liquid fertilisers. The nutrients in liquid fertilisers are more quickly available to the plants. Most liquid types must be diluted before use: follow the directions carefully. You can apply it with a watering can, but for large areas, a dilutor attachment that fits on the end of a hose is useful.

Some chemical liquid fertilisers are made to be absorbed by the plants' foliage. These usually contain trace elements, and they are useful as a fast-acting tonic for nutrient-deficient plants. They can be applied with a watering can fitted with a rose, or by a sprayer or hose-end dilutor.

Slow-release fertilisers. Most organic fertilisers slowly release their nutrients, so that the effects of one application last throughout the growing season. Some chemical fertilisers are made to be released slowly. The rate of breakdown is controlled by soil moisture and temperature, so that the warm, moist conditions that promote growth also allow nutrients to be released. Slow-release fertilisers are less likely to scorch plant roots.

Fertilisers and pollution

The overuse of fertilisers leads to the pollution of groundwater and rivers, with nitrogen stimulating excessive growth of algae and water weeds. Pollution from gardens is small but significant, particularly on light, free-draining soil. Run-off from compost heaps and misuse of compost tea can contribute to water pollution. You should apply fertilisers only when necessary, and use slow-release fertilisers whenever possible.

NUTRIENT DEFICIENCIES

A lack of nutrients can show up as symptoms in vegetables.

Boron: Growing points blacken; hollow stems in cabbage-family plants. Beets form cracks and canker spots; celery has a black heart. On sweet corn, foliage has white stripes; cobs are stunted.

Calcium: Young leaves curl; growing tips blacken. Tomatoes and their relatives develop blossom end rot; tip burn occurs on lettuce; browning occurs inside Brussels sprouts.

Iron: Leaves turn yellow or pale between bright green veins. Young leaves are affected first.

Manganese: Mottled yellowing between veins, with dead patches on leaves. Brown areas may form on seed leaves of peas and beans. It occurs on beans, beet, spinach, peas and cabbage-family plants.

Magnesium: Leaves yellow between veins (interveinal chlorosis), showing on older leaves first. It is common on lettuce, potatoes and tomatoes.

Molybdenum: Leaves are thin and straplike, and growing points die. It is known as whiptail on cauliflower.

Nitrogen: Small leaves, pale, yellowed or with blue or red coloration; stunted plants; poor performance. It is common on cabbage-family plants.

Phosphorus: Stunted growth; blue or bronze tints on older leaves.

Potassium: Older leaves turn pale, with brown scorches at margins; sometimes brown spots on leaves.

Supporting the plants

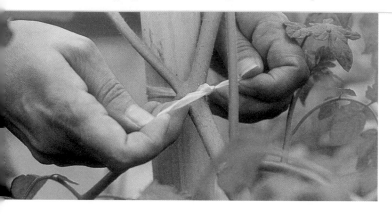

Some vegetables are climbers, some scramble and sprawl and some may be blown over in windy gardens. All of these plants will benefit from a sturdy support system to make sure they produce the maximum yield and are easy to harvest.

VINING PLANTS

You can grow cucumbers, squashes and melons trained up trellises or wigwams of canes outdoors. The fruit of melons, and sometimes squash, are relatively heavy, and they often need the support of individual 'hammocks'. Old nylon tights cut into strips of a suitable length provide the perfect material for these hammocks.

In a greenhouse train these plants up strings suspended vertically from the roof (see pages 80–81).

(see pages 80–81)

Most of the vegetables that we commonly provide with support such as beans and peas would still thrive if left on their own, romping over the ground and only scrambling up trees or bushes when they happened to come across them. However, training them upwards makes sure that the crops they carry are less likely to be misshapen, spoiled by soil contact or eaten by pests such as slugs and snails.

The crops will also be much easier to find and pick during harvest time. Searching through the tangled growth of unsupported pea plants looking for ripe pods can be a backbreaking job. There are a variety of supports, and the ones you choose will depend on the vegetables that need them.

Poles and canes

Perhaps the vegetable best known for needing support is the runner bean. These plants will climb 3m (10ft) or more quite easily, twining their supple stems round anything upright. One of the best ways to support a number of plants is to set bamboo canes or sturdy bean poles in a double row, leaning them together at the tops, and tying them with twine. To keep

To make a wigwam tie together a half dozen or so canes firmly at the top.

the structure secure lay a row of canes along the ridge at the top, tying these firmly in place. Space the canes 15cm (6in) apart if possible, so that you have one cane per plant. If you have lots of beans, this can be an expensive option, in which case, space the canes more widely and run twine horizontally between them to help support the plants. A wigwam is a more suitable option if you are growing only a few plants.

Climbing beans like to cling to a rough surface, which is why bean

A twisting tale

Quick Tip

At planting time twist the tips of runner beans around the base of the supports in the direction they grow – anticlockwise (clockwise if looking down on the top of the bean from above). Twist them the wrong way and they'll just unwind.

poles complete with bark are often preferred to smooth, shiny bamboo canes. However, if beans have trouble clinging to canes, wrap a little garden twine around the base of the canes to give the shoots a grip. Once they get started they won't look back.

Pea sticks

The ideal support for scrambling peas, which cling tightly with tendrils, are pea sticks – twiggy, branching stems of shrubs such as hazel. Cut these in winter and trim them to 0.9–1.2m (3–4ft) high. Push them firmly into the soil every 30cm (12in) or so along the row.

Pea sticks will provide excellent support for your peas while also looking attractively rustic. Smaller versions are useful to support lower growing plants such as dwarf beans.

Netting

Plastic netting that is stretched taut between supporting canes or poles is particularly useful for peas. When used for taller plants such as climbing beans it needs sturdy supports. The netting provides a great deal of wind resistance when covered in plant growth, so it can easily be blown over.

It is often difficult to free the netting from the remains of plant growth at the end of the season, making it awkward to use again. You can try burying the whole bundled net in a compost heap, the theory being that the plant remains will rot away while the plastic netting won't. In practice, you may not get the results you desire.

A wigwam is ideal for supporting beans. They are useful when you want to grow only a small number of plants.

THE BENEFICIARIES

There are several types of plant that can benefit from support:

- Climbers and scramblers such as climbing beans, cucumbers, peas and melons.

- Bushy plants with weak stems such as tomatoes, peppers and aubergines, which lie down under the weight of their crop.

- Sturdy-stemmed plants that are exposed to winter winds such as all the winter cabbage-family plants – strong winds can topple them.

- Smaller plants such as dwarf beans or asparagus peas: twiggy sticks can help to keep the beans off the soil, where they could rot or be nibbled by pests.

Stakes

Some varieties of plants such as tomatoes, peppers and aubergines are stocky enough to be self-supporting, but the majority need help to keep them upright and ensure that the crop is accessible and clear of the ground. A sturdy bamboo cane or stake, pushed several inches into the soil 10cm (4in) away from the main stem, is sufficient. Tie the plant to the cane with twine in a figure-of-eight loop, or use plastic-covered twist ties. In a greenhouse strings can be used to support tomatoes.

In exposed, windy gardens tall winter cabbage-family plants such as Brussels sprouts may be blown over. You can provide support by driving a short, stout stake firmly into the soil 25cm (10in) from the main stem on the windward side of the plant, so that the plant is blown away from the stake rather than into it.

Understanding weeds

Weeds don't just make the garden look untidy – they can also have a significant effect on the quality and quantity of your vegetable harvest.

Telltale weeds

Some weeds can provide useful information about your soil. Sorrel and plantains prefer acidic conditions, but poppies and pansies like chalky soil. Docks indicate that you have a rich, fertile soil; clovers are a sign of poor fertility.

A weed is simply a plant in the wrong place. Weeds are often wild plants, but they can also include cultivated plants that have spread and are growing where they aren't wanted.

Why weeds matter

Weeds will compete with vegetable plants for water, nutrients, light and space – all the essentials of plant life. If allowed to grow uncontrolled they will usually win – vegetable plants are often crowded out. Apart from their competitive effects, weeds can harbour pests and diseases; slugs and snails, for example, find the lush growth of weeds a perfect habitat from which to make their night-time forays to devastate vegetables. Several weeds carry virus diseases, showing no symptoms themselves, but they are spread by insects to cultivated plants.

Annual weeds such as shepherd's purse don't have an extensive root system because they need to last only the one season.

Large taproots or rhizomes on perennials such as dandelion have a long, sturdy root system to survive for years.

Perennials that grow on stolons such as creeping buttercup can spread quickly over a wide area.

Rampant weed growth makes harvesting a tiresome job.

Do weeds have any redeeming features? Wild plants do because they provide food and habitats for a wide range of welcome wildlife. Allowing a corner of your garden to go wild encourages all sorts of creatures, many of which will be your garden's allies, or at least be interesting and fun to watch. However, keep weeds out of the vegetable plot if you want the best from your plants.

Where weeds come from

Turn over a piece of soil and within days weeds start to cover its surface. How do they get there? Any area of fertile garden soil is filled with thousands of weed seeds. They may have been shed from previous weeds that grew and flowered; they may have blown in on a breeze or they may have been carried in by birds and other wild creatures – or even by you, on the soles of your shoes.

These seeds may lay dormant for years, so that the stock in the soil

builds up all the time, waiting for the right conditions to germinate. Plants bought from garden centres or given by friends all contribute fresh stocks of seeds in their soil, and they often bring along a quota of vigorously growing weed seedlings, as well.

Good gardeners compost their garden waste, and much of that waste is likely to consist of weeds. Dumping flowering weeds in the compost heap will lead to you spreading weed seeds around the garden later, too. The weeds themselves usually die as they are smothered in the compost heap, but their seeds are tougher. Even the best-made compost heap will not heat up sufficiently to kill all weed seeds, so by spreading compost over your vegetable plot, you may be distributing weeds.

Dealing with weeds before they start flowering is the best way to cut down the number of seeds in the compost heap. Take care to use the correct composting techniques so there is sufficient heat to kill them (see pages 38–39). However, even if a few weeds are spread with the compost, the benefits provided by the compost far outweigh the inconvenience of the weeds.

Weed wake-up call

Weed seeds are usually small, with little food reserves for the young plant. Most types need to be fairly near the soil surface before the seedlings have a chance of survival: if the seeds are buried too deeply, the germinating seedling runs out of steam before it can get into the light and start fending for itself. For this reason most deeply buried seeds remain dormant. However, once they are brought closer to the surface, they will receive the right signals to start their growth. This is why any soil cultivation is usually soon followed by a good crop of young weeds.

Stems that creep below the ground such as bindweed are some of the most difficult weeds to eradicate.

ANNUAL OR PERENNIAL WEEDS?

There are many different weed species that might invade the vegetable garden, but they can be divided into two main groups: annual and perennial. Annual weeds germinate, flower, produce seeds and die in one season – although some types survive two seasons. Shepherd's purse and hairy bittercress are two successful examples. Annual weeds are easy to manage as long as you deal with them before they flower and seed.

Perennial weeds may continue for a number of years. They can regrow from their roots even when the parts above the ground have been destroyed – sometimes several times. Several types of perennial produce food storage organs such as large taproots or rhizomes to keep them going through periods of poor growing conditions. For example, dock grows deeply into the ground and can be difficult to dig up.

Some perennials produce new plants on stolons, which creep along the ground and root as they go. One extremely invasive type of perennial is bindweed, which has stems that creep below the ground. If these stems are broken every minute piece that remains is capable of growing into a new plant.

93

Controlling weeds

Early action is the key to weed control. Never let weeds get the upper hand, because they will be much more difficult to remove if they become well established.

The longer weeds remain in place, the more time and physical effort will be neccessary to remove them, especially if you allow them to spread. You should always try to remove weeds before they form their seeds.

Weed prevention

There are many methods you can use to help prevent weeds from becoming a real problem.

Clear the ground. When starting a new vegetable plot, make a real effort to get rid of all the perennial weeds. Dig up and remove as much of the roots and stems as possible. If the plot is extremely weedy, you can kill the weeds with a mulch or herbicide (see *Herbicides*, left) before you start.

Cultivate carefully. Remember that soil cultivations bring new weed seeds up near the surface where they can germinate. The no-dig method helps avoid this problem (see pages 42–43), or you can use the stale seedbed technique (see pages 56–57) to cope with the weeds that arise. Always keep soil disturbance to a minimum when carrying out routine care such as hoeing round established plants.

Rotate crops. Some vegetables are much more able to compete with weeds than others. Potatoes, for example, crowd out weeds far more efficiently than onions. Rotating these crops round the plot ensures that weeds are less likely to build up in one particular area.

Mulch. Cover up bare soil to prevent weeds from getting a foothold by depriving them of light. You can use organic mulch such as rotted compost or inorganic mulch such as black plastic sheeting. You can cover a whole bed with plastic sheeting, burying the edges to keep it in place. If you don't intend to plant the area for a while pieces of old carpet can be used instead of plastic, although they tend to look even less attractive.

Organic mulches are easy to spread between the rows after you plant the vegetables. The mulch should be a minimum of 2.5cm (1in) deep, but preferably 7.5cm (3in) deep, to suppress weed growth.

Grow green manure. If you have a spare piece of ground that you don't intend to grow vegetables in for a while, sow a green manure or cover

HERBICIDES

Many gardeners choose not to use chemical herbicides, but they can be valuable in clearing a plot containing difficult perennial weeds, especially if you are unable to hand-dig the plot. An effective chemical option is glyphosate. It is absorbed and distributed around the plant, killing the roots as well as the top growth. Herbicidal soap, based on fatty acids, is an organic option for killing the top growth of weeds, but it does not destroy the roots.

When using herbicides round a growing crop, remember that one slip of your sprayer means you may kill crops instead of the weeds. Even herbicidal soap will kill vegetable plants if sprayed on them by mistake.

Apply all herbicides with care, following the manufacturers' instructions exactly. For the best results choose a dry day with light air movement to avoid spray drifting into other areas.

crop such as rye or buckwheat. Sown thickly, these prevent less desirable weeds from colonising the soil.

Target fertiliser applications. If you broadcast fertilisers over the whole area, weeds will benefit from them, too. If you can, apply fertilisers more selectively near the vegetables.

Weed control

Vegetables and weeds that germinate together can coexist for a while; it usually takes about two to three weeks before the weeds start to compete with the vegetables. However, it is easier to keep the weeds under control if you take action against them beforehand.

Hoeing. One of the best methods of weed control is hoeing – it is effective and is not too strenuous. Use a Dutch or stirrup hoe, and keep the blade sharp. The trick is to push the blade along the soil surface, severing the weed stems from their roots – don't try to dig the weeds up with the hoe. Disturb the soil as little as possible.

Hoe on a sunny day when the soil surface is dry, then the weeds can be left on the surface where they will quickly shrivel up. If the soil is moist, they may re-root. Hoeing works best when the weeds are small. You will need to take care when hoeing near

If you use plastic sheeting as a mulch, you can cut slits into the plastic through which you can plant your vegetables.

vegetable seedlings, because it's easy to slice the vegetable plants off along with the weeds.

Although hoeing weakens deep-rooted perennials, they will probably need to be hoed off several times before they die. Weeds such as annual grasses are difficult to control with a hoe because they don't separate easily from their roots.

Hand cultivators. These tools, usually with three or five tines, don't work as well as a hoe. They are pulled through the soil and loosen the whole weed, complete with root, which must be removed. By disturbing the soil surface, you may encourage more weed seeds to germinate.

Hand weeding. You can pull weeds out of moist soil or loose mulches by hand. It is a satisfying job, but can be backbreaking over a large area. You should pull the weeds out with their roots and remove them from the site. If left lying on the soil surface they could grow again. Where weeds are large, use a hand fork, trowel or garden fork to prise them out of the soil. Again, soil disturbance will tend to encourage more weeds.

CLEARING A PLOT

You can cover a weedy plot with black plastic mulch or old carpet to kill the weeds by depriving them of light. Where weeds are already established, leave the mulch in place for at least a whole growing season to be effective. After you remove the mulch, make sure that you dig out any perennial weeds that are still alive.

A flame gun is a quick and effective way to kill weeds on a spare piece of ground, although it is less suitable for using between crop rows because of possible accidental damage to the vegetable plants. Use a shield on the gun to direct the flame where you want it. Make one pass to wilt the weeds: then take a second pass to burn up the top growth.

Perennial weeds may need more than one treatment to get rid of them, or you can use a fork to remove their roots once you destroy the top growth.

Tug a small weed from the base of the stem. Hand weeding is the best option to avoid accidental damage to nearby vegetables.

95

Preventing pest problems

An inevitable part of growing plants is the appearance of pests, and sometimes vegetables seem to be especially prone to attack. However, there are several simple ways to protect your crops.

A pest is any creature that has a detrimental effect on a vegetable crop. It may be as large as a deer, or a tiny mite that's hardly visible to the naked eye. Sometimes a pest will interfere with the plant's development, weakening it so that it is unable to carry a good crop: other times the pest directly damages the crop itself.

The amount of damage varies, from a few minor blemishes to total destruction. The majority of vegetable pests are insects, although mammals, birds, nematodes and molluscs all make their own contributions.

Pest prevention

Be prepared for inevitable visits from pests by making it harder for them to build up to damaging numbers.

Provide good growing conditions. Sturdy, healthy plants may be no less likely to be attacked by pests, but they

CONFUSE THE ENEMY

Several pests such as carrot fly and onion fly search for plants by smelling their scent. Avoid bruising or handling the foliage of the plants, and perform thinning or weeding operations late in the day to give the flies minimal time to track the vegetables down. Grow carrots and onions next to each other, or alongside a strong-smelling herb such as tansy or garlic to send out confusing scent signals.

Laying shiny aluminium foil alongside rows of lettuce can trick aphids by dazzling them, so they don't land on the plants. Birds are also deterred by shiny, moving objects such as strips of foil or old CDs suspended from a string.

PLANTS TO ATTRACT BENEFICAL INSECTS

Growing these plants near your vegetables can attract pest-controlling insects, including lacewings, ladybirds and hoverflies.

Anthemis tinctoria (golden marguerite): Perennial evergreen, with feathery foliage and golden daisy flowers.

Calendula officinalis (marigold): An easy-to-grow hardy annual with bright orange daisy-type flowers carried over a long season.

Coriandrum sativum (coriander): Carries heads of small white flowers, which set edible coriander seeds.

Fagopyrum esculentum (buckwheat): Fast-growing, medium-height plant with white flowers, popular with hoverflies. Grow it as a green manure.

Foeniculum vulgare (fennel): Tall herb with threadlike foliage.

Limnanthes douglasii (poached egg plant): A low growing, spreading plant with white and orange flowers and light green, fernlike leaves.

Melissa officinalis (lemon balm): A herb with lemon-scented leaves.

A walk-in cage with a roof is ideal for keeping larger animals, including birds, away from your vegetables.

are able to manage the attack better. A strong plant can shrug off a pest infestation that would have a serious effect on a weaker specimen.

Keep the vegetable garden tidy.
Weeds, leaf litter and general plant debris often provide hiding and breeding places for a whole variety of plant pests, but particularly for slugs and snails. A wild area is good for encouraging beneficial species, but keep it to a specific part of the garden, away from the vegetable plot.

Inspect plants frequently. Pest species usually build up on plants quickly. Inspect your plants every two or three days. Look for anything unusual   a plant that is not keeping up with the others, the odd yellowing leaf or a few little holes in the foliage.

If you see something peculiar, investigate it straight away. Check the growing tips of the plants and the undersides of leaves for insects. Look for the slimy trails of slugs and snails or wilting leaves that signify root damage. A pest attack in its earliest stages is simple to manage – you may need to only pick off a leaf or pinch out a growing tip to literally 'nip it in the bud'.

Remember also to inspect new plants for pests before buying them or planting them out.

Grow resistant varieties. Most seed catalogues sell varieties bred for their resistance to certain pests and diseases. For example, the carrots 'Flyaway' and 'Resistafly' are less likely to be attacked by carrot fly (carrot maggot) than other varieties. Lettuce 'Avondefiance' is resistant to the lettuce root aphid.

Time your sowings carefully. Once you know the peak season for a particular pest, sow seeds early or late to avoid the crop developing during that season and decrease the chance of it being adversely affected.

Make use of barriers. Deter animals by using physical barriers. To keep deer out of your garden erect a fence 2.5m (8ft) high – they can leap over lower fences. Keep out burrowing animals such as rabbits by burying the bottom 30cm (12in) of fencing below ground, turning it up in a U-shape on the outside edge of the fence.

You can construct a walk-in cage around the vegetable garden using sturdy stakes and small-mesh netting to completely enclose the area – this is a sure way of keeping larger pests away. In areas where snow is likely, replace the top netting with one of a larger mesh for the winter, or the weight of snow may damage the cage.

Keep out insects, slugs and snails.
You can also keep smaller creatures at bay by using physical barriers. Erect fences of polythene, horticultural fleece or fine-mesh netting about 2–3 feet (60–90cm) high around blocks of carrots to keep out carrot fly, which flies close to the ground to seek out target plants by smell. This type of barrier can also be used round other vegetables as a good deterrent against slugs and snails.

Cloches and horticultural fleece are a boon for keeping plants safe from a wide variety of pests, especially when the plants are young. You can cut off the bases of empty, large plastic drinks bottles and use the top sections (minus the screw caps) to make individual plant covers.

When planting out cabbage-family plants, surround each plant with a disc of material such as card or felt to prevent the cabbage root fly from laying its eggs by the stem. Commercial brassica collars are also available and are easy to use.

Surround the stems of transplants with a collar of aluminium foil to prevent them from being eaten by cutworms. These emerge at night and play havoc with many crops.

Controlling pests

No matter how good your preventive measures are, it is impossible to keep your vegetable garden free of pests. Once they appear, you need to take swift action to limit the damage.

Make your own slug trap by sinking a plastic pot into the ground and filling it with beer. Keep the top rim just above soil level to avoid trapping useful ground beetles.

PESTICIDES

Although there are some organic pesticides, most are inorganic. All the pesticides available today have to pass stringent tests to ensure that they will not harm the user – as long as they are used as instructed. However, most gardeners usually want to avoid using pesticides. One of the main reasons people give for growing their own vegetables is that they want to be sure they are free from pesticide residue.

If all other measures have failed, look for environment-friendly products that have a low toxicity and break down rapidly after use. Among the safest ones to use are those based on fatty acids or insecticidal soap; derris and pyrethrum are short-lived insecticides of plant origin. If you use pesticides remember that even 'safe' pesticides can be harmful to beneficial insects and fish, and they must be used with care.

When a problem arises you'll need to decide which steps to take. If the vegetable in question is near maturity it may be that no action is necessary – the pest may not have time to damage it. However, more often than not, you will have to do something to prevent the harvest from becoming severely damaged.

Pest control measures

There are many ways to control pests in the garden. A combination of these measures will keep your plants healthy.

Hand-picking. If you spot an infestation early enough, you may be able to pick off the pests, or infested leaves or shoots, by hand and destroy them. Caterpillars are easy to pick off when there are only a few of them, and aphids start off clustered on just one shoot – although they soon spread.

Spraying with water. A strong jet of water from a hose is often enough to dislodge pests from plants. However, be careful that the jet of water is not so strong that it damages the plants.

Repellents. Many repellents rely on the pests' sense of smell, using extracts of citrus, garlic or other deterrent plant oils. Slug and snail repellents use substances that make it uncomfortable for the creatures to crawl over them, either because they are irritating or dry up their slime or, in the case of copper tape, contain a small electric current.

Trapping. There are many types of traps for pests, from yellow, sticky strips of card to snare insects to specialised animal traps to capture squirrels and moles. If you decide to use live mammal traps, it is essential that you inspect them at least twice a day. You will also have to decide what to do with the animals once they are trapped. Wildlife experts don't recommend releasing them into the wild because they may have trouble adapting to new surroundings.

Sticky traps are strips of card or plastic coated with a non-drying glue; they are yellow because this colour attracts whitefly. They are useful in greenhouses, but not outdoors because they can trap beneficial insects. Sticky traps are not a complete control, but they keep whitefly numbers down.

Slug and snail traps are sunk into the ground just above soil level and baited with beer or a special slug attractant, which drowns the slugs and snails. Commercial traps are designed to make disposing of the remains less unpleasant.

Biological controls. You can use the natural enemies of some pests to help control their numbers. The first step is to recognise and encourage the useful creatures that already occur in the garden – insects such as ladybirds, lacewings, hover flies, rove beetles and

centipedes, as well as creatures such as bats, frogs, toads and slowworms. You can provide suitable food sources and habitats to help these species proliferate in your garden. Grow the right wild plants as a food source, create a pond, put up nesting boxes or winter shelters – even a pile of stones or logs in a corner of the garden. Although your wildlife areas may harbour a few plant pests as well, the good creatures should outnumber the bad ones. If you are considering using chemical pesticides, remember that most of them are indiscriminate; they kill the beneficial insects along with the harmful ones.

For tailored biological controls you can import pest predators and parasites into the garden (see *Common Biological Pest Controls,* right). A wide variety of controls is available. You can order products direct from the supplier, or buy a pack from a garden centre, which may contain a form to be sent off in the mail, so that the control can be posted directly to you.

It is generally important to get the timing of the order right. For the control to work effectively, the temperature must be at the correct level, and there must also be sufficient numbers of the pest present in your garden to allow the control organism to become established.

(see *Common Biological Pest Controls,* right)

COMMON BIOLOGICAL PEST CONTROLS

Biological controls for specific garden pests are available from speciality suppliers, which usually operate by mail order. Make sure you always follow the suppliers' instructions carefully – some of these controls are for outdoor use, but others are only suitable for use in a greenhouse. Nematodes may require moist conditions to work.

Aphids
Aphidius
Aphidoletes aphidomyza
Chrysoperla sp. (lacewing)
Hippodamia (ladybird)

Red spider mite
Phytoseiulus persimilis

Slugs and snails
Phasmarhabditis
(nematodes)

Vine weevil
Steinernema kraussei
(nematodes)

Whitefly
Delphastus
Encarsia formosa

A wildlife pond, even a small one, is one way to encourage beneficial ceatures such as frogs to make your garden their home.

Understanding plant diseases

Plant diseases can have just as much of a harmful effect on vegetable yields and quality as pests, but good growing techniques will help to keep these afflictions at bay.

Plants are vulnerable to diseases mostly caused by fungi and viruses. However, there are a few bacterial infections that attack plants, and they produce similar symptoms to those of fungi.

Fungal diseases

Because fungi have no chlorophyll, they cannot manufacture food from sunlight, as plants do, so they must obtain their food from other sources. Many of them will tap into the food supply provided by plants.

Some types of fungi grow only on dead plant material, and they are valuable for breaking down plant debris into humus. Other fungi need living plant tissue to survive: these fungi can certainly damage plants but they don't usually kill them, because this is counterproductive to their needs. There are relatively few of this type, but powdery mildew is one that often causes problems for gardeners.

The largest and most troublesome group consists of fungi that will grow on either living or dead tissue. They will continue to obtain nourishment from a plant even if they kill it, and there is nothing to hold them back once an infection is under way.

Fungi produce wide-ranging, threadlike structures called hyphae, which act much like a plant's root system, and they can spread effectively through plant tissues or soil. The hyphae extract nutrients from the plant, either debilitating it, or causing a more serious breakdown of the plant material until it becomes a mushy mass. Instead of seeds, fungi reproduce by spores, which can persist in a dormant state for many years until conditions are right for them to start to grow.

Viral diseases

Viruses are tiny organisms that can cause a huge range of symptoms in plants. Most familiar are the yellow mottling, streaking or mosaic patterns on foliage, and the malformation of leaves and shoots, which can be curled, twisted or crinkled.

Apart from the obvious symptoms, viruses can cause a general reduction in the health and vigour of affected plants, reducing crop yields severely. Viruses are difficult to control: while fungus diseases can be prevented or cured by fungicides, there are no chemicals that will have the same effects on viruses.

FROM THE APHID'S MOUTH

Viruses are spread from plant to plant by touch or through knives or secateurs that have been in contact with infected plant material. However, the most common means by which viruses are spread are aphids.

An aphid actually injects a dose of disease into the sap of a plant with its piercing mouthparts when it moves from feeding on an infected plant to a healthy one. Viruses that affect crop plants can also exist in weeds, which may show no symptoms but form a source of infection for future crops. (For prevention and control, see pages 104–5.)

Powdery mildew occurs late in the season. It spreads by spores, so destroy the plants after harvesting so it won't recur in the spring.

Bringing diseases into the garden

There is a depressingly long list of ways in which plant diseases can sneak into the vegetable garden and attack the plants. There are some diseases we can do little about, but there are others that we have some control over.

Disease spores can literally arrive in the garden on the wind. They may also come in on new plants or plant material from garden centres or other gardens. They could be in the soil round the roots of a plant, or carried in the soil on the soles of your shoes. Several diseases may already be present in the seeds you sow.

Once a plant has been attacked by disease, the debris from that affected plant is a potent source of infection. There may be fallen leaves left lying on the soil surface, scraped up into a pile at one end of the vegetable plot, ready for disease spores to be blown around the garden. Or they can be carried in water splashes on to new plants. Diseased plant remains put on the compost heap will contain spores that are resistant to the composting process, so spreading the compost will also spread the disease.

Diseases that survive in the soil can be persistent – club-root disease can remain dormant for over 20 years. In these cases you'll need to live with the disease and reduce its effects – but you won't be able to eradicate it.

Blossom end rot on the bottom of tomatoes occurs when insufficient water leads to a calcium deficiency; it is not caused by disease.

PLANT DISORDERS

Although a plant may look as though it is suffering from a disease, it doesn't necessarily mean it has been attacked by a disease-causing organism. Nutrient deficiencies in the soil can create a range of symptoms such as pale, mosaic-patterned leaves and blossom end rot on tomatoes – a hard, brown, sunken patch at the base of the fruit that is caused by a lack of calcium and too little water.

Wilting plants may be caused by drought or waterlogging; low temperatures or cold winds can blacken leaves or turn their edges brown. Greenback on tomatoes – a hard area on a part of the fruit that remains green and fails to ripen – can be the result of too much sunlight. Keep these types of disorder in mind when checking plants for symptoms of disease.

Quick Tip

Don't spread it

Don't try to propagate from a diseased plant. Viruses are present throughout the whole system of an infected plant. Propagating from even apparently healthy parts of the plant by cuttings, division or tubers will mean the new plants are infected, too.

Controlling plant diseases

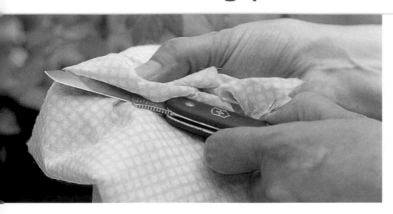

Outbreaks of plant disease are often due to poor cultivation techniques in the garden. Fortunately, there are some simple steps that you can take to reduce the risk.

Where plant diseases are concerned, it is easier to prevent an outbreak than it is to cure one once it has become established. Here are some common-sense rules to follow to prevent diseases.

Practise good hygiene. This is the first essential step when trying to maintain a healthy vegetable garden. Always clear up any plant debris promptly, especially if a crop has been suffering from some type of ailment. Diseased plant material is best burned, because while some diseases will be destroyed in a well-made compost heap, plenty of others will survive and continue to spread the infection.

Make sure you always keep your gardening equipment clean. Wash pots and seed trays in hot water at the beginning of the season, and occasionally wipe over the blades of knives and secateurs with a garden disinfectant. Use a sterile compost for raising plants in containers.

Provide the right conditions for rapid growth. Sowing or planting vegetables too early, when the soil is wet and cold, will increase the amount of time they take to become established,

leaving them more prone to attack by disease organisms. The same applies to trying to grow plants that are not suited to your particular climate. It's always an enjoyable challenge to see how far you can push the boundaries, but a plant that thrives in hot, dry conditions will be more prone to problems in a chilly, damp area – and vice versa. You can try it but be prepared for disappointments.

If you want to get an early start with your vegetables, try raising the plants in containers in a frame, a greenhouse or a conservatory. You should only set them outside once growing conditions are more suitable for the plants.

Plant healthy stock. If you can, raise your own plants from seeds sown in sterile mix and clean seed trays. Buy the seeds from a reliable source, too – some plant diseases are seed borne. If you have limited space to raise your own plants, cabbage-family plants are probably the most important ones to concentrate on. It's easy to import club-root disease with newly purchased cabbage-family seedlings – and once you have club root in the soil, it is there for good.

DISEASE CONTROL

There are not too many options for controlling diseases once they have broken out. Diseases generally develop quickly, so prompt action is essential to avoid a major problem.

Remove all affected parts on a plant as soon as you notice signs of disease and destroy them, preferably by burning. This will help to prevent the disease from worsening on the affected plant, and will also help to prevent it from spreading to other plants. If a plant is badly affected, destroy the whole plant.

You can use fungicides to treat diseases. Two fungicides suitable for organic use are copper and sulphur. Although a wide range of non-organic fungicides is available, the use of these is generally restricted to plants not used for human consumption, so it is particularly important to check the label of any product before using it on vegetables. One non-organic fungicde that can be used safely on vegetables is mancozeb; however, this works better as a preventive than as a treatment for existing disease.

If you have to purchase vegetable plants, you should make sure you buy them from a reputable supplier whose stock looks healthy and well maintained. If certified disease-free stock is available (as with seed potatoes, for example), buy only that type. At least you'll know that you're starting out with healthy plants.

Make conditions unfavourable for diseases. Some plant diseases need specific conditions to thrive, and you can manipulate these to your advantage. Club root, for example, requires an acid soil, so reducing soil acidity by adding lime to your cabbage-family plot will help keep club root away. Conversely, potato scab likes alkaline soil, so make sure you don't lime the area where you plan to grow potatoes.

Rotate crops. Growing the same type of vegetables in the same patch of soil year after year will give disease organisms the ideal opportunity to build up. Following a crop rotation plan (see pages 18–19) will help to avoid this, particularly where the diseases are soil borne.

Avoid overcrowding. Most diseases thrive in a humid atmosphere – the same type of conditions that are created by overcrowded plants. Thin seedlings out as soon as they can be handled easily, and make sure the plants are set out at the recommended spacings. A good airflow is essential. Don't forget that weeds will create a humid micro-climate around your vegetable plants, too – another good reason for getting rid of them.

Keep the plants happy. Keep your vegetable plants growing strongly by practising good growing techniques. Putting plants under any type of stress – whether it's by overcrowding, a lack of nutrients, too high or too low temperatures or a lack of water – will make them less able to withstand a disease attack.

Water carefully. Because many plant diseases like humid conditions, take extra care when watering. Don't splash water round too freely when it's not really necessary. Overhead watering, particularly in cool conditions where moisture stays on the leaves, is much more likely to promote disease than applying water direct to the soil. Water splashes may also carry disease spores from one plant to another.

Be aware of the weather. Certain weather combinations create the ideal conditions for various diseases. Warm, wet summers, for example, are ideal for potato blight to develop, whereas warm, dry conditions are favourable for powdery mildews. Downy mildew on lettuce tends to appear in cool, damp weather, which is also loved by grey mould disease, especially in greenhouses. By knowing which diseases are most likely to appear and by keeping a close eye on plants, you can take action as soon as a problem arises.

Control aphids. One of the best steps you can take to prevent the spread of viral diseases (see pages 100–1 and pages 104–5) is to keep aphids under control.

Grow resistant varieties. Read seed catalogue descriptions for details on disease-resistant varieties.

Use fungicides. Unlike insecticides, fungicides can have a preventive effect by coating the leaves of plants to stop disease spores from germinating. (See *Disease Control*, left, for more information about fungicides.)

Provide proper spacing between your vegetable plants – this is especially important in hot, humid weather to help prevent disease.

Identifying pests

Soil pests

Includes: Cutworm, millipede, wireworm

Symptoms: These pests feed on the roots or stems of plants, causing the leaves to turn yellow and wilt; young plants often die. The stems of seedlings and transplants may be severed at soil level. Pest larvae are responsible; look for curled white or brown grubs in the soil. Adult millipedes also cause the damage.

Prevention and control: Dig soil in autumn and winter to expose the pests to birds and the weather. Keep vegetable plants weed free to discourage adults from laying eggs. Clear away plant debris. Use collars against cutworms.

Chemical control: None.

Beetles

Includes: Asparagus beetle, flea beetle, pea and bean weevils

Symptoms: Beetles generally feed on leaves and stems of plants, although some species such as wireworms and cockchafers have larvae that are soil pests.

Flea beetles attack young seedlings, often cabbage-family plants, biting small holes in the leaves; pea and bean weevils eat the leaf edges of pea and bean plants. Asparagus beetles eat foliage and distort young shoots.

Prevention and control: Encourage rapid growth of vulnerable seedlings and young plants by providing the correct conditions. Hand-pick beetles where seen. Remove plant debris, which shelters adults and allows them to overwinter.

Chemical control: Bifenthrin, rotenone, pyrethrins.

Flies

Includes: Cabbage root fly, carrot fly, celery leaf miner, onion fly

Symptoms: Cabbage root fly attacks all cabbage-family plants; the first sign is often wilting of lower leaves in warm weather. Small white larvae feed on roots, which checks or kills plants.

Carrot fly feeds on roots of carrots, celery, parsley and parsnips; leaves on affected plants have a red tinge. Celery leaf miner attacks the leaves, causing patchy white areas, and weakens plants. Onion fly attacks stems and bulbs; plants will rot.

Prevention and control: Dig soil in autumn and winter to expose pests to birds and the weather. Clear away plant debris, which gives cover for adults. Destroy affected leaves on celery.

Protect cabbage transplants by placing a card or fabric disk around stems.

Carrot fly finds carrots by smell, so avoid bruising the foliage; sow seeds thinly to reduce hand thinning. Sow late in the spring or early summer to avoid worst attacks. Lift and store mature carrots.

Chemical control: None.

Caterpillars

Includes: Cabbage caterpillar, pea moth, tomato moth

Symptoms: Cabbage caterpillars reduce healthy cabbage-family plants to lacework in a few days.

Pea moths feed on the developing peas that are unseen within the pod. Tomato moth caterpillars eat holes in both the leaves and the fruits, and are most common in greenhouses.

Prevention and control: Inspect the undersides of cabbage-plant leaves for egg clusters; destroy affected leaves. Pick or hose off caterpillars as they appear. Cover cabbage-family plants with horticultural fleece or grow them in a fruit cage to keep egg-laying butterflies off the plants. Pick brown tomato moth caterpillars off tomato plants. Clear up plant debris.

Sow peas early or late to avoid plants growing during the peak caterpillar season.

Chemical control: Bifenthrin, rotenone, pyrethrins.

The following chart lists some of the major pests that are fond of vegetables. In addition to the preventive and control measures listed here, some gardeners may want to use chemical pesticides (see pages 98–99) – always follow the product label exactly.

Mammals and birds

Includes: Deer, rabbits, mice and voles, badgers, cats

Symptoms: Deer and rabbits will eat almost anything green, and badgers are particularly fond of sweet corn. Mice and voles eat seeds, especially peas and beans, and stored produce. Cats foul beds.

Many birds are useful pest predators, but pigeons attack cabbage-family plants in winter and jays may steal peas and beans.

Prevention and treatment: Put down traps for mice and voles; keep garden clear of debris that provides shelter.

Put up fencing to keep out larger mammals and birds (see pages 96–97). Various scaring devices can be used to deter them, and netting or horticultural fleece help to protect vegetables.

Cover freshly prepared seedbeds with plastic netting, to prevent cats from digging, or keep soil moist.

Repellents may have some affect against these pests.

Chemical control: None.

Aphids

Includes: Black bean aphid, cabbage aphid, mealy cabbage aphid, potato aphid

Symptoms: These small insects are often green or black but may be grey, brown, or pink, depending on the species. All are sapsuckers: they weaken plants, make crops unpleasant to eat and spread viral diseases.

They develop in dense colonies on shoot tips and leaves and reproduce rapidly. Females give birth without mating, but there are also winged females that do mate. Aphids exude a sticky honeydew when feeding.

Prevention and control: Clear plant debris promptly, especially old cabbage-family plants where aphid eggs overwinter.

It is impossible to keep aphids out of a garden, so be vigilant and deal with outbreaks as soon as they occur. Pick off and destroy the infested shoots and leaves, or knock the aphids off plants with a strong spray of water.

In greenhouses you can use biological controls.

Chemical control: Bifenthrin, fatty acids, rotenone, pyrethrins.

Greenhouse pests

Includes: Red spider mite, whitefly
(Note: These pests are not limited to the greenhouse.)

Symptoms: Red spider mite infests tomatoes, cucumbers, aubergines and peppers, causing white flecks on the leaves and webbing at tips. Look for tiny mites.

Whiteflies look like tiny white moths; they like cucumbers but attack all greenhouse plants and cabbage-family plants outdoors. They cluster on the undersides of leaves and rise up when plants are disturbed. Both pests are sapsuckers and weaken plants.

Treatment and control: Red spider mites thrive in dry conditions; to deter them, keep the atmposphere in the greenhouse moist. Try the biological control *Phytoseiulis persimilis*, a predator.

Use *Encarsia formosa*, a parasite, to control whiteflies. Yellow sticky traps help to keep numbers down.

Clear away plants as soon as harvesting is over to reduce populations of both pests.

Chemical control: Bifenthrin, pyrethrins, rotenone, fatty acids; imidacloprid for peppers, aubergines and tomatoes.

Slugs and snails

Includes: Field slug, garden slug, keeled slug, garden snail

Symptoms: Slugs and snails eat leaves and stems, leaving just a network of veins, with telltale slimy trails. Damage is generally done at night. Tender young plants are most at risk – seedlings may be entirely consumed overnight.

Prevention and control: They are most evident in moist, warm weather. Keep areas surrounding the vegetable garden clear of weeds and debris because slugs and snails shelter there during the day. Use traps (see pages 98–99) and empty them regularly.

You can hunt for slugs and snails at night, by torchlight, to remove large numbers; wear gloves to pick up slugs because slime is difficult to remove from your fingers.

You can use a microscopic nematode, *Phasmarhabditis,* a form of biological control.

To protect individual plants, surround them with a circle of sharp sand, crushed eggshells or diatomaceous earth, or cover with plastic bottles.

Chemical control: Aluminium sulphate, metaldehyde.

Identifying diseases

Blight

Crops affected: Potatoes, tomatoes

Symptoms: Blight occurs in warm, wet weather. It progresses rapidly on potatoes. First signs are dark blotches on the leaves, followed by rapid wilting and yellowing of foliage and stems, then a collapse of the plant, often in a few days. Spores wash down to infect the tubers, which develop a brown rot.

Blight is less dramatic on tomatoes but is serious, with leaves collapsing and fruits developing brown rotting patches.

A different organism is responsible for early blight, which causes brown spots on the leaves, but it is much less serious.

Prevention and control: Warnings are often given by official bodies when the right combination of humidity and temperatures can lead to a risk of blight.

If the disease is spotted on potato foliage, remove and burn the haulms (top growth). If you harvest the crop right away, the tubers may be unaffected. Destroy infected or suspect crop remains by burning, or bury them deeply and well away from the vegetable garden.

Greenhouse tomatoes are slightly less vulnerable to attack than outdoor ones.

Chemical control: Mancozeb, copper sulphate, copper oxychloride.

Blossom-end rot

Crops affected: Tomatoes, peppers

Symptoms: A hard, sunken brown rot forms at the blossom end of the fruit, furthest away from the stem.

Prevention and control: This is a disorder caused by a shortage of calcium; it occurs when there is a water shortage at fruit development.

A plant that wilts while flowering and fruiting is liable to carry fruits with blossom end rot later on.

It mostly affects plants growing in small containers that dry out quickly. Keep the soil around the roots moist at all times. Add a handful of garden lime to the watering can occasionally.

Chemical control: None.

Canker

Crops affected: Parsnips

Symptoms: The shoulders of the roots are dark brown or black and shrivelled.

Prevention and control: This disease is worse in damp seasons and acid soil. Look for resistant varieties such as 'Avonresister' or 'Gladiator'. Do not sow seeds too early – mid- to late spring is fine. Lime the soil where necessary and follow a crop-rotation plan.

Chemical control: None.

Botrytis (grey mould)

Crops affected: Many, especially lettuce and tomatoes

Symptoms: This fungus starts on dead tissue but spreads to live parts. It produces a fluffy grey mould growth: under this growth the plant tissue rots. It is most often found in greenhouses.

Prevention and control: It prefers cool, damp conditions.

Clear all dead and dying plant debris away. As soon as you see grey mould, cut out and destroy affected parts.

Keep greenhouses ventilated and avoid overcrowding of plants. Water early in the day, and do not splash water.

Chemical control: Copper sulphate can control an outbreak.

Club root

Crops affected: Cabbage-family plants

Symptoms: Plants wilt in warm weather and growth is stunted and may die. Roots swell and are distorted.

Prevention and control: Club root likes moist, acid soil. Lime the soil and improve drainage on heavy soils.

Grow plants from seeds: don't buy plants or accept them as gifts.

Dormant spores can persist for 20 years, so there is no benefit from crop rotation. There are no fungicide treatments.

If the garden is infected, raise plants in pots of sterile compost; plant out with roots in a good ball of compost.

Chemical control: None.

The following chart lists some of the major diseases that attack vegetables. Preventive and control measures are listed below; however, some gardeners may want to use chemical fungicides (see pages 100–3).

Damping off

Crops affected: All seedlings

Symptoms: The seedlings collapse, sometimes with a lesion on stems. This often occurs in circular patches in seed trays.

Prevention and control: It thrives in overcrowded contions, usually in pots and trays rather than the open garden.

Clean trays and equipment at the start of the season – use a disinfectant. Use sterile compost; sow seeds thinly. Keep trays ventilated when seedlings appear. Do not overwater.

Chemical control: Copper sulphate and copper oxychloride when signs first appear.

Leaf and pod spots

Crops affected: Beans, cabbage-family plants, cucumbers

Symptoms: Anthracnose on beans causes sunken, reddish brown spots on pods and dark stripes on stems. Chocolate spot on broad beans forms brown spots on foliage and stems. Halo blight on beans causes dark spots surrounded by a pale ring.

Cucumbers with anthracnose have spreading spots on leaves and stems and sunken areas on fruits. Many organisms cause spots on cabbage-family plants.

Prevention and control: Practise garden hygiene: give plants enough space. Destroy affected leaves. Do not save seeds.

Chemical control: Mancozeb.

Mildew

Crops affected: Cabbage-family plants, peas, onions, lettuce, spinach

Symptoms: Powdery and downy mildew produce a white or grey mould, often in round patches, not as fluffy as botrytis.

Downy mildew appears on undersides of leaves in cool, damp conditions; powdery mildew forms on top in dry conditions.

Prevention and control: Look for mildew-resistant varieties. Do not overcrowd plants, and do not overwater. Remove plant debris promptly.

Mildew appears late in season so it may not need treatment.

Chemical control: Mancozeb (for downy mildew), green and yellow sulphur (for powdery mildew).

Scab

Crops affected: Potatoes

Symptoms: Tubers have brown, roundish corky areas on the surface.

Prevention and control: Scab thrives in alkaline soil, so never lime before growing potatoes. The disease is worst on light, free-draining soils, which should have plenty of organic matter added.

Keep potato plants watered during prolonged dry spells.

Chemical control: None.

Virus

Crops affected: Cabbage-family plants, lettuce, potatoes, tomatoes

Symptoms: A streaking, mosaic or mottling pattern on leaves, or malformed leaves with crinkled or rolled edges.

Common viruses include cauliflower mosaic, cucumber mosaic, lettuce big vein, tomato mosaic and potato leaf roll.

Prevention and control: Aphids are the main way viruses spread, but any contact can transmit disease. Control aphids: keep tools and equipment clean.

Remove and burn affected plants as symptoms appear. Buy certified virus-free stock: look for virus-resistant varieties in seed catalogues.

Chemical control: None.

Wilt

Crops affected: Tomato- and cabbage-family plants

Symptoms: Fusarium wilt is the most common type. Young plants become pale and stunted. Lower leaves yellow and wilt, sometimes on only one side of the plant. The symptoms move upward, and plants may die. If you cut across the stem of an affected plant, there may be a brown stain.

Verticillium wilt causes similar symptoms but without one-sided effects. Wilt diseases are worst in hot weather.

Prevention and control: Wilt diseases stay in the soil, so if a garden is infected, grow resistant varieties. Clear away plant debris and rotate crops.

Chemical control: None.

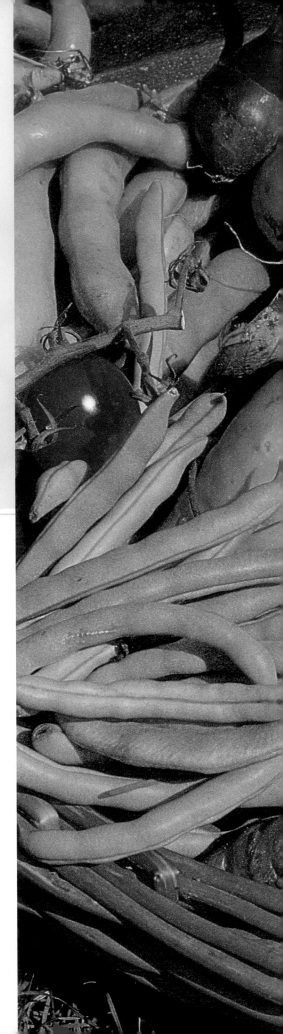

5 Harvesting and storing

One of the major benefits of growing your own vegetables is that you can pluck them from the plant or take them out of the ground when they are absolutely at their peak and enjoy them ultrafresh and bursting with nutrients.

Vegetables are usually at their best when eaten within minutes of harvesting, but you can also store many of them for later use. Knowing the right way to store them will ensure that the flavour, texture and nutrient value of your vegetables are all preserved.

Harvest time is the moment when you reap the benefits of all your hard work in the garden.

The right time to harvest

Relatively few of the vegetables we eat are grown until maturity. In fact, most of them are gathered young, when they are tender and sweet. To be able to achieve a balance between the greatest yields and the best-quality crops, it's important to understand when each type of vegetable is in its prime.

How and when a vegetable is harvested depends on whether it belongs in the leafy vegetable or fruiting vegetable group or if it is a stem or root.

Leafy vegetables

Among the leafy vegetable group are cabbage, kale, spinach, Swiss chard, lettuce and other salad greens. You can grow some plants – cabbages and many lettuce varieties, for example – until they form a firm head. When the head is large enough, cut the whole plant.

To check that a lettuce heart is firm and dense and ready for harvest, press it gently with the back of your hand – don't pinch it with your fingertips because you can bruise the leaves. Try to cut lettuce as soon as it reaches a usable size; if left too long, it will run to seed.

You can eat summer cabbages as soon as they look large enough. Don't wait until they are enormous, because supersize heads can split and be ruined. Autumn and winter cabbages are hardier than summer ones, and in most places, you can leave many varieties in the ground for harvesting throughout the winter. However, some varieties are better cut and stored in a cool place before the worst of the cold weather arrives.

For other leafy vegetables such as spinach, Swiss chard, kale and some lettuce varieties, harvest gradually over the season. If you take just a few well-developed leaves from the outside of each plant per picking, the plants will continue to grow and crop.

Fruiting vegetables

Tomatoes, peppers and melons are the obvious fruits, but this category also includes cucumbers, aubergines, tomatillos, okra and squash, as well as the seed producers – peas, beans and sweet corn.

Vegetable plants produce fruits, cobs and pods for only

When to pick

Quick Tip

Harvest times can vary widely according to the variety grown, so always check the seed packets for details.

Pick string beans before you can feel bumps in them, which are a sign that the beans are too ripe.

Leave tomatoes on the plant until ripe and ready to eat. They will develop more flavour when ripened on the vine.

STEMS AND ROOTS

You can enjoy new potatoes, baby beets, salad turnips and young carrots at a relatively immature stage, so you can harvest root vegetables as soon as they become large enough. Otherwise, leave roots in the ground until the end of the season. In fact, some roots can remain there throughout the winter (see pages 116–17).

Kohlrabi, which is not a root but a swollen stem base, becomes tough and woody when it reaches about tennis-ball size, so harvest it while still young.

Harvest **celery** and **Florence fennel** when the heads reach a suitable size. Keep an eye on fennel – if left too long it will run to seed. You can keep some varieties of celery in the ground until midwinter.

Asparagus shoots start to push their way through the soil in mid-spring; cut them when they are 15–20cm (6–8in) tall, before the bud scales start to open. Continue harvesting for about eight weeks, then stop to allow the plants to build up their reserves for next year.

one reason – to contain seeds that will ensure the continuation of the species. As soon as some of the seeds are fully ripe, they send the parent plant a message, which signals the end of fruit and seed production for the season. For maximum crops harvest frequently, so that the seeds never have a chance to ripen and switch the production system off. (The exception is when a mature crop is required – haricot beans for drying, for example, or pumpkins for winter storage.)

Most pod and cob vegetables are eaten young, when tender and sweet. The first sign of ripening is when the sugars in developing seeds begin to turn to starch. This is familiar to anyone who has eaten corn or peas beyond their prime. The pods holding them become tough and fibrous. For French and string beans, asparagus peas, snap peas and others in which the pods are eaten, pick the pods while they will still snap cleanly, without any stringiness.

You should pick summer squashes and cucumbers while they are young and tender – and remember, the more you cut, the more new fruits will be produced. Allow winter squashes to ripen into the autumn for the flesh to develop its characteristic sweetness – this is one case where you'll have to accept trade-off of a lower yield. You should also allow tomatoes to ripen on the plant. However, for sweet peppers, pick the first fruits while still green to encourage heavier crops.

How to harvest

Gathering your crops is one of the most satisfying and enjoyable tasks in the whole process of vegetable gardening. By making sure you do the job properly you'll also ensure a high-quality product with a long shelf life.

DIGGING AND LIFTING

A garden fork is more useful than a spade to prise crops from the ground, but be careful to avoid spearing them on the prongs. When digging crops such as Jerusalem artichokes and potatoes use the fork to loosen the soil, then work through the soil with your fingers to unearth the roots.

Main crop carrots, parsnips, salsify and scorzonera often have long roots, so push the fork down a good depth before levering it up, or you might snap the roots. In light soil you can sometimes pull up these crops by hand. However, unless the roots are shallow such as those on radishes, loosening the soil with a fork is the safest option.

You can also use a fork to lift non-root crops that are partly buried such as leeks and blanched celery and onions.

Harvesting can be as simple as picking a few leaves off a plant, or it may require a knife for cutting or a fork for digging. No matter which method you use, it won't take much effort to harvest your crop.

Harvesting a leafy crop

A good, sharp knife is useful to cut many leafy crops cleanly, particularly those that form a heart or head such as many varieties of lettuce and cabbage. You can also use a knife (or sharp scissors) to cut individual leaves of spinach, kale or chard. You can pick leaves by hand, but you run the risk of tugging up the whole plant by the roots if you don't do so carefully.

Sprouting broccoli has a much longer cropping season if the young flowering shoots are cut high up so that several leaves remain at the base of the stems.

New shoots will then grow from each leaf axil to multiply the harvest.

Wield the knife carefully when cutting asparagus. Harvest spears as soon as they are long enough, cutting the stems at soil level with a sharp

When picking a leaf by hand, hold the stem of the plant with one hand and pull carefully with the other.

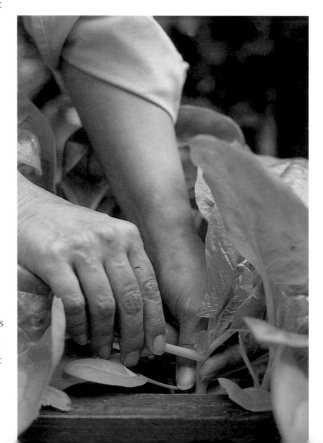

blade. Be careful not to damage developing shoots close by, hidden below the soil. Special forked asparagus knives are available to make the job a little easier.

Cut-and-come-again crops

You can grow many varieties of leafy vegetables as cut-and-come-again crops, including kale, salad leaves, Swiss chard, beet greens and spinach. Harvest the plants leaving stumps about 2.5–5cm (1–2 inches) high. A fresh flush of leaves will regrow and be ready for picking a few weeks later. In a good growing season you may even be able to get a third picking from the same plants.

Hand-picking

Pick most fruiting vegetables – peas, tomatoes, aubergines, peppers and beans (see pages 110–11) – as they are ready. Always try to remove the entire pod or fruit cleanly; damaged crops don't keep for long after picking, and any portion left on the plant provides an entry point for disease. When pulling off peas and beans, hold the stem with one hand to make sure you do not loosen the plant in the soil as you tug.

Pick tomatoes with the spidery green calyx still attached; snap the fruit away at the knuckle that is found just along the stem. Use any fruits that come away without the calyx first, because they may not keep as long as those with the calyx intact.

Peppers and aubergines don't have a knuckle like tomatoes do, but they should also be picked with a short length of stem attached. You may need a sharp knife or pruning shears because the stems can be tough.

Pick Brussels sprouts as soon as the first buttons are large enough, starting at the bottom of the stem and moving upwards. Remove old, yellowed leaves

Courgettes, cucumbers and other squashes have sturdy, prickly stems, which should be cut with a sharp knife just below the base of the fruits.

for easier access and push the buttons off sideways. Leave the leafy tops on the plants to protect the maturing sprouts below them from the weather. As soon as you pick the last sprout, cut the tops and eat them too.

Quick Tip

Extra pickings

After you cut a large head off a cabbage plant, leave the stalk in the ground and cut a shallow cross in the top. After a few weeks, another crop of leafy greens will sprout from each corner of the cut.

Keeping harvested vegetables fresh

It's not always practical or possible to eat harvested vegetables right away. In these situations follow the appropriate storing method to slow down the inevitable fall in quality that occurs once a vegetable is harvested.

Spray beans and peas with fresh, cold water to cool them quickly.

Being able to eat fresh crops as soon as you pick them is one of the joys of having a garden. As a rule of thumb, pick crops only when you want to eat them or when they are in danger of becoming overripe. The best place to store vegetables is in the ground or on the plant.

Once vegetables reach the point when they will start to spoil if left any longer, there is no choice. You'll have to harvest them, even if you already have all the beans or lettuce you need for the next few days. If you have a real glut (and it happens in even the best-planned gardens), you should consider a long-term storage method (see pages 116–23). However, for smaller surpluses a few days' grace is usually all that is needed.

Stopping deterioration

Once vegetables are picked, their quality begins to deteriorate because they are cut off from their supply of food and water and, therefore, have to start using up their own stores. Sugar will begin to turn to starch; the leaves will lose their crispness and become limp and wilted; and various micro-organisms will begin to cause rotting in the plant tissue.

You can slow down or halt the deterioration process by carrying out the following simple steps:

Check for damage. Even if only slightly damaged, eat the produce right away. The disease-causing micro-organisms will soon multiply in damaged areas – and they can spread to adjacent, undamaged produce, too.

Cool down the crop. It is extremely important to keep the temperature of your harvested crop low, because warmth can speed up the rate of deterioration. Try to pick vegetables for short-term storage early in the morning, while they are still cool and fully charged with moisture from the night. Bring them into a cool, shaded place immediately after picking, and spread the produce out instead of piling it up in a heap.

Reduce water loss. As soon as a vegetable is removed from the plant or the soil, it can no longer replace the moisture it loses by evaporation.

Soft, leafy crops such as spinach and lettuce – with their large surface areas – are affected most rapidly by moisture loss.

Water loss is accelerated by heat, so it is best to cool down susceptible crops quickly. You can spray leafy crops with freshly drawn cool water to help to rehydrate them, as well as bring the temperature down. Use a gentle spray to avoid damaging the leaves. After cooling, shake or blot excess water from the produce and move it to a cool place such as the salad box of a refrigerator to protect it from further moisture loss.

Wrap asparagus in a damp kitchen towel and store it in the refrigerator.

STORING VEGETABLES IN A REFRIGERATOR

The cool environment of a refrigerator is ideal for many vegetables, but be careful – some crops can be spoiled by low temperatures. You should never refrigerate tomatoes, for example, because it ruins their flavour, even if they are allowed to come to room temperature before being eaten. Keep them in a cool room or larder.

Store squashes, peppers and cucumbers in a refrigerator at 3–4°C (37–39°F) for two to three days, and keep all crops above freezing unless you first prepare them for freezing (see pages 118–19). Most refrigerators have a crisper or salad box that maintains higher humidity. You can also put produce in plastic bags or containers, or roll it up loosely in a damp towel. Check the produce often – the high humidity can encourage mould and rot.

Quick Tip

Protecting roots

Root crops are best left in the ground until needed. However, if you do have to lift them in advance, don't wash off the soil clinging to the roots until the last minute because it protects them from drying out and wrinkling.

Long-term storage

It's always a bonus to save some of summer's bounty to enjoy through the leaner winter months. Some crops need only minimal preparation to stay in good condition for many weeks, well into the winter.

Crops that are natural storage organs – including roots (carrots and turnips), tubers (potatoes) and bulbs (onions) – are easy to store with a little preparation. Leeks and winter-hardy, cabbage-family crops are also easy to store into winter.

Most of these crops will remain in good condition because they have natural protection against excessive moisture loss, whether it is their tough, waxy outer leaves, protective skins or their small surface area in relation to their density. You can help prolong their useful life even further by taking extra precautions to prevent moisture loss. Remember that the crops chosen for storage should be healthy and undamaged. There are several storage options for these vegetables.

In the ground

Often the best way to keep crops in good condition is to leave them in their growing positions; however, there are drawbacks. Crops in the ground are prone to attack by pests and diseases, and, depending on the climate, they can be damaged by excessive cold, rain or wind. They can also be impossible to harvest where winters are harsh and the soil is frozen for long periods.

Because potatoes and sweet potatoes can be damaged by frost, harvest them well before the cold weather. They are also prone to slug damage if left in the soil too long.

Depending on the severity of the winter, roots such as beetroot, carrots, swedes and turnips are usually sufficiently hardy to be left in the ground. However, some varieties are hardier than others, so check the seed packet. In cool areas provide extra protection by piling straw or leaf

A perfect place for storing parsnips and other root vegetables is in sand in a box.

litter over the rows once the leaves die down. Parsnips, celeriac, salsify and scorzonera are the hardiest of the root vegetables, and they can usually remain in the ground throughout winter in milder areas.

Quick Tip

Stake sense

Brussels sprouts, winter cabbages, sprouting broccoli and kale shrug off low temperatures. On exposed sites, tie these plants to a stout stake to keep them from being blown over by autumn and winter winds.

STORING IN CLAMPS

A root clamp – a pile of roots covered in an insulating layer of straw and soil – is a traditional storage method.

Root clamps are seldom used now, but they are worthwhile if you have a lot of roots to store. Build a clamp in an unheated cellar or garage, or in a sheltered spot in the open. Start with a 15-cm (6–in)-thick layer of light soil, sand or straw, then build a neat stack of roots on it, sloping the sides to form a conical pile about 75cm (30in) high and the same across at the base. Cover the stack with a thick layer of straw, then top that with another 15-cm (6-in) layer of slightly moist, sifted soil or sand, patting it down smooth with the back of the spade. Finally, pull a handful of straw through the soil at the top of the stack for ventilation.

The roots must be cold before they are piled up, so wait until early winter to build the clamp.

Take roots out through the side of the clamp, then replace the covering.

be left on the soil surface to dry for a couple of hours, after lifting and before bagging up. Close the tops of the filled bag and store them in a cool, dark place. Exposure to light causes potato tubers to turn green and produce poisonous, bitter alkaloids.

Shelves, nets and ropes

Slatted wooden shelves in a cool, dry shed or cellar will allow a good flow of air around vegetables, which helps prevent rotting. Place mature vegetables such as pumpkins and winter squashes, onions and autumn cabbages on the shelves, but be aware that they sometimes start to rot underneath where they press against the wood. Hanging them up in nets or old nylon stockings avoids this problem.

Onions and garlic are traditionally plaited into ropes, using the dried foliage of the bulbs, and hung in an airy place.

Leeks are another hardy crop that can often remain in place. However, where winters are long and harsh, lift a proportion of leeks, and all the root crops already mentioned, before the low temperatures arrive. Store them in boxes as described below – this way you can ensure that you'll have some vegetables available when the rest are frozen into the ground.

In boxes

Store roots in frost-free cellars, sheds or garages in boxes layered with moist soil or sand. Wooden boxes are best, but stout cardboard boxes will do. You should place them in their storage positions before filling – they may be too heavy to move afterwards.

Store potatoes in strong paper bags – don't use plastic bags because they encourage rotting. Harvest potatoes on a dry day so they can

Leave potatoes to dry, before you store them in a large paper bag. Remove any damaged potatoes before storing.

Freezing

Freezing is one of the most successful and popular methods for storing vegetable crops. Remember that it's worth taking a little time to prepare the produce before freezing – it can make all the difference to the quality of the end product.

IS FREEZING FOR YOU?

PRO

• Freezing is one of the best methods for home preservation.

CONS

• There may not be enough space in a standard freezer for everything you want to keep in it.

• There is the initial expense of buying a freezer and its running costs to take into account – and a power cut can be inconvenient.

• Freezing inevitably damages vegetable texture to some extent, so it is not suitable for produce that you plan to eat raw.

The micro-organisms that cause decay and deterioration are rendered almost completely inactive by the cold temperatures involved in freezing. Frozen vegetables retain virtually all their nutritional value, and their flavour and appearance are also usually well preserved.

Don't waste freezer space on vegetables that will keep well enough by other simpler methods such as those already discussed on pages 116–17. Save this technique for young and tender vegetables that cannot be preserved as successfully by these other methods. As always, use fresh, undamaged produce.

Blanching

Before freezing vegetables for long-term storage, it is important to blanch them to destroy micro-organisms and enzymes, which are responsible for the deterioration of their texture, colour and flavour. You may be tempted to skip the blanching process,

Freezing vegetables

Prepare the vegetables for cooking, then blanch them in boiling water and cool them. Most vegetables need two to three minutes' blanching time; root crops and corn cobs need four to seven minutes, depending on their size. Package the vegetables in plastic freezer bags or containers. To save space and prevent deterioration, remove as much air as you can by depressing the lid on a container or squeezing out air from a bag before sealing them.

1 Prepare the vegetables as you would for a recipe: for example, trim the ends of green beans or cut into pieces. Place them into a wire basket (no more than 250g/9oz at a time).

To freeze a leafy herb rinse and finely chop it with a sharp kitchen knife. Place 15ml (1tbsp) of herb into each compartment of an ice-cube tray, cover with water, then freeze. Once frozen, remove the ice cubes from the tray and store in a plastic bag in the freezer. Simply add the cubes of frozen herbs when needed to stews or soups.

but it improves the quality of frozen vegetables. However, if you plan to eat the frozen produce within two or three weeks, it is not essential to blanch.

Leafy herbs

Among the leafy herbs suitable for freezing – in ice cubes – are basil, mint, chervil, parsley, tarragon and chives. These can lose their taste and aroma shortly after being picked, but freezing helps retain them (but the leaf texture and colour will be altered).

Quick Tip

Power cut

Don't open the freezer door to check the contents during a power cut. Most older freezers allow food to stay frozen for at least 11 hours without power and modern ones for up to 29 hours – but only if the door remains closed.

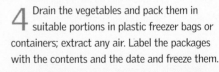

VEGETABLES FOR FREEZING

You can freeze vegetables such as cabbage, Brussels sprouts and root crops if it's easier than keeping them in the ground or in clamps (see pages 116–17). Vegetables with a high water content such as courgettes and tomatoes tend to collapse when thawed and are usually best cooked in a ratatouille or similar dish before freezing.

Other vegetables suitable for freezing are:

Asparagus

Beans: broad, French and string

Broccoli

Carrots (young)

Cauliflower

Peas and mangetout

Spinach and Swiss chard

Squashes (young)

Sweet corn

2 Plunge the basket into a pot of rapidly boiling water. Bring the water back to a boil as quickly as possible, then start timing from the moment it boils again.

3 As soon as you reach the end of the blanching time, remove the wire basket and plunge the vegetables into plenty of ice-cold water to cool them as rapidly as possible.

4 Drain the vegetables and pack them in suitable portions in plastic freezer bags or containers; extract any air. Label the packages with the contents and the date and freeze them.

Drying vegetables and herbs

Drying, one of the most ancient forms of food preservation, has enjoyed a renaissance in recent years. Think of sun-dried tomatoes! In our climate sunshine can't be relied on for drying, but don't despair – there are other ways of achieving tasty results.

By removing moisture from your vegetables, you deny micro-organisms a vital component. Without a supply of moisture, they can no longer grow – or spoil food.

Getting ready for drying

Prepare vegetables in the usual way for eating or cooking. Cut large or dense vegetables into pieces thin enough to allow thorough drying.

Blanching improves the storage life and quality for some vegetables. Blanch as if for freezing (see pages 118–19), but line the basket with muslin for chopped vegetables. Once blanched, dip the vegetables in ice-cold water briefly to stop them from cooking. Drain well and blot with a paper towel, then put them on to racks for drying. (Use racks, not solid trays, so air can circulate.)

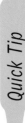

Making a rack

Stretch muslin or cheesecloth across a wooden frame to make a drying rack. You can use metal racks (such as cake cooling racks), but line them with muslin to prevent produce from falling through or being marked by the grid.

Oven-dried tomatoes

Heat the oven to 95°C (200°F), and leave the door propped open slightly. The amount of time required for drying tomatoes depends on the variety you use. The higher the moisture content, the longer they'll need in the oven.

2 The tomatoes take about 24 hours to dry; you may need to experiment. Check them often. When done, they should be leathery and exude no juice if squeezed.

1 Put a single layer of sliced tomatoes on a baking tray lined with baking parchment; then put it in the oven.

3 Store dried tomatoes in olive oil in an airtight jar with a tightly fitted lid. Keep in a dark, cool place.

Microwaving herbs

A microwave is excellent for drying herbs. Because they contain little moisture in the first place, they are able to dry out without cooking. (However, microwave drying is not suitable for vegetables.) Adjust the timing to suit your microwave oven and use a high setting. If the leaves are not dry and brittle when removed, heat for another 30 seconds.

1 Lay the herbs on a piece of paper towel, then place a second piece on top. Heat in the microwave for two to three minutes.

2 Crumble the herbs and pack them into an airtight container with a tightly fitting lid. Keep in a cool, dark place for up to a year.

STORING AND USING DRIED VEGETABLES

Let dried produce cool down completely before storing it in airtight containers – glass jars with screw lids are ideal. Keep them in a cool, dark place: sunlight fades the vegetables' colour and destroys vitamins. Dried produce can keep for up to a year at 10°C (50°F): warmer conditions reduce the storage life.

Use dried vegetables by adding them to soups, stews or other liquid-based dishes, simmering until they are rehydrated. Or soak them in water or stock for one to two hours and drain.

Drying methods

Gentle warmth is all that is needed for drying vegetables – enough to remove their moisture, not cook them. There are several ways of providing the warm, dry conditions necessary.

Sun. A reliably hot, dry climate with a minimum air temperature of 85°F (30°C) and humidity below 60 per cent for several days is ideal. It's worth a try during a heatwave.

Warm indoor space. A warm, dry place in the house such as a shelf near the central heating boiler can be used.

Domestic oven. An oven is fine as long as you keep the temperature low.

Dehydrator. Proprietary dehydrators provide ideal drying conditions.

Drying times vary from six hours in a dehydrator to three to four days outside, depending on the temperature, humidity and airflow. Check every four to five hours, and stir the produce for an even result.

Whatever the method, when ready, peas, beans or diced vegetables will be crisp. Tomatoes will be dry and leathery.

PREPARING VEGETABLES

Cut vegetables into slices, or dice, before blanching.

PRODUCE	PREPARATION	BLANCHING
Aubergines	Slice 6-mm (¼-in) thick or dice.	3 minutes
Beans, French	Leave whole if small and slender, otherwise slice like string beans.	2 minutes
Beans, string	Slice as if cooking.	2 minutes
Carrots	Slice 3-mm (⅛-in) thick or dice.	3 minutes
Celery	Trim and slice across stalks 6-mm (¼-in) thick.	2 minutes
Okra	Slice across 6-mm (¼-in) thick.	Not needed
Onions and garlic	Peel and slice onions 3–6-mm (⅛–¼-in) thick. Chop garlic finely.	Not needed
Peas	Shell.	1–2 minutes
Peppers	Remove seeds, white parts; slice into 6-mm (¼-in)-thick strips.	Not needed
Tomatoes	Halve or quarter if small, or slice 6–12-mm (¼–½-in) thick.	Not needed

Pickles, preserves and condiments

There is something very satisfying about filling larder shelves with jars of home-made pickles, preserves and condiments. You don't need to be a first-class cook – just follow a few simple rules for guaranteed success.

Several preservation techniques come under the heading of 'pickles and preserves', but the aim is the same – to prevent food spoilage organisms (bacteria and fungi) from developing. There are two methods to stop micro-organisms in their tracks: heat and chemicals. (The chemicals used are natural ones: sugar, vinegar and salt.) However, not all methods are suitable for all vegetables.

This is a quick overview of the most common methods. Consult a cookbook for detailed instructions.

Bottling

In the bottling process produce is packed into special jars, covered in syrup or water, and heated to sterilise it. The jar is then vacuum-sealed to prevent further contamination.

Bottling is fine for fruits because their acidity prevents the growth of heat-resistant bacteria. However, most vegetables do not have enough acid, so botulism-causing bacteria can escape heat sterilisation – and if eaten the results can be fatal. Tomatoes are the exception because they have enough acid. It is essential to use proper jars fitted with rubber rings and spring clips or screw bands that enable a vacuum to form in the jar after heat processing.

Pickles, chutneys and sauces

Vegetables can be preserved by the acidity of vinegar. Pickles are made from vegetables that remain crisp and

---

HERB-FLAVOURED OILS

Bay, chives, oregano, sage, rosemary, tarragon and thyme are all herbs ideal for adding flavour to a good-quality olive oil. Place sprigs of your chosen herb (or combination of herbs) into a bottle and fill with the oil. Seal the bottle and store it in the refrigerator for two weeks to allow the flavours to transfer to the oil. You can also add chillies or peeled garlic cloves. Strain the oil; refrigerate and use within three weeks. Herb-flavoured oils are ideal for salads, breads and sauces.

A simple no-cook mixed pickle

Pearl onions, green beans, peppers and cauliflower are just a few of the vegetables that can be pickled. Soak them in a salt-water solution before adding them to a vinegar of at least 5 per cent acidity (check the bottle label) – this firms them up and allows the vinegar to penetrate.

1 **Prepare the vegetables** as you would normally for a recipe, peeling them and trimming off the ends, if needed, then cutting them into florets, strips or wedges.

2 **Soak the vegetables** for one to two days in a mixture of 450g (1lb) of salt and 4.5 liters (8pt) of water. Drain the vegetables, rinse them and dry them thoroughly.

3 **Pack the vegetables** in an airtight container, leaving a 2.5-cm (1-in) gap at the top: cover completely with a spiced vinegar (see box, above right) mixed with sugar. The quantity of sugar depends on the volume of vinegar and your taste. Place a layer of waxed paper or cling film on top; then tightly secure the lid. You can eat it right away or store it for up to six months.

ADDING FLAVOUR TO VINEGAR

Spiced vinegar adds flavour to pickles and chutneys and is made by adding whole spices such as cinnamon, cloves, mace, peppercorns and chillies to a bottle of vinegar and allowing them to infuse for two months.

Herb vinegars can be made in the same way, adding a large handful of bruised herb foliage to a bottle of white-wine vinegar or cider vinegar for six weeks – strain it before use. Tarragon is a favourite for this treatment, but you can also use rosemary, sage, thyme or mixed herbs.

recognisable, and they are used raw or are cooked for a short time. Pickles are made with vinegar or a mixture of vinegar and sugar for sweet pickles.

Chutneys are made from a mixture of vegetables and fruits chopped small and cooked slowly until soft and the right consistency. Sugar is always used along with the vinegar, so chutney has a sweeter flavour than pickles. Peppers Beetroot, squash, and sweet corn are suitable for making a chutney.

Sauces have a pouring consistency. They are cooked with spices and are sieved before sugar and vinegar are added. Tomato and red pepper sauces are two of the most popular types.

Jams and jellies

Fruit is the main component for jams and jellies, but you can also find recipes using carrots, pumpkins or tomatoes. You can add herbs such as mint and rosemary to jellies, too. Jams and jellies use the preservative power of heat and sugar. Cook the produce in an open pan until soft. Add sugar and boil the mixture until it reaches setting point.

Part 2

THE
VEGETABLES

6 Lettuce and greens

A simple salad will never be boring when your garden includes a bed containing some of the many varieties of lettuce available to inspire creative salad-making. You can also include a range of other spicy and tasty salad leaves, as well as vitamin-rich spinach and Swiss chard.

For delightful salad mixes, grow premixed mesclun blends or experiment with mixing your own for unique salads crafted to your taste. Easy-to-grow rocket, chicories, radicchio and endive add a tantalising flavour and colourful accent to salads – and they can be delicious heated, too.

Swiss chard comes in a rainbow of colours and is just one of a huge variety of lettuces and greens.

Lettuce

Great salads start with freshly picked lettuce. Plant a mixture of butterhead, crisphead, loose-leaf and cos (romaine) lettuce. With a little luck and experience, in most regions you can enjoy crispy, sweet lettuce for at least six months of the year.

Sowing and planting

Soil Lettuce will grow best in rich, loose soil with a pH between 6.0 and 7.0. Spread a 5-cm (2-in) layer of organic matter over the soil and work it in. Before sowing seeds, rake the bed to remove any clods. When planting lettuce as a successional crop, you should add compost or a balanced organic fertiliser to renew soil fertility between plantings.

Sowing Lettuce doesn't keep long after being picked, so make small, frequent sowings. Sow 10 seeds every two weeks (or weekly). You can sow seeds in garden beds, but it is often better to sow seeds in pots or trays.

The germination of delicate lettuce seeds can be disappointing. The seeds will generally germinate well in soil temperatures of 4–21°C (40–70°F), but poorly in warmer temperatures. Potted seedlings grow quickly and will be ready to transplant within three weeks.

Growing spring crops Cover planting areas with plastic to warm the soil a few weeks before planting. You can sow hardy varieties in late winter, or in autumn in mild areas.

Planting summer lettuce Lettuce may bolt to seed or develop a bitter taste in high temperatures and during long days. To counteract this you can choose heat-tolerant and bolt-resistant varieties, plant lettuce in partial shade or use shade cloth or shading devices. Add extra compost or leaf mould as you dig planting holes for transplants so the soil will retain more moisture. Mulch the soil surface. Water often, which may mean once or twice a day.

Interplant lettuce among tall crops such as tomatoes, corn and trellised melons or runner beans.

BEST OF THE BUNCH

'Buttercrunch' Dependable, heat-tolerant butterhead lettuce with a buttery texture.

'Lakeland' Crisphead type with large, well-filled, deep green heads and relatively few outer leaves.

'Lollo Bionda' Loose-leaf lettuce with frilly edge, pale green leaves produced over a long period.

'Red Sails' Good loose-leaf variety for hot conditions, with frilly, reddish maroon outer leaves.

'Rouge d'Hiver' Rounded leaves with reddish-bronze blush that is good harvested for baby leaves; it has a buttery texture and tolerates heat and cold well.

'Salad Bowl' Frilly, deeply notched leaves that resists bolting, with a sweet flavour.

'Winter Density' Compact cos type with loose heads of dark green leaves; it is good for overwintering.

PLANTING GUIDE

What to plant Seeds or transplants.

Starting indoors Sow seeds early to extend the season.

Site preparation Add organic matter to improve moisture-holding capacity.

When Frequent small sowings while weather is cool or in autumn.

Spacing *Butterhead* and *cos* Sow 15–25cm (6–10in) apart, 45–60cm (18–24in) between rows. *Crisphead* Sow 25–30cm (10–12in) apart in rows 45–60cm (18–24in) apart. *Looseleaf* Sow 2.5–5cm (1–2in) apart; set transplants or thin seedlings to 10–15cm (4–6in) apart.

How much For each person, two to four plants every two weeks.

Temperature alert
Lettuce grows best in cool conditions, and seeds will not germinate reliably in hot weather. Keep seed drills moist and shaded.

Planting for autumn Keep sowing lettuce in small amounts throughout the summer to extend the harvest into autumn. Take care to sow seeds in cool, shaded, moist soil during the hottest months, as too-high temperatures cause seed dormancy – sowing in the early afternoon should enable germination to take place in the coolest period, at night. Lettuce usually takes six to eight weeks from sowing to harvest, so in late summer, start selecting hardier varieties to mature in autumn.

After the first frost, hardy varieties will keep well in the garden. Cover the plants with horticultural fleece when temperatures below 25°F (-4°C) are predicted, but lettuce will survive at surprisingly low temperatures. Plastic tunnels provide even greater cold protection.

Overwintering lettuce You can sow varieties such as 'Valdor' and 'Loboits Green Cos' outside in autumn and overwinter them to provide a crop in early spring. Horticultural fleece will protect the plants, and in cold areas you willl have better results by growing these varieties in a tunnel or frame. You can also grow varieties such as 'Kwiek' in an unheated or slightly heated greenhouse. You shouldn't expect dense hearts from overwintered lettuce.

When harvesting a full head of lettuce, use a sharp knife to cut cleanly at soil level. Discard damaged and dirty outer leaves after cutting.

Harvest overwintered lettuce plants on the small side – they will bolt quickly in response to spring warmth and longer days.

Care

Watering Don't allow the plants to dry out, especially in hot weather. Water if the top 5cm (2in) of soil becomes dry. Don't water in the autumn unless there is prolonged dry weather.

Fertilising When you transplant lettuce, side-dress the plants with a high-nitrogen fertiliser, sprinkling it in a strip 2.5cm (1in) wide. For long-growing crispheads, you can spray with a liquid organic fertiliser once a month until the autumn.

Harvesting

Begin harvesting baby lettuce leaves two weeks after setting out transplants. Pick leaves from the outside edges of plants. The plants will continue producing new leaves from the centre.

In the autumn harvest entire heads – there won't be much new growth. Harvest hearting lettuce when the heads are firm. If they are elongated they will taste bitter. If a long heat wave is predicted, harvest small heads to avoid bolting.

Storing Lettuce is best eaten just after you pick it. To store lettuce refrigerate it unwashed (unless you need to rinse the leaves immediately after picking to cool them in hot weather, but then dry them) in plastic bags. Loose-leaf lettuce will last only a few days; iceberg-type lettuce will keep for up to three weeks.

 PROBLEM SOLVER

Curled, distorted areas on leaves. Dislodge aphids with a strong jet of water. Spray persistent infestations with insecticidal soap. Protect new plantings with horticultural fleece sealed at the edges with soil.

Twisted and stunted or mottled leaves. Destroy plants infected by viral diseases. (Aphids can spread them; see above.)

Holes in leaves. Look for caterpillars, slugs or snails. Cover new plantings with horticultural fleece. For slugs and snails, use slug traps or spread a band of sharp sand, crushed eggshells or diatomaceous earth around plants.

Edges of internal leaves turn brown. A calcium deficiency causes tipburn of head lettuce; it is worst in hot weather. Choose resistant varieties. Undamaged areas of leaves are usable.

Silvery streaks on leaves. Spray plants with insecticidal soap, especially leaf undersides, to get rid of thrips.

Cottony growth on lower leaves. Plants infected by mildew, a fungal disease, which is worst in cool, damp weather. Give plants sufficient space to avoid overcrowding.

Rusty lesions on leaves; slimy or wet rot at base of plants. Various fungal disease can cause rotting in wet condtions. Do not overwater the plants.

Quick Tip

Cool lettuce

For a convenient supply of lettuce during the height of summer, plant some lettuce in containers on your patio so that you can move the containers into the shade on hot afternoons.

Types of lettuce

Try planting attractive ruffled leaf lettuce and deep red lettuce in beds with annual flowers. Add crisphead, cos, loose-leaf and butterhead lettuce to your vegetable garden, and there will be a steady supply of ever-changing salad fixings.

▶ **Crisphead lettuce**

This type has crinkled leaves, firm hearts and a good flavour; one of the oldest varieties is the still-popular 'Webbs Wonderful'. Iceberg lettuces, a more recent development, are a type that forms a dense, tightly packed heart. They are popular with shoppers because of their good keeping qualities, but they are more difficult to grow successfully at home. Iceberg varieties need a longer growing season and more fertile soil than other crispheads, and must never be allowed to go short of water.

▼ **Batavian lettuce**

Batavian lettuce is a loosely headed type of crisphead lettuce that tends to be more flavourful than iceberg types. Many Batavian varieties have purplish or rosy outer leaves.

◀ Loose-leaf lettuce

Loose-leaf lettuce (leaf lettuce) is a catchall term for lettuce that doesn't form a head even when mature. The lettuce is easy to grow and the plants are beautiful, with a wide range of leaf colours and forms. Leaves may be smooth or crinkled, ruffled, notched or curled. They range from green and yellowish green to reddish and bronze. Some varieties are ready to harvest 40 days or less after planting.

◀ Cos lettuce

Also known as romaine lettuce, cos varieties will form upright heads of sturdy leaves that have thick midribs. The heads range from 20cm (8in) to over 30cm (12in) tall when ready for harvest. The leaves may be smooth or ruffled, and some varieties have red-tinged or red-speckled leaves. At its best, cos lettuce is the sweetest of all lettuce.

▲ Butterhead lettuce

Buttery is the perfect way to describe the colour and texture of the inner leaves of butterhead lettuce. This type of lettuce forms heads of loosely folded, soft leaves. Butterhead lettuce doesn't store or transport well but it isn't hard to grow, so it's a good choice for the home gardener. Freshly picked butterheads are infinitely better than the tired, limp heads from the supermarket.

Rocket

Young rocket, or arugula, leaves have a nutty or tangy flavour that becomes peppery and more piquant as the plants grow or the temperature rises. Use its soft, lobed leaves fresh from the garden in salads or pesto, or sauté it lightly.

Sowing and planting

Soil Loosen the top few inches of soil, and spread a 2.5-cm (1-in) layer of compost over it and work it in. Rake smooth to remove clods.

When Sow rocket every one to three weeks from early to mid-spring (depending on how often you want to harvest the leaves). Rocket tends to run to seed quickly in hot weather, so try sowing the seeds in the shade of tall crops.

In late summer and early autumn, you can make sowings in a frame for a winter harvest. Crops growing in the garden can be covered with horticultural fleece in autumn to extend the harvest.

Care

You should water the plants regularly to prevent the flavour from turning too strong or hot. Make sure you keep rocket well watered in hot weather if you want to enjoy tender, tasty leaves.

Allow a few of the plants to go to flower. The flowers are edible, and the seeds will self sow. Let the seedlings spring up in the garden where you want them to grow, or you can try carefully transplanting them from one spot to another.

Harvesting

Baby leaves will be ready to harvest within a few weeks of sowing. When the leaves grow to about 7.5cm (3in) long, use a pair of sharp scissors to snip off the leaves about 2.5cm (1in) above the soil level. The plants will resprout and provide a new crop.

If you allow the leaves to grow large, sample them often to make sure their flavour is not too hot. Once the flavour turns, pull out the plants and move on to new plantings.

Wash rocket leaves by swishing them in a bowl or sink full of cool water. The leaves may require three or more washings to remove all traces of soil.

Storing For best results, you should use rocket immediately after picking. If you must store it wash and dry the leaves thoroughly, then place them in a plastic bag in the refrigerator. They will keep for up to two days.

PLANTING GUIDE

What to plant Seeds.

Site preparation Add organic matter to improve moisture-holding capacity.

When Early to mid-spring and through the summer.

Spacing Sow seeds 2.5cm (1in) apart in rows 15cm (6in) apart. Don't thin if growing for baby leaves; thin to 15cm (6in) for standard-size plants.

Intensive spacing Sow seeds lightly in a band 5–10cm (2–4in) wide.

How much Per person, 30–60cm (12–24in) of row per sowing.

Temperature alert
Rocket grows best in cool conditions. Hot weather can change the flavour of rocket leaves from savoury to 'skunky'.

PROBLEM SOLVER

Small holes in leaves. Flea beetles may be attracted to rocket, especially during hot weather. Cover plantings with horticultural fleece after sowing.

Endive

Lend a new flavour to salads with endive. Curly endive has narrow, frilly leaves and a tender, tightly packed heart. Broad-leaved endive (or escarole or Batavian endive) forms an open rosette of broader, wavy leaves with a blanched heart.

PLANTING GUIDE

What to plant Seeds or transplants.

Starting indoors Sow seeds four weeks before the desired outdoor planting date.

Site preparation Add organic matter to improve moisture-holding capacity.

When From mid-spring to late summer.

Spacing Sow the seeds lightly; thin the seedlings or set the transplants 20–30cm (8–12in) apart in rows spaced 30–60cm (12–24in) apart.

Intensive spacing Broadcast seeds in wide rows; thin to 15cm (6in) apart on centres for curly endive, 30cm (12in) apart for escarole.

How much Per planting, two plants per person.

BEST OF THE BUNCH

'Moss Curled' Deep green leaves that have a good flavour when blanched.
'Pancalieri' An ornamental type with dark green, frizzy leaves; long cropping season.

Sowing and planting

Soil Spread a 5-cm (2-in) layer of organic matter over the soil and work it in. Before sowing seeds, rake the bed well to remove all clods.

When Sow endive in a greenhouse or frost-free frame in early spring for planting out in summer, or sow directly where it is to mature from late spring and early summer onwards.

If there is a cold spell after a spring sowing outdoors, cover the seedlings with cloches or horticultural fleece to protect them, as low temperatures may cause young plants to bolt.

Care

Blanching endive will help prevent bitterness. About one week before harvesting, gather the leaves into a clump and tie twine or slip a rubber band around them. Alternatively, you can cover the plant with an upended pot, with the drainage holes sealed to prevent light from reaching the plant. During cool, autumn conditions, blanching will take longer, generally up to three weeks.

Endive can survive temperatures as low as -12°C (10°F) with protection. Although broad-leaved types may suffer some damage, the undamaged parts will still be edible.

Extending the season Try a succession planting of endive from mid- to late summer. As temperatures fall below freezing, protect the plants by using either plastic tunnels or frames. They should continue to grow slowly for harvest through autumn and into winter.

In the wet conditions that are typical in autumn and winter, endive is prone to rot, especially under covers used for blanching. You should ensure the plants are not too wet before the covers are put in place.

Harvesting

Pick leaves, or cut heads 2.5cm (1in) above ground level. The plants may resprout. Flavour will be sweeter after a frost, and blanched endive hearts are sweeter than outer leaves.

Storing You can store endive leaves in plastic bags in the refrigerator for up to 10 days.

Quick Tip

Inner beauty
The secret to enjoying endive is to pull away the outer leaves, which can be bitter, to reveal the light green, mild-flavoured inner leaves.

Chicory

The plump, pointed blanched chicons for winter salads are the most familiar type of chicory, but there are others that have beautiful leaf forms and a lively flavour, including sugarloaf, grumolo and Italian dandelion.

Sowing and planting

Soil Chicory grows best in rich, loose soil. Work in a 5-cm (2-in) layer of organic matter. Rake the bed well to remove clods before sowing.

When Sow chicory from mid-spring onwards until mid- to late summer. Cold weather after sowing in spring may cause plants to bolt prematurely, so you should delay sowing until the weather is mild.

For an early crop, sow the seeds in a heated greenhouse or frame and plant out in late spring. Sow witloof chicory for blanching in late spring or early summer.

Care

Maintain even soil moisture at all times. Blanching improves flavour. Sugarloaf chicory blanches itself naturally. For other types cover them with a flower pot (with the drainage holes plugged) when the leaves are 25cm (10in) long.

For witloof chicory lift the roots in autumn, cutting the leaves back to 2.5cm (1in), and plant the roots in a deep box or pot of sowing compost or peat substitute. Cover the tops with a depth of 25cm (10in) of compost, or an upturned pot to keep out all light. Keep in a warm, completely dark place until the chicons have formed.

PROBLEM SOLVER

Ragged holes in leaves. Combat slugs and snails with slug traps and spreading a band of sharp sand, crushed eggshells or diatomaceous earth round the plants.

Harvesting

You can use the cut-and-come-again method to snip leaves as you need them; alternatively, cut whole heads. After a frost the outer leaves of sugarloaf chicory may be mushy, but you can still use the heart.

Storing You can keep sugarloaf heads in a cool place or refrigerator for up to a month. For other types of chicory, you can store the leaves in a plastic bag in the refrigerator for as long as 10 days.

Chicory is a perennial, although it is often grown as an annual.

PLANTING GUIDE

What to plant Seeds.

Site preparation Add organic matter.

When From mid-spring to late summer.

Spacing *Sugarloaf chicory* and *Italian dandelion* Sow the seeds about 5cm (2in) apart in rows set 45–60cm (18–24in) apart; thin the seedlings to 25–30cm (10–12in) apart. *Grumolo chicory* and *Belgian endive* Sow the seeds about 2.5cm (1in) apart, with 45cm (18in) between rows; thin the seedlings to 15–20cm (6–8in) apart.

How much Per planting, two plants per person.

BEST OF THE BUNCH

Italian dandelion 'Red Rib' Green leaves with a red stem; slightly bitter flavour.
Sugar loaf 'Pain de Sucre' Forms a dense, mild-flavoured heart.
Witloof 'Apollo' When forced, compact white chicons with a good flavour.
Grumolo 'Rosso' Red rosette-like head.

Radicchio

Red heads with white accents make raddichio an eye-catching crop. Chioggia types form rounded heads. Treviso raddichio looks like cos lettuce, but it has pink to red leaves and a distinctive radicchio flavour – a bitter taste that mellows in cool conditions.

Sowing and planting

Soil Radicchio grows well in most soils. Dig a 5-cm (2-in) layer of compost into the soil before you begin planting.

When You can sow seeds in a heated greenhouse or frame in early spring for planting out in late spring or early summer. Otherwise, sow the seeds where the plants are to be grown from mid-spring to late summer.

In most areas late sowings can be overwintered in the garden, but covering the plants with cloches will help to protect them and maintain their quality, especially in colder areas.

Care

You should never allow the soil to dry out, because moisture stress leads to bitter flavour. Mulch to control weeds and keep the soil moist. Fertilise radicchio every three to four weeks with compost tea or a balanced fertiliser (but fertilise less or not at all in autumn).

Heirloom varieties may produce a lot of green leafy growth with no sign of a cabbage-like head. You can force them to produce a head by cutting back the tops to 5cm (2in) above the soil level. The plants will resprout and form heads.

PLANTING GUIDE

What to plant Seeds or transplants.

Starting indoors For a spring crop, start the seeds from six to eight weeks before the last expected frost.

Site preparation Add organic matter.

When From mid-spring to late summer.

Spacing Sow the seeds 2.5cm (1in) apart with 45cm (18in) between the rows; set the transplants or thin the seedlings to 20cm (8in) apart.

How much Up to five plants per person per planting.

BEST OF THE BUNCH

'**Palla Rossa Bella**' Burgundy-red leaves with contrasting white veins. Leaf colour improves in cold weather.
'**Posso di Treviso**' Upright heads with bold white midribs and leaves that turn deep red in cold weather.
'**Cesare**' Dense, round, deep red heads with a fine flavour.

PROBLEM SOLVER

Brown tips on outer leaves. Tipburn is due to heat; change planting time of crops. Undamaged parts are edible.

Elongated core of head. The start of bolting, triggered by heat or long days. Adjust the planting time of future crops.

Heads slimy or rotten at base. Bottom rot occurs in wet conditions. Destroy infected plants. Replant in another spot with good drainage; water less often.

Harvesting

Harvest young leaves for mixed salads, or allow heads to form. Squeeze the heads at the base: they are ready to cut when firm. Remove the outer leaves to reveal red heads. With protection, radicchio keeps in the garden for a long time; harvest as needed.

Storing Store radicchio heads in the refrigerator in a perforated plastic bag for up to three weeks.

Temperature alert
Too much heat can make radicchio unpleasantly bitter. In warm areas time sowings to avoid plants maturing in hot periods.

Mesclun (salad leaves)

Create simple, unique salads by growing mesclun, a mixture of mild, spicy and bitter greens. Loose-leaf lettuce is a common ingredient, but it's only the starting point. Mesclun is easy to grow in the garden, in containers or in a frame.

PLANTING GUIDE

What to plant Seeds.

Site preparation Add organic matter; prepare a fine seedbed.

When From early spring to late summer. Sow small amounts every two to three weeks.

Spacing Sow seeds lightly in rows 7.5–15cm (3–6in) apart, or broadcast them lightly over a wide row.

How much Plant an area that is 30–60sq cm (12–24sq in) for each person.

Temperature alert
Most mesclun mixes grow best in cool weather. In summer heat some bolt; others have an unpleasantly hot or bitter flavour.

Sowing and planting

Soil Spread 5cm (2in) of compost over the planting area and work it into the top several inches of soil. Rake the planting area until you remove all the clods.

Sowing prepared mixes The easiest way to grow mesclun is to purchase packets of premixed seeds – many different blends are available. You should shake the packet well before sowing to make sure the seeds are evenly blended. You can sow mesclun mixes in rows, but broadcasting the seeds lightly over a wide bed will make harvesting easier.

Creating a custom harvest You can concoct your own custom blend by buying a packet of each of your favourite lettuces and salad greens. Mix a small amount of seeds from each packet in a container; then sow the mix in rows or broadcast the seeds. Bear in mind that some fast-growing varieties may be more prevalent than others in your mix.

Another way to create custom blends is by planting each component in its own short row. Then you can harvest individual leaves in whatever combinations and proportions you like, depending on whether you want a milder or spicier mix.

Extending the season A mesclun mix will grow well in a frame. Sow the seeds a week or two before the first expected autumn frost. The mix will grow slowly and keep fresh for weeks. If you have limited space in your frame, regard your planting as a treat for a fresh salad once a week. Sow the seeds in drills 2.5cm (1in) apart. Make sure you ventilate the frame if temperatures inside rise to 18°C (65°F) or above.

Care

Water as needed to keep the top several inches of the soil moist at all times. Fast-growing mesclun doesn't need fertilising.

Harvesting

Mesclun will be ready for harvesting four to eight weeks after sowing. You should cut the plants 2.5cm (1in) above soil level. In good weather conditions the plants will resprout for an additional harvest, although the subsequent cuttings may be more uneven than the first. If the stand seems too crowded, pull out some plants entirely at the time of the first harvest to leave more space for regrowth. Harvest mesclun in frames on the small side – when leaves are 7.5–10cm (3–4in) tall.

You should carefully wash the leaves to remove all dirt and grit. Handle the mix gently as you work because the leaves are fragile. Spread the leaves on a clean towel to dry after washing.

Storing Because some components of mesclun will keep better than others, it's best to harvest only as much as needed. You can store mesclun in plastic bags in the refrigerator for up to two days.

PROBLEM SOLVER

Ragged holes in leaves. Handpick slugs and snails, set out slug traps, or spread a band of sharp sand, crushed eggshells or diatomaceous earth round the patch.

Plants slimy or rotten at base. Various diseases cause rot, especially in cold, wet weather. Destroy infected plants. Re-sow in raised beds to improve drainage.

To wash the leaves swish them in a bowl of cool water and repeat as often as needed.

WHAT'S IN THE MIX?
Mesclun mixes can include everything from dandelion greens to fresh herbs and edible flowers.

Bitter greens Curly endive (see page 133), some leafy chicories (see page 134) and radicchio (see page 135) are excellent bitter greens for mesclun.

Cultivated dandelion greens are another bitter green worth trying (these seeds are often labelled as 'French dandelions'). The leaves are broader and smoother than those of typical weedy dandelions.

Pick young dandelion leaves for best flavour. If your cultivated dandelions go to flower pick off the flowerheads before they set seed, or they may become a weed problem in your garden.

Spicy greens Rocket (see page 132), mustard greens and cress add a hot, peppery flair to mesclun. Mustard greens and cress are generally hardy and disease resistant. Sow and grow them as you would other greens.

Mild greens Loose-leaf lettuces (see page 131) and spinach (see page 138) are common mild greens for mesclun. You can

also add Asian greens such as mizuna and tatsoi (see pages 182–83).

Corn salad Also known as lamb's lettuce or mache, this is an iron-rich green that makes a nice addition to mesclun. It forms low rosettes of spoon-shaped dark green leaves. Unlike other greens, corn salad leaves don't turn bitter even after the plants form seed stalks.

Corn salad germinates slowly, so sow it separately and add it to your mesclun at harvest. Soak seeds before planting to speed germination, and keep the seedbed moist. Thin plants to 7.5cm (3in) apart.

Other greens You can clip young beet greens (see pages 194–95), Swiss chard (see pages 140–41) and kale (see page 178) leaves to add rich colour and texture to a mesclun mix.

Herbs and flowers For a mix with more complex flavour, you

A mixture of greens from a variety of plants will provide a blend of colours, flavours and shapes that will add spark and intensity to your salads.

can add a small amount of fresh basil (see pages 259–61), chervil or fennel leaves (see page 257). Edible flowers such as pansies, calendulas, nasturtiums and 'Scarlet Emperor' runner bean blossoms add contrast of colour and form, as well as flavour.

Spinach

Tasty spinach is one of the most nutritious greens – and one of the most cold-tolerant. Some gardeners think spinach is hard to grow, but choosing varieties that are resistant to bolting helps overcome one of the major problems.

PLANTING GUIDE

What to plant Seeds.

Site preparation Add plenty of compost because spinach is a heavy feeder.

When From early spring, as soon as the soil is suitable, to early autumn.

Spacing Sow the seeds about 2.5cm (1in) apart with 45cm (18in) between the rows; thin the seedlings about 10–15cm (4–6in) apart.

Intensive spacing Sow seeds 10cm (4in) apart on centres.

How much Per planting, about 60cm (2ft) of row, or five plants per person.

Temperature alert
Temperatures above 24°C (75°F) and longer days in late spring can cause bolting. You can choose more heat- and cold-tolerant savoy types.

Sowing and planting

Soil Spread 2.5–5cm (1–2in) of compost over the planting area and add a dressing of a high nitrogen fertiliser. Work these into the top several inches of soil.

Successional sowing From the early spring you can sow spinach in succession every three weeks or so. You should try to choose a partially shaded spot if possible.

Avoiding bolting problems As the days gradually become longer in the spring, the plants will receive a signal to stop producing leaves and send up a flower stalk. When a warm spell occurs, the heat will provide even more of an 'incentive' for the plants to send a stalk, causing them to bolt rapidly and leaf growth to decline.

Premature bolting is a common problem, particularly on dry soils. Make sure you keep the beds well watered after sowing and all through the plants' development.

To help plan sowing times for future years, make a note of which sowings do best and which bolt. Note the weather conditions too, as hot, dry weather encourages bolting. Where bolting is a frequent problem stop sowing in late spring and start again in mid- to late summer.

Late sowings For sowings made from early summer onwards, choose varieties that are recommended for summer and autumn sowing.

In many areas plants of the right varieties, covered with cloches or horticultural fleece, can be harvested through the winter months, although pickings may be sparse. You should have a heavier harvest when they start into growth again in spring. However, bolting is often a problem with overwintered plants, too.

Care

Mulching will keep the soil cool and prevent it from spattering onto leaves when it rains. If your spinach doesn't seem to be growing vigorously, you can feed the plants weekly with a solution of balanced fertiliser.

Quick Tip

Cool success
Where spinach proves particularly difficult to grow successfully, you should try growing one of the spinach substitutes (see opposite page) instead of battling against the odds.

HEAT-TOLERANT SPINACH SUBSTITUTES

If you yearn for fresh spinach (a cold-tolerant plant) in the summer, try growing a spinach substitute. New Zealand spinach and Malabar spinach are heat-tolerant plants with leaves that have a spinach-like appearance and flavour.

New Zealand spinach is a frost-tender plant with branching, sprawling stems. Its seeds are dried fruits with multiple seeds in each. Soak the seeds in warm water before sowing to speed germination. Start the seeds indoors in spring and transplant them outside after danger of frost is past. Or sow the seeds directly in the garden from mid-spring through early summer. Set the plants 30–38cm (12–15in) apart in rows that are about 60cm (24in) apart. Harvest the young tender leaves at the growing tips (cut about 7.5cm/3in of stem and leaves) and use them as you would spinach. The plants will resprout, and the harvest should continue until the first hard frost.

Malabar spinach is a tender vine that produces thick, glossy, succulent leaves and thrives in warm, humid conditions. It is an attractive ornamental plant.

Spinach beet is also known as leaf beet and perpetual spinach, and it produces a good crop of tasty, spinach-like leaves. It does well on dry soils where true spinach would bolt quickly.

Swiss chard (see pages 140–41) is another good spinach substitute and is much less fussy about its growing conditions. The thick leaf stalks can be cooked spearately from the spinach-like leaf blades.

Harvesting

You can harvest baby leaves for salads, or use the more mature leaves for cooking. For the best flavour, harvest spinach early in the morning. You can pick individual outer leaves, cut whole plants 2.5cm (1in) above the soil surface or pull up whole plants and trim the roots.

Swirl the leaves in a bowl or sink full of water to remove all the soil and grit. Remove the leaves, replace the dirty water with fresh water and repeat as often as needed until the leaves are clean and ready for use.

Storing Refrigerate unwashed spinach in a plastic bag for up to one week. Spinach freezes well.

Smooth-leaved spinach is the best type to grow if you want spinach for a salad.

Spinach leaves may be savoy (crinkled), semi-savoy or smooth.

BEST OF THE BUNCH

'Bloomsdale' A heavy cropping type with deep green, tasty leaves.
'Melody' Produces big, semi-savoy upright leaves that are disease resistant.
'Olympia' A productive type with smooth, dark green leaves and that is slow to bolt. It has excellent flavour.
'Space' Forms smooth leaves and is good for planting in spring and autumn; it freezes well.
'Scenic' An F1 hybrid variety with good mildew resistance. It is upright growing with dark green leaves.

 ## PROBLEM SOLVER

Small round holes in the leaves. Flea beetles cause this damage. To prevent holes cover planting areas with a fleece immediately after sowing seeds.

Irregular lines or blotches on leaves. Leaf miners (larvae of small flies) tunnel through the leaves. If damage is minor, pick and destroy damaged leaves. Cover future plantings with fleece. Check under the fleece occasionally – pupae in the soil can emerge and attack plants.

Yellow patches on leaves. If you find gray or purple mould on leaf undersides, the problem is downy mildew. Pull up and destroy infected plants. Replant in a new location in raised beds to improve drainage; plant mildew-resistant varieties.

White areas on leaves. Leaf scorch is due to heat and moisture stress. Mulch and water more often. Time plantings to avoid hot periods.

Stunted plants with mottled leaves. Mosaic disease is caused by a virus that is spread by aphids. Destroy infected plants. Cover new plantings with horticultural fleece to prevent aphids.

Swiss chard

A relative of beetroot and spinach, Swiss chard is also called seakale beet. Swiss chard is full of vitamins, and there are many varieties in an exciting range of colour combinations, making this crop a great candidate for any garden.

PLANTING GUIDE

What to plant Seeds.

Site preparation Add organic matter to poor soils.

When From mid- to late spring and summer use, and again mid- to late summer for a spring crop.

Spacing Sow the seeds 5cm (2in) apart with 30–60cm (12–24in) between the rows; thin the plants 15–30cm (6–12in) apart.

How much Three to five plants per person.

Sowing and planting

Soil Well-worked fertile soil needs no special improvement. However, if your soil is sandy or infertile, you should dig in a 5-cm (2-in) layer of compost before planting.

When to sow Make the main sowing of Swiss chard in mid-spring. This will provide plants that will crop right through the summer, and they will often persist through the winter to give an early spring crop. Spring-sown plants may run to seed quickly in their second spring. You may have more success with a sowing made in mid- to late summer that is specially for overwintering. In particularly cold areas cover overwintering plants with horticultural fleece.

Care

Thinning Like beet seeds, Swiss chard seeds are dried fruits, each containing several seeds. The seedlings will emerge in clusters. When the plants are a few inches tall, thin each cluster to one plant.

Watering Maintaining soil moisture is critical for Swiss chard. Check the soil moisture regularly, and water whenever the top several centimetres of the soil becomes dry. In hot-summer areas you can mulch in early summer to conserve soil moisture.

This striking variety of Swiss chard has vibrant red veins running through the bright green leaves.

BEST OF THE BUNCH

'Bright Lights' Multi-coloured yellow, orange, pink, violet and white stalks, with a mild flavour.

'Yellow' Yellow stems turn to a rich golden shade as the plants mature; yellow-green leaves; has an excellent mild flavour.

'Rhubarb' Large red stems, with dark green leaves with red veins. Cook stems like asparagus; use leaves like spinach.

Fertilising If you plan to harvest from the same sowing through the season, fertilise the plants once a month with a balanced or high-nitrogen fertiliser.

Harvesting

You can cut all the stems on a plant at once, but leave 5cm (2in) of the plant at the base intact. The plant should resprout, producing a fresh crop of young leaves. You can also harvest individual Swiss chard stems: pick them from the outer edges of the plant. Baby Swiss chard leaves are excellent for adding to a mesclun mix. In general don't let leaves grow too large – leaves longer than 25cm (10in) may have poor flavour.

If the outer leaves turn yellow or the stalks seem tough, remove them from the plant and compost them –

they won't have good eating quality. Remove any flower stalks that appear.

Storing Refrigerate Swiss chard stems and leaves unwashed, but use them as soon as possible. If you harvest a large quantity at one time, you can freeze it (see pages 118–19).

Harvest the leaves using a sharp knife. Use the leaves as you would spinach; you can steam or stir-fry the stems.

Unique foliage and eye-catching colours will make Swiss chard an ideal addition to an ornamental garden.

PROBLEM SOLVER

Ragged holes in leaves. Look for slugs and snails. Hand-pick the pests, set out traps and surround the plants with a band of sharp sand, crushed eggshells or diatomaceous earth.

Irregular lines or blotches on leaves. Leaf-miner larvae tunnel through the leaves. Cover plants early in the season to prevent adults from laying eggs on them. Pick and destroy damaged leaves.

White areas on leaves. Leaf scorch is due to heat and moisture stress. Mulch the soil and water more frequently during hot periods.

Plant sends up premature flower stalks. Moisture stress is the factor most likely to cause bolting. Check the soil moisture more often, especially during periods of hot weather.

Quick Tip

A winning green

Swiss chard handles heat better than most greens. Many gardeners find that a spring planting of this crop will last through summer and into autumn without bolting or losing quality.

7 Peas and beans

Prolific and easy to grow, peas and beans belong in every garden. These nitrogen-fixing legumes need less fertilising than other crops and can even help to improve the garden soil. Plant a sampling of shelling-pea varieties, snap peas and mangetout in the spring. Once the weather warms it's bean-planting time, and the choices are almost unlimited. Enjoy a bounty of green beans, French beans, broad beans, shelling beans and more. Some gardeners like fast-producing dwarf varieties, while others prefer long-season climbing varieties – you may want to try both.

Peas start the season in spring and are ready to harvest as early as two months after sowing.

Peas

Plump pea pods sweeten the dreams of gardeners in the spring. Once you've tasted the incomparable sweetness of home-grown peas, you'll find yourself checking your pea vines daily for more of these sugary treasures.

Sowing and planting

Soil Peas grow well in average garden soil. Prepare your pea bed in autumn, working a 12.5-mm (½-in) layer of organic matter into the soil. Shape the soil into a raised bed so that it drains better and warms up faster in spring.

When to sow Spread out the harvest of peas by sowing suitable varieties at different times throughout the season. Not all varieties do well at the various seasons, so check the catalogues to choose the right peas for your needs.

The earliest crops can be obtained by sowing a hardy, fast-maturing variety in autumn or late winter. This sowing will only succeed in reasonably mild, sheltered areas and in light, free-draining soil. The peas will do better if the rows are covered with cloches or low polythene tunnels.

The main crop of peas, harvested from early to midsummer, are sown from early to mid-spring. For a late summer and early autumn crop, choose a fast-maturing variety and sow in midsummer.

Choosing a variety The sweetest varieties of peas have wrinkled seeds, so these are the ones to select where possible. However, the wrinkles in the seeds hold water, so in cool, damp conditions, wrinkled-seeded peas are more likely to rot. For autumn and early spring sowings, round-seeded peas are the better choice. Most catalogues indicate whether a variety is wrinkled- or round-seeded.

The catalogues also group peas as early or maincrop varieties, and they may be split into a number of groups such as first early, second early, early, maincrop and late maincrop. These labels will help you to choose the right variety for the right sowing time, but they are slightly misleading – the peas are grouped by their speed of maturing rather than their cropping season. Therefore, a 'first early' variety is not restricted to early-season crops; it is also a good choice sowing in summer to give an early autumn crop, because it will mature quickly.

Wide rows and double rows For better yields and a more uniform planting, try sowing peas in a wide row or double row. For wide-row planting, open a 15-cm (6-in)-wide drill 2.5cm (1in) deep down the bed, and broadcast the seeds lightly in the drill. Set up a support along the centre of the drill. Peas will grow up both sides of the support. Thin as needed.

For double rows, open two 2.5-cm (1-in)-deep drills about 15cm (6in) apart. Sow the seeds 2.5cm (1in) apart and cover. Set up a support to run between the two drills. Thin as needed.

PLANTING GUIDE

What to plant Seeds.

Site preparation Work in organic matter; prepare in autumn for early spring planting.

When From early spring to mid-summer; in mild areas also in autumn and early winter.

Spacing Sow seeds in 15-cm (6-in)-wide drills, 2.5cm (1in) deep; thin seedlings to 5–10cm (2–4in) apart.

Double rows Sow the seeds 2.5cm (1in) apart in two rows 15cm (6in) apart; allow 75–90cm (30–36in) between double rows; thin the seedlings 5–10cm (2–4in) apart.

How much *Shelling peas* Allow 6m (20ft) of row per person (for freezing and fresh eating). *Mangetout and snap peas* Plan 30–60cm (12–24in) of row per person for fresh eating.

Temperature alert
At the height of summer, check your pea plants daily. Harvest pods extra young, because quality may decline quickly in the heat.

Care

Watering Avoid overwatering the young plants. Cold, wet soil will slow root development and may lead to disease problems. When the plants start flowering, water once weekly. Apply water to moisten the soil 23–30cm (9–12in) deep. Deliver the water at soil level, close to the base of plants, and avoid wetting the foliage.

Supports Support is essential for tall varieties, and even peas that grow only 90cm (36in) tall can benefit from it. Use chicken-wire fencing or twine attached to sturdy stakes. You can insert pea sticks – twiggy prunings from trees and shrubs – among the vines as a traditional way to support peas.

Harvesting

Because the sugars in pea seeds start turning to starch immediately on picking, home-grown peas will be at their sweetest just after picking. The critical factors for all types of peas are to harvest before the pods become too mature and to harvest often to encourage continued production.

Shelling peas will be ready for harvest when they are bright green and full, almost rounded. The same is true for petit pois; however, the pods will be only about half the size of regular shelling peas. Mangetout are at their best and ready to harvest when 5–7.5cm (2–3in) long, with small seeds. Mangetout should be flat, bright green and crisp.

For all types of pea, make sure to harvest before pods begin to lose their sheen. As harvest draws near, visit the pea patch daily to sample a few pods of each variety. Harvest thoroughly when the peas are at the right stage, and then check again a few days later to see how the crop is progressing.

Storing You can store unwashed fresh peas in the refrigerator for two to three days. Keep in mind that they continuously lose sweetness, so you should eat them as soon as possible.

To prepare mangetout for freezing, blanch pods for one minute in boiling water; snap peas or shelled peas, for two minutes (see pages 118–19).

PROBLEM SOLVER

White, powdery coating on leaves. Some varieties are prone to powdery mildew, a fungal disease that likes high humidity with warm days and cool nights. Pull out and destroy infected vines. Replant resistant varieties. Grow peas early in the season to avoid the disease. Sulphur or fungicide may prevent it.

Plants turn yellow and die. Root rot is often the cause. Grow future crops in well-drained soil; practise crop rotation.

Distorted growth and sticky sap. Look for clusters of aphids (small, round green insects), especially at growing tips. Wash plants with a strong stream of water or spray with insecticidal soap.

Small, creamy maggots in peas. Pea moth is not visible until the pod is opened, when you find the peas eaten and a sticky brown 'frass' excreted by the maggots. Sometimes only one or two peas in the pod are affected but often the whole pod is ruined. Prevent problems by sowing early or late, so that the peas are not flowering in mid-summer, peak egg-laying season for the moths. Fleece covers at flowering time may keep the moths away.

BEST OF THE BUNCH

'Green Arrow' Small dark green peas on semi-bush plants.

'Felthan First' A dwarf, early variety; very reliable. It is suitable for autumn sowing.

'Kelvedon Wonder' Early variety with a heavy crop of well-flavoured peas. Resistant to mildew.

'Oregon Giant' 5-in (12.5-cm) mangetout pods remain sweet even when the seeds are visible; disease resistant; 90-cm (36-in)-tall vines.

'Sugar Snap' Thick-wall snap peas on 1.5-m (5-ft)-tall vines.

Regardless of the type of pea, harvest the pods before they become overly mature, while they can still provide the best flavour.

Types of peas

All peas – shelling peas, snap peas, mangetout and petit pois – need the same conditions and care. When prime for picking, the tiny seeds of flat mangetout will barely bulge in the pods, while the meaty snap pea pods will have a smooth, rounded profile.

▼ Shelling peas

This is the classic garden pea. There are early, mid-season and late varieties, as well as bush and tall types. Harvest pods when they are full of round seeds but before the pods lose their sheen and bright colour. Some varieties produce petit pois – small peas in pods that are only 5–7.5cm (2–3in) long.

▲ Mangetout

Crispy, sweet mangetout pods are superb served raw in salads or lightly stir-fried. At their prime, mangetout pods will be 5–7.5cm (2–3in) long, and the tiny seeds will be barely bulging in the pod. Mangetout pods may have fibrous strings, similar to string beans, which are best removed before eating raw or cooked. Snap off one end of the pod and pull the string to remove it. Mangetout are available in both dwarf and tall varieties.

▲ Snap peas

Snap peas offer you the choice of eating the pods when they are young, like mangetout, or allowing the pea seeds inside to enlarge partially before harvesting and eating them, pod and all. The pods are meatier than mangetout pods. It's best not to let the seeds grow as large as peas for conventional shelling, or their sweetness may be lost. Eat snap peas raw or lightly steamed. Most snap pea varieties grow 90cm (36in) high or taller.

ASPARAGUS PEAS

The plant is a member of the legume family, but it belongs to a different genus from either peas (*Tetragonolobus purpurea*) or beans (*Lotus tetragonolobus*). This plant is beautiful with a low, bushy form, and with its grey-green leaves and brick-red flowers. The asparagus pea makes a great addition to either a flower garden or ornamental kitchen garden.

Seeds can be sown where the plants are to grow in mid-spring or early summer, so that the seedlings do not emerge until after the risk of frost is over. In cold areas or exposed gardens, start seeds in containers under cover, planting them out in early summer. After about two months of growth, the plants will begin to produce pods that have four raised ridges, or wings, with frilly edges.

The entire pod is edible if picked young, when about 2.5cm (1in) long. Older pods become stringy and fibrous, with hard ridges, and are not edible, so it is important to check the plants over daily and to remove all pods that are of edible size. The plants may bear pods for as long as three months if you keep picking them regularly.

The flavour of the pods is similar to asparagus, and they're best cooked as you would asparagus spears – steam lightly, drain, add a little butter and enjoy.

French and broad beans

French and broad beans are favourite crops for gardeners. These French beans are dwarf varieties – climbing French beans are on pages 150–51. Broad beans produce succulent young beans from late spring, while French beans crop throughout the summer.

Sowing and planting

Soil Beans will grow well in average soil. Plant a green manure the preceding autumn, dig it into the soil in spring and let it break down several weeks before planting.

Sowing beans Always sow fresh bean seeds, because seed quality declines quickly. Broad beans are hardy, and in mild gardens some varieties (such as 'Aquadulce Claudia') can be sown in autumn for a late-spring crop. They need a sheltered spot and do better under a cloche. You can also sow seeds under cloches in late winter. The main sowing of broad beans in the open garden begins in early spring; if you sow in succession every three to four weeks you can pick pods all through the summer.

French beans are less hardy than broad beans. If your soil is light and free draining and you have a sheltered spot, you can sow them outside from mid-spring under cloches. Otherwise, the main sowing is from late spring to early summer. A final sowing can be made in midsummer and covered with cloches in early autumn.

Successional sowing To spread the harvest and prevent your crop of beans maturing all at once, make succession sowings every two weeks.

For later sowings when the soil is warm and dry, sow seeds 5cm (2in) deep to keep them moist. Stop sowing 60 days before the first expected frost.

Care

Beans usually have few problems, as long as you plant them in healthy soil and care for them properly. However, broad beans are prone to attacks by black bean aphids, which cluster on the growing tips in spring and can stunt the plants' growth. To prevent this, pinch out the tips of the plants in early summer. If they are not already infested with aphids, you can use the shoot tips – they are delicious cooked.

Thinning When thinning bean plants, preserve only vigorous plants and thin out all weak plants. Weak plants are more prone to disease, and once disease gets a foothold, it can spread to healthy plants too.

Fertilising Be cautious about fertilising beans. Too much nitrogen can cause excess leaf growth at the expense of pods. In addition, succulent foliage is more attractive to pests. As legumes, beans will provide some of their own source of nitrogen. Your crop may not need any fertiliser, but if you are concerned about nutrient deficiencies, try a liquid fertiliser.

PLANTING GUIDE

What to plant Seeds.

Site preparation Ensure site is well drained.

When *Broad beans* Early spring through summer. *French beans* Late spring to early summer.

Spacing Sow the seeds about 2.5–5cm (1–2in) apart in rows 45–75cm (18–30in) apart; thin to 15cm (6in) apart.

Intensive spacing Sow 15cm (6in) apart on centres.

How much Per planting, 1.5m (5ft) of row.

Harvesting

As the time of maturity approaches, sample some beans for readiness. The pods of French beans should be crisp enough to snap in two at the centre when bent, but pod tips should be flexible and bend without breaking. Seeds inside the pods should be tiny. Don't let the pods become overly mature, because their quality declines fast and the plants stop producing pods.

For fast, easy harvesting, pull up an entire plant by the roots, turn it upside down and pull off all the pods. The yield will be a little lower, but you'll save the strain of stooping to pick the beans from low-growing plants. Compost the plants (or destroy them if there are signs of diseases or insects). To harvest selectively, use two hands to pull the pods off the plants without breaking the stems or damaging the foliage. Never harvest when plants are wet, or you may spread disease.

Broad beans are picked for shelling when the beans have swollen and are beginning to show as bulges in the sides of the pod. The scar on the bean (where it is attached to the pod) should still be pale green; if it has darkened to brown or black, the beans are past their best and could be tough. You can still use the pods if you trim away the edges and slice them like runner beans before cooking them. For a treat, try picking broad bean pods when they are young, up to 7.5cm (3in) long, and cooking them whole.

For dried beans, wait until much of the foliage has died. The beans should rattle loosely inside the brown or blackened pods. Shell the beans and separate them from the chaff.

Storing Most fresh beans last for up to a week in the refrigerator, and both broad and French beans freeze well (see pages 118–19). Frozen beans will keep for almost a full year.

Before storing dried beans, test their moisture content by putting several beans in a closed glass jar, then check 24 hours later. If you see condensation inside the jar, the beans need additional drying. Keep dry beans in airtight jars in a cool, dry place.

BEST OF THE BUNCH

BROAD BEANS:
'Green Windsor' Classic broad bean variety for spring or autumn crop.
'The Sutton' Dwarf variety suitable for small spaces. Can be sown both in spring and under cloches in autumn for an early crop.
'Jubilee Hysor' Heavy cropping, early maturing variety for spring sowing; it produces large, white beans that have a good flavour.

DWARF FRENCH BEANS:
'The Prince' Well-established, early variety that produces heavy crops of flat, podded beans.
'Safari' Very slim 'filet' type beans; excellent flavour.
'Golddukat' Bright golden pods make a welcome splash of colour both in the garden and on the plate.
'Tendergreen' A good crop of round, stringless, well-flavoured pods. Good for freezing.
'Purple Teepee' Another interesting colour variation. The dusky purple beans are carried at the top of the plant, making them easy to pick and resistant to soil splashes and slug damage.

Broad beans can provide a tasty harvest from late spring right through the summer on plants that are largely trouble free.

Climbing beans

Great taste and texture – plus harvesting over a long season from a single planting – motivate many gardeners to choose climbing beans instead of dwarf beans. Climbing beans are also space-saving and easy to pick because they grow vertically.

PLANTING GUIDE

What to plant Seeds.

Site preparation Choose a well-drained site; average fertility is fine.

When After all danger of frost is past in late spring and early summer.

Spacing *Fence or trellis support* Sow the seeds 7.5–10cm (3–4in) apart; thin the seedlings to 15–23cm (6–9in) apart. *Pole support* Sow six seeds at the base of each pole; thin to two to three plants per pole.

How much Per person, about 10 plants.

BEST OF THE BUNCH

RUNNER BEANS:
'Lady Di' Long, straight, stringless beans produced over a long period.
'Scarlet Emperor' Runner bean with sweet, rich flavor; scarlet-orange flowers.

CLIMBING FRENCH BEANS:
'Cobra' Long, deep green, round pods follow violet flowers; heavy cropper.
'Blue Lake' Round, stringless pods with white seeds; good flavour. You can let the seeds mature to use as haricot beans.
'Kentucky Wonder' Butter-coloured pods, brown seeds; grows well in cool climates; harvest as green beans and shelling beans.

Sowing and planting

Soil Good drainage is important, but average fertility is fine, because – as with dwarf beans – climbing beans produce some of their own nitrogen. However, for the best results, grow a green manure the preceding autumn. Work it into the soil in spring and allow it to break down before planting the beans.

Or you can work in a shovelful of compost at each planting hill where you plan to provide some type of pole support. Allow several weeks for the compost to finish breaking down – unless it is already fully mature.

Supporting the vines Climbing beans can stretch as high as 4.5m (15ft) if you provide a tall support. You can set up poles or a trellis of stakes and heavy twine before you plant. Many gardeners use wigwams for climbing beans; however, it can be difficult to harvest bean pods from the upper areas of a wigwam. You should set individual poles 15–30cm (6–12in) apart.

Climbing beans grow well on a chain-link or wooden fence if you run twine from the top of the fence down to the ground for the vines to wind around. Or use cylinders of wire fencing such as tomato cages to support the vines.

Sowing seeds Sow the seeds outside in late spring or early summer, after all risk of frost is past. In cold, exposed gardens you can raise the seeds in individual pots or trays under cover, sowing from mid-spring onwards. Do not sow the seeds too early – the seedlings will grow fast and their climbing shoots will become tangled, if you have to wait too long for the weather to warm up before planting out the beans.

Care

Watering Keep the top 5cm (2in) of soil moist, but don't let the soil get soggy. Moisture is especially important for germination and, once the flowers appear, for seed formation in pods. Once the plants are established, you can apply a 2.5–5-cm (1–2-in) layer of grass clippings or straw to conserve soil moisture.

Quick Tip

Variety choice

Runner beans are by far the most popular type of climbing bean, but there are also climbing varieties of French bean. The beans may be round, like the typical French bean, or flat in shape, and they are heavy cropping.

Harvest the beans while they are still young, so that the plant continues to produce more flowers and pods.

Climbing beans will make an eye-catching feature when trained up a wigwam or canes.

Fertilising Because climbing beans produce a crop over a prolonged period, they'll benefit from some supplemental fertilising but avoid supplying too much nitrogen.

Ending the season Pick the pods and water the plants regularly to extend the season right through the summer. As soon as the first frost is forecast, pick all the remaining beans and dismantle the trellis or wigwam. Discard the twine and store the poles for next year. Don't compost the vines unless you're certain they are free of pests and diseases.

Harvesting

With climbing beans, it's important to pick pods on the young side (except for dried beans), because when pods mature on the plant, it signals the vine to stop producing more flowers and pods. Follow the harvesting guidelines for various types of beans described on page 149 and pages 152–55.

PROBLEM SOLVER

Pale speckles on leaves. Red spider mites can sometimes affect plants during hot, dry conditions. Spray the plants with insecticidal soap.

Brown and black blotches on pods. Bacterial blight is the cause, especially during warm, wet weather. Pull up and destroy the infected plants. For future crops, you can use a copper spray to prevent the disease.

Black insects thickly clustered on shoots. Aphids (small, round insects) can be dislodged from the plants by spraying them with a strong jet of water, but make sure the spray isn't so strong that it damages the plants.

Leaves turn yellow and die; stems rot at the base. Foot and root rot, which is caused by a fungus, will produce these symptoms. The affected plants must be destroyed as soon as these symptoms are noticed to try to prevent its spread. Make sure you practise crop rotation for future crops.

No flowers form. A lack of flower production is usually due to excess nitrogen in the soil, which causes healthy leaf growth but poor flowering. Feed the plants potash.

No beans form. If the plants are flowering but the pods are not setting, this is most often due to lack of water at flowering time. Water the plants thoroughly at the roots if a dry spell coincides with flowering, soaking the soil several inches deep. There is no need to spray the flowers with water – it doesn't help setting. Another possible cause is that sometimes birds pick off the flowers. Growing a white or pale-flowered variety can help to avoid this problem in the future.

Types of beans

There's no end to the possibilities when growing beans. Choose beans based on whether you want to grow dwarf-type plants or climbing beans, and whether you want to harvest immature pods, enlarged bean seeds (shelling beans) or dry beans.

▼ Shelling and dry beans

The terms 'shelling beans' and 'dry beans' refer to the stage at which beans are picked, not a specific type of bean. You should pick beans for shelling when the seeds have enlarged but are still soft. The pods will be green but no longer edible. When bean seeds are mature, the pods will turn brown or black and the dry beans will rattle inside. After picking, separate the seeds from the pods and chaff.

▲ Dwarf French bean

These are also sometimes known as snap beans. The beans that you pick are actually immature pods. As the beans age they can devleop a 'string' along the ridge of the pod, which won't soften even after cooking. However, if you pick the pods when they are still young, most won't have a noticeable string. Modern varieties also tend to remain string free for much longer than older ones. Many different varieties are available, and when they are regularly picked they can produce heavy crops.

◀ Filet bean

Filet beans are a gourmet type of French bean, also sometimes known as Kenyan beans or fine beans. They are bred to produce long, very slender beans that have a sweet flavour and delicate texture, which need only very brief cooking. These beans are best for eating fresh – and they may not freeze well. One of the most poular varieties is 'Safari'.

▼ Climbing French bean

These beans may be round, like normal French beans, but there are also stringless, flat-podded varieties with a distinctive flavour and texture. They can produce heavy crops.

▶ Coloured bean

Yellow and purple French beans are sometimes known as wax beans, but this is a misnomer because there's nothing waxy about these crisp, tasty beans. A major benefit of coloured varieties is that it is easy to spot the young beans among the green foliage when picking them. Purple varieties turn green on cooking, but the yellow types keep their colour. 'Purple Queen', 'Purple Teepee', 'Berggold' and 'Gollddukat' are good varieties to try.

Types of beans (continued)

▼ Runner bean

Although it can be grown as a perennial in warmer climates, the runner bean is a frost-tender plant and is normally grown as an annual in the UK. Most varieties are good climbers, capable of growing up to 3.7–4.6m (12–15ft) tall. However, there are some short, non-climbing varieties available ,too. The attractive flowers may be red, white, red and white or pink, according to the variety. The seeds are black or black mottled with dark red. Pick the pods while they are young and slice them before cooking.

▶ Broad bean

Broad beans, or fava beans, grow well in cool conditions and can withstand frost. The plants grow 0.9–1.2m (3–4ft) tall, with pods 30cm (12in) long. The pods at the bottom of the plant will ripen first. In reasonably sheltered gardens, sow a suitable variety such as 'Aquadulce claudia' in autumn to overwinter for the earliest crops; othewise sow in early spring. The beans may have a tough seed coat; if so, slip it off after cooking. If you are of Mediterranean, African or Southeast Asian descent, you may suffer a serious reaction to eating these beans called favism. Consult a doctor to test your susceptibility.

▼ Yardlong bean

Another unusual crop for the UK, yardlong bean (*Vigna unguiculata sesquipedalis*, also called asparagus bean or dow ghok) is a tropical plant that is a real heat lover. In mild, sheltered areas of Britain it can be grown outside under horticultural fleece or with similar protection; in cooler gardens it can be grown in a greenhouse or polythene tunnel. The vigorous vines, which sport pale blue flowers, need the support of a sturdy trellis. The pods are unlikely to reach a yard long in the UK, but can be harvested at about 30–45cm (12–18in). Each pod should bear 10 to 20 seeds, which will have a sweet, beany flavour.

▲ Soya bean

Soya beans do not usually grow in the UK, but there are a few varieties such as 'Ustie' that have been developed for British conditions. With a mild and nutty flavour, they can be used in any dish that calls for dry beans. In general, soya beans are grown like French beans; they produce a taproot so they are drought tolerant and tend to be free of pest and disease problems. Harvest and store soya beans as you would other dry beans, but remember that before they are eaten, all dry beans must be boiled rapidly for at least 10 minutes to destroy toxins.

8 The onion family

Many a memorable recipe begins with onions and garlic sautéed in olive oil. When those dishes are prepared with home-grown onions and garlic, the results are even more delectable. It's easy to tuck onions, garlic and salad onions into your garden.

Leeks, an onion cousin, take a little more space and effort, but the superb flavour of their white fleshy stems is an excellent reward. Delicate chives are equally at home in a vegetable garden bed, herb garden or flower border.

Onions are sweet, mild or pungent; white, yellow or red; and globe- or torpedo- shaped or flattened.

Onions

Full sun and a fertile soil will enable you to get the best results from growing onions. Whether you grow from seeds or from sets, it's not difficult to get a good harvest of sizeable bulbs that will store right through the winter.

Sowing and planting

Soil Onions generally need a fertile, well-drained soil that is not too dry. They do not like acid conditions, so it may be necessary to add lime to the soil. You should use a pH testing kit to find out (see pages 32–33).

To provide good drainage, you'll need to make a raised bed that is approximately 10cm (4in) high (see pages 22–23). To prepare the bed for onions, spread a 3.75cm (1½-in) layer of compost over the soil and dig it into the soil.

When to sow seeds For a harvest in late summer and early autumn, sow the seeds where they are to grow in late winter or early spring, as soon as you can work the soil. For an early sowing, you can cover the sowing area with a cloche from mid-winter onwards. This will allow the soil to dry out and enable you to work it earlier than would have been possible without the protection.

You can also sow seeds in mid- to late summer for a crop that will overwinter and be ready for harvesting in early summer of the following year. You will need to choose a hardy variety specifically bred for overwintering such as the Japanese variety 'Senshyu Yellow' (see *Best of the Bunch*, opposite).

In areas where the soil is unlikely to be ready for sowing early enough, you can start the plants off in either a heated greenhouse or indoors. Sow the seeds in trays or modules and harden the plants off for setting outside in mid- to late spring.

When to plant sets Sets are small, specially produced bulbs that are easy to grow and give a quicker harvest than growing plants from seeds. Heat-treated sets are less likely to bolt than untreated sets.

Plant the sets in mid-spring for lifting in mid- to late summer. Make a drill approximately the depth of the sets, and place the sets in the drill with the tip of the bulb pointing up. When you fill the drill, the pointed

PLANTING GUIDE

What to plant Seeds, sets or transplants.

Starting indoors Sow 8 to 12 weeks before planting outdoors.

Site preparation Add compost and lime if soil is acid.

When Early spring, and again in late summer.

Spacing *Seeds* Sow 12.5mm (½in) apart in rows that are 30–45cm (12–18in) apart; thin to 10–15cm (4–6in) apart. *Sets or transplants* Plant 10–15cm (4–6in) in rows 30–45cm (12–18in) apart.

Intensive spacing 10–12.5cm (4–5in) apart on centres.

How much About 3–4.5m (10–15ft) per person.

Quick Tip

Shop around

Buy fresh seeds each year; they don't last in storage. Buy sets from a reliable garden centre or mail-order catalogue. Sets that haven't been stored properly may bolt early, producing poor yields.

ONION DAYS

Shallots form clusters of smaller bulbs than onions that have a mild but distinctive flavour. Each cluster consists of 6 to 10 bulbs, round or elongated, according to variety. Use them raw in salads, for cooking like ordinary onions or for pickling. Shallots can be sown in early spring, but they are often grown from sets planted between late winter and mid-spring, as soon as the soil can be worked.

Open a drill and space the sets evenly along the length, 10–15cm (4–6in) apart, with the pointed end up.

Carefully fill the drill so that the tips of the sets are barely visible or just below the surface of the soil.

ends should be barely visible or just under the soil surface.

Care

Watering and weeding Water the onions often but lightly at soil level. You should avoid wetting the foliage, because this can lead to disease. Make sure you cultivate gently to remove weeds without damaging the roots of the onions.

When the soil is warm, you can apply a mulch of chopped leaves or grass clippings to suppress weeds and conserve moisture. Pull back the mulch when bulbing begins, to allow them to mature.

Fertilising Water the plants with a balanced fertiliser every three to four weeks from three weeks after planting. You should stop fertilising about six to seven weeks before the bulbs are ready for harvesting.

Harvesting

You can begin pulling the onions as soon as they are large enough for your needs. Overwintered Japanese onions will mature in early summer and should be used straight away, as they do not store well.

For onions that will store through the winter, wait until the foliage turns yellow and flops over. You can then lift the bulbs carefully using a fork, and allow them to dry thoroughly before storage.

In fine, dry weather you can leave the bulbs to dry on the soil surface, as long as you turn them regularly. However, you can obtain better results by putting the bulbs in single layers on wire mesh or a similar material to allow air to circulate all round them.

You should use damaged bulbs, or those with thicker necks than normal, as soon as possible after harvest because these do not often keep well.

Storing You should store onions in a cool place with low humidity. You can use the dried tops to plait onions together into a traditional rope for hanging. Alternatively, you cut off the tops and put the bulbs in mesh bags, knotting the bag between each onion, or lay them in single layers in wooden trays.

 PROBLEM SOLVER

Yellowed and wilting leaves. Onion fly maggots tunnel into the bulbs. Roots rot. To avoid problems, use fleece to cover crops after sowing. Plants from sets are less likely to be damaged.

Rusty stripes and mottling on leaves. Thrips feed on the leaves, especially during hot, dry weather. Spray the plants with either insecticidal soap or neem.

Mould on plants; rotting plants. Downy mildew can occur in warm, damp seasons, producing fluffy grey mould spreading from the tips of the leaves; remove the affected plants or spray them with a fungicide. More serious is onion white rot. Bulbs rot and produce fluffy white growth at their base, and foliage yellows and wilts. Remove and burn affected plants; the disease is carried in the soil for many years, so in following years grow onions in raised beds of uncontaminated soil.

Young plants bolt. Premature bolting occurs if sets are stored at 4.5–10°C (40–50°F); transplants are exposed to prolonged temperatures below 7°C (45°F); root damage occurs during cultivation; or there is moisture or nutrient stress. The bulbs are edible but cannot be stored.

Doubled bulbs. Two half-bulbs may form if a plant suffers moisture stress.

BEST OF THE BUNCH

'Ailsa Craig' Large, sweet onion; long-day variety; stores well.
'Bedfordshire Champion' Large, yellow onions with excellent storage qualities.
'Brunswick' Medium size, with red skin and mild-flavoured, white flesh.
'Kelsae' Large, globe-shaped onions with a sweet flavour. Very reliable.
'Pikant' Shallot with a strong flavour and resistance to bolting.
'Red Baron' Large, red-skinned bulbs with a good flavour and storage qualities.
'Senshyu Yellow' Flat bulbs with a yellow skin; sow in late summer to overwinter.

Types of onions

Onions are available in a wide assortment of varieties, differing in shape, colour and season. Shallots are a tasty treat that's easy to grow, and for fun why not try one or two plants of the unusual Egyptian onion.

◀ Red onion

Red-skinned onions may have white, red or bicoloured flesh. As well as being used for cooking, they can be served raw in salads, sandwiches and on beefburgers. Some long-keeping red varieties are available, but it can be difficult to get red onions to develop large bulbs.

▲ Yellow onion

Yellow storage onions are good all-purpose onions and are especially well suited for cooking in soups and stews. Many yellow varieties are easier to grow than other types of onions because they have a tougher skin that is more resistant to attack by insects or disease organisms.

▶ Pickling onion

Sometimes called silverskin or cocktail onions, these varieties are sown in spring and lifted in midsummer for pickling, when they reach the size of a large marble. The most popular variety is 'Paris Silverskin'.

▼ Shallot

Shallots are a special type of onion often prized by cooks. Shallot bulbs have a coppery skin and a tapered shape. There are some varieties available from seeds. From each shallot bulb you plant, a cluster of up to a dozen baby bulbs will develop. Usually, each bulb consists of two cloves. The flavour of shallots is described as a mixture of sweet onion and garlic.

◀ Egyptian onion

These interesting onions have several other names, including tree onions, walking onions and topsetting, multiplying onions. The plants produce small purplish red bulblets at the top of their tall stems. These bulblets aren't seeds – they are tiny bulbs, up to 2.5cm (1in) long. The bulbs are good for pickling or in soups, and they will keep well in storage.

If you leave Egyptian onion plants to their own devices, the heavy head of bulblets eventually bends over to the ground, where the bulbs root and a new cluster of shoots appear. Let the plants spread, or pick individual bulblets and plant them where you want new plants to grow. You can buy Egyptian onion plants from herb nurseries or mail-order suppliers.

Chives

Bushy clumps of bright green chives (*Allium schoenoprasum*) are a welcome addition to both kitchen and flower gardens. A sprinkling of chopped chives will lend a light touch of onion flavouring to salads, soups and cooked vegetables.

PLANTING GUIDE

What to plant Seedling clumps, divisions or potted plants.

Starting indoors Sow clusters of seeds in individual pots.

Site preparation Add compost.

When Spring, late summer or autumn.

Spacing Set seedling clumps, divisions or potted plants about 20–30cm (8–12in) apart.

How much One plant per person for culinary purposes.

GARLIC CHIVES

For a taste of mild garlic in the form of chives, try garlic chives (*Allium tuberosum*). They are as easy to grow as chives. Older leaves are coarse, so trim them even if you don't need them. New, tender leaves will resprout quickly. You can grow garlic chives for their white flowering ornamental quality; in this case don't trim the foliage. Cut off flowerheads before they go to seed to prevent weedy seedlings.

Sowing and planting

Soil Dig individual holes for each plant about twice the width of the root ball. Mix the removed soil with a handful of compost.

Starting seedlings Always use fresh seeds, and sow several seeds per pot. Keep them in dark conditions at 15.5–21°C (60–70°F) until the seeds eventually germinate. Move the seedlings under lights or to a frame.

The clumps of seedlings will be ready for planting outside in four weeks. They may grow slowly at first, but they should be ready for regular harvesting by the second year.

Planting outdoors Chives are hardy plants that die down in autumn and regrow in spring. Whether you plant seedling clumps, divisions or potted plants, make sure the chives are set at the same depth as they were growing beforehand, and water them well after planting.

Care

Chives need little care once they're established. Mulch them with grass clippings to suppress weeds and give a little nitrogen boost. Chives often die back during hot summer weather. However, if you keep them watered they will send out new growth when temperatures cool down.

Dealing with flowers Remove flowers to get the best crop of leaves, but you can allow one or two to develop and use them in salads.

Dividing In the autumn cut back the tops and dig up the plants for dividing. Pull each plant apart into small sections and replant. You should divide the plants every three years to keep them growing vigorously.

Extend the harvest in winter by potting up divisions in 20-cm (8-in) pots. Leave the pots outdoors until after the first frost, then move them to a cool light position indoors, where you can continue to snip the leaves as you need them.

Harvesting

Use sharp scissors to clip chive leaves near the base – do not take just the tips. Harvest as needed when plants are growing vigorously. If the leaves become yellow and strawlike, give an application of liquid fertiliser to boost their growth.

Storing Rinse chive leaves and use them right away. Try storing chopped chives in the freezer in ice-cube trays (see pages 118–19).

Salad onions

Any young garden onion (*Allium cepa*) can be harvested as a salad onion (also known as spring onion, or scallion), but varieties specially bred for the purpose tend to have a better shape and a milder, more pleasant flavour.

Sowing and planting

Soil Loosen the soil several inches deep and work compost into it, then shape a low raised bed.

Starting seeds indoors For an early crop, you can sow seeds in a bed in a heated greenhouse or frame in midwinter.

Sowing outside Sow short rows every two weeks or so from early spring onwards, as soon as the soil is in a workable condition. Continue sowing through the summer for a successional harvest. Mid- to late summer sowings can provide an overwinter crop.

Welsh onion The Welsh onion, *Allium fistulosum*, is a little different from the typical salad onion. It is a perennial with round, hollow leaves and forms a spreading clump growing to 60cm (24in) or more tall.

Space the plants about 23cm (9in) apart and cut the leaves as required. At the end of the summer, you can lift the clump, divide it into smaller sections and replant it.

Modern Japanese varieties of *A. fistulosum* such as 'Ishikura' are usually grown as annuals – you can pull the seedlings and eat them at a young stage like other salad onion varieties.

Care

Mulch the plants with grass clippings to conserve moisture and provide nitrogen. If the plants need a growth boost, you can water them with a high-nitrogen fertiliser.

Salad onions should not need thinning. However, if seedlings look overcrowded at an earlier stage, thin them out to improve air circulation and help prevent downy mildew.

In cold areas mulch overwintering plants with straw or leaf litter to protect them, or cover rows with horticultural fleece.

Harvesting

You can begin harvesting salad onions when they are about pencil thickness. Keep harvesting them as you need them for fresh eating. You will need to lift the plants with a trowel rather than pulling them, because the stems will break very easily.

With the Welsh onion, remove as many stems as you need. The flavour of Welsh onion leaves is mild, and the leaves can be cut and used in the same way as salad onions. You can slice larger stems into rings for use.

Storing Salad onions will not keep well for longer than about one week in the refrigerator.

PLANTING GUIDE

What to plant Seeds, plants.

Site preparation Add compost.

When Sow in early to mid-spring, as soon as the soil is workable, and through the summer. Sow in mid- to late summer to overwinter.

Spacing Sow seeds thinly and start to pull onions as soon as they are a usable size, to avoid thinning at a later stage. Thin young seedlings if they become overcrowded. *Welsh onion* Set plants 23cm (9in) apart.

How much 30cm (1ft) of row per person per sowing.

BEST OF THE BUNCH

'Ishikura' A Welsh onion without bulbs, with long stems and a good flavour.
'White Lisbon' Quick, reliable grower. From midsummer to autumn, sow the hardier 'White Lisbon–Winter Hardy'.
'North Holland Blood Red' A variety with red stems; mild flavour.
'Guardsman' Vigorous, straight-stemmed variety; good for a long harvest.

Leeks

It takes a little special care to establish leeks in a bed, but their beautiful white stalks add a unique mellow flavour to a wide variety of dishes, including soups, stews and salads. Leeks have long been a favourite of home growers – for good reason.

PLANTING GUIDE

What to plant Transplants.

Starting indoors Sow seeds in mid- to late winter; harden off for a spring planting.

Site preparation Prepare a bed with deep, loose fertile soil, adding a layer of compost.

When Sow in a seedbed in mid-spring for planting out in early to midsummer.

Spacing Set the transplants 10–15cm (4–6in) apart, with 30–45cm (12–18in) between the rows.

How much For each person, grow about 10 plants; you can grow more if a prolonged harvest is planned.

Sowing and planting

Soil Leeks don't require much special preparation. Work a 5-cm (2-in) layer of compost over the planting area.

Starting seeds indoors Sow seeds in containers that are at least 7.5cm (3in) deep. Keep the containers at 13–24°C (55–75°F) – the temperature in which the seeds germinate best. Feed the seedlings a solution of balanced fertiliser every two weeks. Begin hardening off the plants for a spring planting one week before transplanting.

Sowing outdoors Sow seeds in a well-prepared seedbed outdoors in mid-spring, and thin the seedlings so that they are 2.5–5cm (1–2in) apart. Transplant to their final positions in early to mid-summer. They are ready for transplanting when they are rather less than pencil thickness.

Planting methods Make individual planting holes for each transplant with a large dibber. Water the seedbed the day before lifting, and use a fork to prise up the seedlings. Lay a bunch of seedlings with their bases together and trim the roots with a pair of sharp scissors; also trim the tips of the leaves so that the plants are about 15cm (6in) long. Drop the seedlings into their planting holes, ensuring that they

contact the soil at the base. Water the row after planting; this will wash down enough soil to cover the roots. Leave the planting holes open – the leeks will fill the space as they grow.

An alternative method is to open up a 15-cm (6-in)-deep trench and set the transplants in it. Cover the roots and stem bases with soil; as the leeks grow, gradually fill the trench with soil, straw or chopped leaves.

Care

Watering Leeks require frequent watering. If you earth up soil around the plants (see below), don't water the plants directly or you will wash away the soil. Instead, let water pool between the rows and soak into the soil. To avoid disease try not to water the foliage or stems directly.

Blanching If you plant leeks in a trench, once it is filled, earth up soil around the stems as they grow to blanch them. This keeps the stems white and tender. Be careful not to push soil up to where the leaves branch out from the stalk, or the leeks will be difficult to clean later on.

Even if you planted leeks in deep holes, you can still earth up soil round the stems as they elongate. Or slip a 15-cm (6-in) length of plastic pipe round each leek to shade the stem.

Before planting leeks grown together in containers, use a pair of sharp scissors to trim the tangled roots – they will be easier to plant.

Plant the leeks in individual holes made by a dibber; alternatively, plant the leeks in a trench (you won't need to trim their roots).

Fertilising Apply a balanced fertiliser or compost tea once a month.

Harvesting

Use a garden fork to loosen and unearth leeks when they reach the size you desire. If you have a large planting, harvest some early, slender baby leeks. Many varieties produce stems up to 5cm (2in) in diameter.

Take the harvested leeks away from the growing crop before shaking the soil off the roots, or you are likely to shower soil over the rest of the crop and you will find your leeks full of grit when you prepare them.

Storing In most areas of the country, leeks will keep well in the garden through the winter and enable you to harvest them in cold spells. In cold areas cover them with a deep straw mulch to protect them from frost.

After digging the leeks, carefully pull down the outermost leaf to reveal the clean white shank, then trim the roots and leaves. The leeks generally keep for several weeks in the crisper drawer of a refrigerator or in moist sand in a root cellar (see pages 116–17).

Before storing leeks, make sure you trim the roots and cut back the dark green leafy tops.

Succulent leek stems and leaves require lots of moisture. Make sure you water leeks well as they grow.

BEST OF THE BUNCH

'Carlton' An F1 hybrid producing early crops of long, straight, tightly formed stems. Good flavour.
'King Richard' Fast-growing; long stalks; good for harvest of baby leeks or full-size leeks.
'Musselburgh' Reliable, hardy old favourite, producing thick white stems.

Garlic

Autumn planting sets the stage for a successful garlic harvest. Plants sit dormant or grow slowly through the winter. Once the weather warms up in spring, the plants produce plenty of straplike green leaves that will feed the developing bulbs.

PLANTING GUIDE

What to plant Single cloves.

Site preparation Plant a cover crop in spring or enrich soil with organic matter before planting.

When From autumn to early spring.

Spacing *Softneck* Set the cloves 15–20cm (6–8in) apart in rows 30cm (12in) apart. *Hardneck* Set the cloves 10–15cm (4–6in) apart, with 30cm (12in) between rows.

Intensive spacing Set cloves at standard in-row spacing, but in rows 15–20cm (6–8in) apart.

How much Per person, about 3m (10ft) of row.

Quick Tip

Buying cloves
While it is possible to grow a crop of garlic from cloves bought in the supermarket, you will get better results by buying garlic from a specialist mail-order nursery. They will have a wider range of varieties and can give cultivation advice.

Sowing and planting

Soil Pick an area in the garden with excellent winter drainage, because cloves will generally rot in cold, wet soil. To improve drainage, you can mound up the soil into a raised bed. Garlic has shallow roots, so you will need only a 10-cm (4-in)-high bed (see pages 22–23).

Planting a green manure crop in spring and digging it into the soil in late summer is good preparation for garlic. If you plan to plant in a spot where another vegetable crop grew during the summer, you should spread a 5-cm (2-in) layer of compost over the planting area and work it into the soil.

Planting cloves Don't separate the cloves from the bulbs until just before you plan to plant them. You should discard any damaged, diseased or puny cloves. (Big cloves will produce big bulbs.) Make a planting drill or, if your soil is loose, you can simply push the cloves into the soil to the proper depth.

In mild areas you should set the top of the clove 2.5–5cm (1–2in) below the soil surface. In colder areas make sure you plant them deeper, 5–10cm (2–4in) below the soil. Water the cloves thoroughly and mulch with straw or chopped leaves.

Spring planting In areas with very cold, wet winters you can try planting garlic in spring, as soon as you can work the soil. Yields will be lower than for autumn-planted garlic, but you will avoid bulbs rotting in cold, wet soil.

Care

Watering After the first watering in autumn, you may not need to water garlic plants again until spring, depending on the weather.

GARLIC TYPES

Garlic is available in hardneck (or topsetting) and softneck varieties. Softneck garlic comes from the Mediterranean but is adaptable to many conditions. The bulbs form multiple layers of cloves, and they will last well in storage.

Hardneck garlic grows well in cold-winter areas. The bulbs produce one layer of cloves, which are larger than those of softneck and easier to peel. The cloves have a stronger flavour than softneck. Most of the varieties available are softneck types, but hardneck varieties are available from specialist suppliers. Hardneck garlic will not keep long in storage.

From spring onwards, you should keep the plants well watered. However, don't allow them to become soggy or the bulbs will rot.

During the last four weeks of growth, you should cut back on watering, which will allow the bulbs to mature. The roots will still need some moisture, but it's best if the soil stays dry to the depth of the bulbs. Stop watering altogether about two to three weeks before the plants should be ready to harvest.

Weeding Because garlic has upright foliage that doesn't shade out weeds, you will need to maintain a weed-suppressing mulch around them. Apply the mulch when planting, and keep it in place until the last few weeks before harvest (but pull back the mulch if it seems to be holding moisture around the bulbs). Cultivate as needed to keep the stand clear of all weeds.

Fertilising If your soil isn't rich enough to support strong foliage growth, begin fertilising the plants in spring when growth starts. You can either spray or side-dress plants with a balanced fertiliser. You should stop fertilising by late spring, or you may ruin the flavour and quality of the developing bulbs.

Harvesting

For garlic that was planted in autumn, you can expect to harvest it in late spring or early summer. Garlic that was planted in spring is not usually ready for harvest until mid- to late summer – or even early autumn in some places.

Yellowed, dry lower leaves are a sign that the garlic bulbs are approaching maturity. In general, plants will have only four to six green leaves left at harvest time. However, there are some early varieties that will be ready for harvest when the foliage has barely started to die back.

When about one-quarter of the foliage has dried up, the garlic will be ready for checking. Unearth a couple of bulbs and unwrap them. Bulbs that are ready to harvest will have tight outer leaves. Inside these leaves, the cloves should be fully separated. If your bulbs are ready for harvest, don't delay it too long, or the outer leaves will deteriorate.

You can either pull out the bulbs by hand or use a garden fork to unearth them. To dry the bulbs you will need to spread out the plants in a single layer on screens in an airy shed, garage or greenhouse – or even on a covered patio. If the atmospheric conditions are very humid, you should set a fan on low speed to blow across the plants – the breeze will help to dry out the bulbs. Curing generally takes one to four weeks.

Storing When the garlic is fully dry, clip the leafy tops to about 12.5mm (½in) long. If there is any sign of moisture when you cut the tops, the plants haven't finished curing. Cut the roots back to about 12.5mm (½in), too. Use a toothbrush or fingernail scrub brush to gently brush soil off the bulbs.

Store the bulbs in baskets, sacking or net bags in a dark place at room temperature and low humidity. Or store them at 0–4.5°C (32–40°F) and low humidity. Avoid temperatures between 5.5–11°C (42–52°F), which may prompt the bulbs to sprout.

When garlic plants are cured, the outer skins of the bulbs will be completely dry, so that the necks of the plants form a tight barrier to protect the cloves inside.

PROBLEM SOLVER

Silvery streaks and blotches on leaves. Feeding onion thrips will reduce the plant's vigour and can also spread disease. Thrips are generally worst during hot, dry conditions. Spray the plants with a strong stream of water. If the problem persists you can spray the plants with insecticidal soap. Destroy the crop remains after you harvest the bulbs.

Yellow leaf tips; white mould appears on plants; bulbs rot. Fungal infection can cause rot and white mould. It occurs most often in cold, poorly drained soil. Try replanting garlic in a different area in the garden. You can improve soil drainage by building up a raised bed about 10cm (4in) high.

Stored cloves rot or shrivel. These symptoms can occur on garlic that has been harvested prematurely or stored in poor conditions. Wait for some of the foliage to die back before harvesting. Make sure the cloves are fully dry before storing them at the correct temperature.

9 The cabbage family

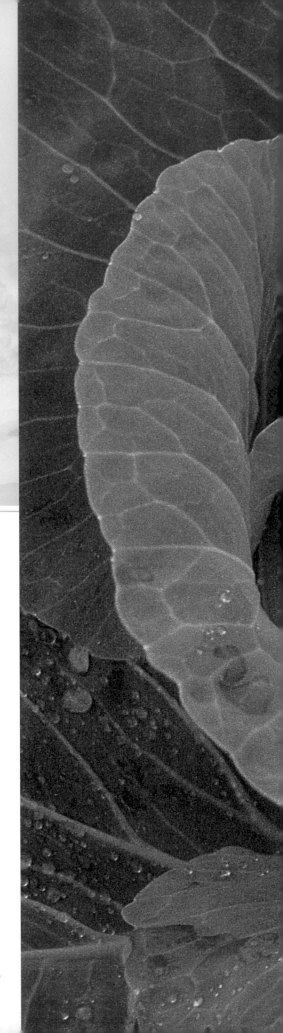

Nearly every vegetable garden is home to at least one member of the cabbage family. Even if you're not a cabbage lover, chances are you do like some of its relatives, which include broccoli, cauliflower, Brussels sprouts and kale.

These crops are collectively called brassicas or crucifers because they belong to the botanical family known as Brassicaceae or Cruciferae. This chapter also includes growing advice for some Asian relatives of the cabbage, including Chinese cabbage, pak choi and tatsoi.

Cabbages and other brassicas are at their best when freshly picked from the garden.

Cabbage

What kind of cabbage should you grow? There are types to suit all tastes, uses and growing conditions, and cabbages can be available fresh from your garden all year round. There are also varieties that can be stored for many weeks through the winter.

PLANTING GUIDE

What to plant Transplants or seeds.

Starting indoors Sow two to four weeks apart to spread the harvest; or sow a few varieties with different maturity dates.

Site preparation Either plant a cover crop the preceding autumn or add well-rotted compost before planting.

When Depends on variety.

Spacing *Large heads* 45cm (18in) or more apart. *Small heads* About 30cm (12in) apart. *Spring greens* About 15cm (6in) apart.

How much Per person, 5 to 10 cabbages, depending on variety.

BEST OF THE BUNCH

'Hispi' Early summer cabbage with a pointed head. Reliable; resistant to bolting.
'Offenham 2 – Flower of Spring' Spring cabbage with pointed heads; also good for growing as spring greens.
'Ruby Perfection' Large, deep red heads. Stores well.
'Savoy King' Crinkled, dark green leaves. Suitable for planting in any season.

Sowing and planting

Soil Cabbage plants need rich, fertile soil. You can boost soil fertility by growing a green manure and turning it under. Alternatively, spread a 5-cm (2-in) layer of compost and work it into the soil.

Check the soil pH where you plan to plant cabbages. It should be at least 6.0, but ideally 6.5 to 7.0, to reduce the risk of club root.

When to plant You can grow cabbages to mature all year round, and sowing dates vary according to the season in which they will be harvested. Most seed catalogues have a good selection of varieties for different seasons, with heads of different shapes and leaves of varying colours and textures.

Sow early summer varieties under cloches, in a frame or in a greenhouse in late winter or early spring and transplant in mid-spring. You can sow cabbages for the main summer season in the open in a seedbed in mid-spring and plant them out in late spring and early summer.

For cabbages to cut from late summer and through the autumn, sow outdoors from mid-spring to mid-summer and plant out from early to late summer. You should also sow winter varieties between mid-spring and midsummer, depending on the variety. These are usually planted out in mid- to late summer.

Sow spring cabbages in mid- to late summer and plant them out in early to mid-autumn for overwintering. They provide leafy greens in early spring, and firm heads a few weeks later.

Direct sowing You can sow cabbages directly where they are to grow if space allows, particularly quick-maturing summer types. Also sow spring greens (non-hearted, leafy greens, sometimes known as collards) where they are to mature; thin the seedlings to 15cm (6in) apart.

Care

Watering Cabbage need even moisture, particularly when the weather is hot and when the plants are forming heads. If the soil dries out and heavy rain falls, the sudden rush of water into the plants can cause the heads to split.

Despite your best efforts, you may find that the soil round your cabbages has become too dry. Don't flood the area with water because that will make the heads split too. Instead, apply a small amount of water each day – 475–700ml (16½–24½fl oz) per plant – to gradually restore the soil moisture.

To conserve soil moisture, you can spread a 5-cm (2-in)-thick layer of organic mulching material around the cabbage plants. However, do not allow the mulch to touch the heads, or it may encourage rot.

Weeding Competition with weeds will slow cabbage growth, so cultivate as necessary to prevent weeds. Because cabbages are heavy feeders, you should spread a shovelful of compost round each plant after weeding and work the compost into the soil, providing a nutrient boost for your cabbages.

Fertilising For the first four weeks after transplanting, water weekly with a balanced liquid fertiliser.

Harvesting

You will know when cabbages are ready to harvest because the heads will be firm. Use a sharp knife to cut through the stem below the heads. It is best to cut the heads in the morning, when the sugars will be at their highest, which yields the best flavour.

If several heads mature at the same time, spread the harvest by breaking a portion of the roots on some of the plants. This reduces water uptake and lessens the risk of split heads during the harvest period. Use both hands to twist a cabbage head about one-quarter turn, or plunge a shovel into the soil at one side of the head.

If a head does split, harvest it right away. Cut away any deteriorating portions and cook the remaining healthy cabbage immediately.

Leave stumps of cut plants in place so they can produce small side heads. Removing all but one side shoot will promote a bigger size of the remaining head. Cut the side heads when 5–10cm (2–4in) across.

Remove cut stumps from the garden after the harvest is complete. Otherwise, diseases and pests may persist in the stump and roots.

Storing Cut off any soiled outer leaves but don't wash the cabbages. Store them in the refrigerator in plastic bags for two weeks (longer for late varieties). Late-season cabbages store well in a cool shed or garage.

Cabbage heads may be red or green, round, pointed or flat, with smooth or crinkly leaves.

PROBLEM SOLVER

Plants wilt in hot weather. The first sign of either club root or cabbage root fly attack. Tunnels in roots indicate cabbage root fly larvae. Prevent attack by placing discs of felt, underlay or similar material (available from garden centres) round the bases of plants after transplanting, Alternatively, cover the plants with horticultural fleece while they are young. Plants affected by club root have swollen and distorted roots and should be destroyed by burning. To help prevent club root, follow a crop-rotation plan and keep the soil pH between 6.5 and 7.0 by liming where necessary.

Deformed or distorted leaves. Look for clusters of aphids, particularly the waxy, grey, mealy cabbage aphid, on the undersides. Spray the plants with a strong jet of water to dislodge the aphids, pick off badly infested leaves or use insecticidal soap.

Small holes in leaves. Protect young plants from tiny flea beetles with horticultural fleece; older plants aren't harmed by an attack.

Large holes in leaves. Cabbage caterpillars can reduce leaves to a network of veins. Hand-pick caterpillars; cover plants with horticultural fleece to protect them from cabbage white butterflies. Pigeons also attack cabbage-family plants, especially in winter. Cover plants with netting or grow them in a fruit cage. Slugs and snails are especially damaging to young plants; see pages 104–5 for controls.

Temperature alert
You should plan to plant cabbages so heads will mature in cool conditions.

Brussels sprouts

Eating home-grown Brussels sprouts for the first time is a revelation. Freshly harvested sprouts have a tender texture and nutty sweetness that are completely different from those bought in a supermarket.

Sowing and planting

Soil Brussels sprouts need rich, moist soil. Work a 5-cm (2-in) layer of compost into the soil and rake in an application of general fertiliser.

When For a late summer or early autumn harvest, sow in a greenhouse, frame or under cloches in late winter or early spring, transplanting in early summer. For late autumn and winter crops, sow in a seedbed outdoors from early to mid-spring; transplant in early to midsummer.

Select varieties according to their maturity dates. Most gardeners grow at least two varieties, an early and a late, for a cropping season that extends from autumn through the winter.

Brussels sprouts need firm planting. Loose soil and insufficiently firmed plants will lead to loosely formed sprouts instead of firm, tight buttons.

Care

Watering Keep the young transplants well watered until they are established. Thereafter, plants need watering only during very dry spells.

Fertlising On poor soils, apply a high-nitrogen fertiliser in midsummer.

General care Keep the plants free of weeds and watch out for cabbage-family pests (see page 171). Provide

Keep Brussels sprouts in the garden well into winter. Most people believe that their flavour improves after a frost.

(see page 171)

PLANTING GUIDE

What to plant Transplants only.

Starting indoors Sow seeds indoors or protected under cover in early spring for an early autumn crop.

Site preparation Enrich the soil with a layer of compost before planting.

When Between early and late spring, depending on the variety and its maturity date.

Spacing *Short varieties* Set plants about 45cm (18in) apart on centres. *Tall varieties* Set plants about 60cm (24in) apart on centres.

How much Two to three plants per person.

Temperature alert
Brussels sprouts become sweeter after a frost, so early maturing varieties may not have as good a flavour as later ones.

tall plants in exposed gardens with a stake to prevent them from being blown over by winds.

Harvesting

Start picking sprouts when they are 2.5–3.75cm (1–1½in) in diameter, starting at the stem base. Snap off the sprouts or cut them free with a sharp knife. To reach them easily, remove lower leaves as you harvest. Pick the sprouts every week or two as needed.

To force sprouts to mature at the same time, cut off the top 15cm (6in) of the plant five to six weeks before your first average frost date. The sprouts will mature six to eight weeks after the plant top is removed.

The loose, leafy plant top is edible, too. Cook the small leaves as you would spring greens or cabbage.

Storing Harvest sprouts as you need them. They remain in good condion on the plants through the winter. You can store unwashed sprouts in the refrigerator for one or two days.

BEST OF THE BUNCH

'Jade Cross Hybrid' Blue-green sprouts with mild flavour.
'Oliver' Produces firm sprouts; vigorous and early bearing.
'Peer Gynt' Well-known reliable F1 hybrid with well-formed, tight green buttons on compact plants. Heavy yielding.

PROBLEM SOLVER

The sprouts are loose and tufty. The soil was not firmed enough at planting time; for future plantings make sure you firm in the soil.

Tiny grey or black insects in the sprouts. These are aphids, which will suck juices from tender sprouts. During the growing period, you can dislodge aphid clusters by spraying them with a hard stream of water.

Broccoli

Home gardeners can enjoy broccoli over a long season by planting a combination of varieties to crop from very early in the spring right through until late autumn.

PLANTING GUIDE

What to plant Transplants.

Starting indoors Fairly easy; seedlings grow fast.

Site preparation Enrich the soil well before planting.

When Depending on the variety, early spring to mid-autumn.

Spacing 45cm (18in) apart; 60cm (24in) between rows.

Intensive spacing 38cm (15in) on centres.

How much About three plants per person.

BEST OF THE BUNCH

'Green Comet' Calabrese with very large, almost cauliflower-like green heads but few sideshoots.
'Decathlon' A vigorous, heat-tolerant calabrese that grows well on poor soil; suitable for successional cropping.
'Claret' Strong-growing, heavy cropping purple sprouting type suitable for a mid-spring harvest.

Sowing and planting

Soil Soil pH should be at least 6.0 – 6.5 to 7.0 is ideal. Enrich the soil with a green manure, or work a 5-cm (2-in) layer of compost into the soil.

When From early spring sow calabrese, or green sprouting broccoli, under cover for transplanting in early summer, or sow it where it is to mature in mid- to late spring. Sow purple and white sprouting broccoli in late spring in a seedbed outdoors and transplant in early to midsummer.

Care

Watering Keep calabrese plants moist, and apply a high-nitrogen fertiliser as the heads form. Water purple and white sprouting broccoli until the plants are established.

Protection Cover young plants with fleece to protect them from pests such as flea beetle. In exposed gardens, stake purple and white sprouting broccoli before winter to prevent them being blown over in windy weather.

Harvesting

Calabrese types form a large, central head in mid- to late summer. Cut it as soon as you can use it; a further crop

PROBLEM SOLVER

Calabrese plants form heads too soon. Known as buttoning, this can be caused by overhardening of transplants, too little water or hot or cold temperatures.

Hollow stems. Too much nitrogen or boron deficiency. Feed plants mature compost or a balanced organic fertiliser. Heads with hollow stems are edible.

See page 171 for additional solutions.

of smaller sideshoots will follow, extending the harvest into autumn.

Purple and white sprouting broccoli have smaller shoots with a more intense flavour; harvest between late winter and late spring or early summer. Picking the central shoot on each stem encourages a prolonged harvest of smaller sideshoots. White sprouting broccoli is less hardy and lighter cropping than purple, but has a more delicate flavour. All broccoli should be picked while the flower buds are still tight, before the petals start to show.

Storing Broccoli lasts about one week in the refrigerator, stored loosely in a plastic bag. For the best quality, cook broccoli as soon as possible after harvesting or freeze it (see pages 118–19).

Broccoli rabe

Broccoli rabe, or broccoli raab or rapini, is a popular vegetable in parts of Europe and the USA but is an unusual choice in Britain. The tender shoots have a sharp, spicy flavour. They look like broccoli, but the plant is more closely related to turnips.

Sowing and planting

Soil Enrich the soil by working in 5cm (2in) of compost. Or dig a trench 15cm (6in) deep and 7.5–10cm (3–4in) wide, and fill it with compost to 2.5cm (1in) below the soil level. Add 1.25cm (½in) of soil and sow the seeds; cover with soil to ground level.

When Sowing times depend on the variety, but start in early spring and continue until midsummer. Some varieties are ready for picking more quickly than others; those that take longer may have a better flavour. Broccoli rabe bolts to seed quickly in hot weather, so time sowings to avoid the hottest period if possible.

Sowing for overwintering Try a late sowing for overwintering. Sow in early autumn, two to three weeks before the first frost is due. Cover the seedlings with low polythene tunnels, horticultural fleece, cloches or a straw mulch, and they should survive the winter to give an extra-early crop the following spring. This works best in well-drained soil.

Care

Improving yields Broccoli rabe is generally easy to grow. Keep the soil moist and apply a nitrogen-rich organic fertilizer for a better yield. Make sure you keep the plants well watered in hot weather.

See page 171 for solutions to pest and disease problems.

Harvesting

You can harvest the young leaves and stems to add to a salad mix, or allow the flowering shoots to develop and use them like broccoli. Pick the stems before the flowerbuds show any sign of opening. Harvesting the main stems should encourage the production of further sideshoots.

The flavour of broccoli rabe has a sharper bite and is more spicy than ordinary broccoli – it has been likened to a cross between broccoli and radish. One of the most popular ways to cook it is to steam or lightly boil the shoots before stir-frying them – this mellows the flavour.

Storing Place unwashed shoots in a plastic bag; they will keep fresh in a refrigerator for up to three days.

PLANTING GUIDE

What to plant Seeds.

Site preparation Enrich the soil before planting.

When From early spring to mid-summer, depending on variety.

Spacing Sow seeds 2.5cm (1in) apart, with 45cm (18in) between rows; thin to 15 (6in) apart.

Intensive spacing Broadcast seeds in wide rows; thin to 7.5cm (3in) apart.

How much Two to four plants per person.

BEST OF THE BUNCH

'Cima Di Rapa' Both early and late selections of this type are available. A reliable grower with a pleasantly spicy flavour.

'Sessantina' Thick but tender shoots; good for a late summer crop or to overwinter.

Temperature alert
Broccoli rabe grows best in cool conditions and will do well in partial shade.

Cauliflower

Cauliflower is broccoli's temperamental cousin. Conditions that are too hot, too cold or too dry can result in disappointing head development. However, with perseverance and luck, you can grow delicious cauliflower to harvest almost all year round.

PLANTING GUIDE

What to plant Transplants.

Starting indoors Germination is fastest at 26.5°C (80°F). Harden off after four to five weeks.

Site preparation Provide rich soil conditions.

When Depends on the variety.

Spacing Set plants 38–60cm (15–24in) apart; 60–90cm (24–36in) between rows.

Intensive spacing 45cm (18in) on centres, or 15cm (6in) on centres for 'mini' cauliflower.

How much About five plants per person.

Quick Tip

Buttons

The formation of small premature heads is known as 'buttoning'. It occurs if there is a check to the growth of young plants caused by overcrowding, cold or lack of water or nutrients. Try to keep them developing steadily at all times.

Sowing and planting

Soil The pH should be at least 6.0 but 6.5 to 7.0 is ideal. Enrich the soil with a green manure, or work a 5-cm (2-in) layer of compost into the soil.

When to plant Choose the varieties carefully when growing cauliflowers to mature at different times. The temperature and weather conditions required by different varieties vary.

Sow cauliflowers under cloches or in a frame in mid-autumn, or under cover in a heated greenhouse in mid- to late winter for transplanting in early to mid-spring. You can harvest them in early to midsummer.

Sow outdoors in a seedbed in mid-spring and transplant in early summer for a crop in late summer and early autumn; sow in mid- to late spring and transplant in early to midsummer for crops in autumn and winter. Choose a sheltered position for winter crops.

Transplanting Transplants are ready to set out when they have five leaves. If they become too large before transplanting, they can 'button'. Early varieties are prone to buttoning.

Sow 'mini' cauliflowers with small heads where they are to grow as a successional crop for a longer harvest.

All cauliflowers should be firmed in well on transplanting.

Care

In cold areas protect spring transplants from low temperatures by covering them with horticultural fleece or cloches. Keep the soil moist at all times, and, after the first month, feed plants with a balanced or high–nitrogen fertiliser every two or three weeks. (The exception is winter cauliflower, which does not need extra feeding.)

Pest protection Cauliflowers are prone to attack by a number of familiar cabbage-family pests. Covering the crops with horticultural fleece will keep many of them at bay, but in summer use a lightweight fleece to ensure the plants do not become overheated.

PROBLEM SOLVER

Thin, straplike leaves and poor head formation. Caused by a deficiency of molybdenum known as whiptail. It occurs on acid soils. Spray affected plants with a foliar feed containing trace elements, and ensure soil is limed for future crops.

Curds turn brown. This may be sunburn; protect crops from sun. Downy mildew, a fungal disease, occurs in humid conditions.

See page 171 for additional solutions.

'Snow Crown' Fast and easy to grow. White heads form up to 20cm (8in) wide.
'Fremont' Self-blanching; good in a variety of soil and weather conditions.
'Violet Queen' Purple head turns green when cooked.
'Maystar' Overwintering type with a white head.

Prevent sun scorch by bending the large leaves over the head and securing them in place.

Purple-head varieties do not require blanching to protect their heads from sunburn.

Blanching White cauliflower curds require protection from the sun to retain their snowy colour, otherwise they will turn yellow. Some varieties are described as 'self-blanching' because the foliage wraps the curd tightly to protect it. However, if the head is exposed to sun, snap one of the outer leaves halfway so that it covers the curd. You can also use twine or rubber bands to fasten the leaves round the head.

Harvesting

As soon as the cauliflower is large enough to use, cut the stem just below the head and with some leaves enclosing it. Make sure you harvest the plants while the heads are still tight, before the florets begin to separate. Harvest mini cauliflowers all at once because their quality deteriorates quickly; you can freeze surplus heads.

Storing
Cauliflower heads will keep fresh in the refrigerator for up to four weeks, if they are covered in plastic wrap or stored in plastic bags.

Temperature alert
Too much heat or cold can lead to poor production of cauliflower heads.

Kale

This particularly hardy member of the cabbage family has deep green, curly leaves that provide a delicious treat through the autumn and winter. Packed with vitamins, kale is as healthy as it is tasty.

PLANTING GUIDE

What to plant Seeds or transplants.

Starting indoors Start the seeds in midsummer for an autumn crop.

Site preparation Cover crop the previous season or add compost to the soil.

When Mid-spring, for transplanting midsummer.

Spacing Sow the seeds 7.5cm (3in) apart, with 45cm (18in) between the rows; thin the plants to about 30–45cm (12–18in) apart.

Intensive spacing Sow the seeds about 20cm (8in) apart on centres.

How much Above five plants per person.

Temperature alert Kale can tolerate cold conditions, and it will taste best harvested after a frost.

Sowing and planting

Soil Kale thrives in rich, moist soil. Enrich the soil with a green manure, or work 7.5cm (3in) of compost into it.

When to plant Sow in mid- to late spring, and transplant young plants to their cropping positions in early to midsummer. Kale is a hardy crop and is ideal for even the coldest areas.

You can also sow kale in spring and summer for harvesting as baby leaves for salads and mesclun mixes (see pages 136–37).

Care

Water plants well after transplanting until they become established. In cold areas do not water after this unless it is essential; too much water will make the plants produce soft growth that is less able to survive cold weather.

Feeding in early summer with a high-nitrogen fertiliser may improve yields, but in cold areas take care not to promote too much soft growth late in the season.

In autumn earth up round the stem bases for extra stability. In exposed gardens provide tall plants with a sturdy stake to prevent them being blown over by autumn and winter winds, and try the compact, dwarf varieties rather than the tall types.

Harvesting

Many people regard kale as strong-flavoured, bitter and tough – but this reputation is undeserved. It has come about in part from growing old varieties instead of the more modern, sweeter and tender-leaved types, but also from harvesting the older leaves of the plants instead of those growing from the centre of the crown.

Pick the young leaves from late autumn onwards, throughout the winter and early spring. Don't bother picking the older, lower leaves of plants – they are not worth eating.

To harvest for salads, cut the young seedlings when they are about 8-10cm (3-4in) tall.

Storing You can keep leaves in a plastic bag in the salad section of the refrigerator for a few days.

BEST OF THE BUNCH

'Dwarf Green Curled' Tightly curled leaves; good flavour. Cold resistant.
'Red Bor' Decorative type; curled, purple leaves. Crops through cold conditions.
'Starbor' Rich green, tightly curled leaves on compact plants.
'Pentland Brig' Tasty, crinkle-edged leaves. Forms sideshoots as spring approaches; cut when 10cm (4in) long and eat like broccoli.

Kohlrabi

The swollen above-ground stems of kohlrabi are delicious whether eaten raw or cooked, and they have a mild, sweet flavour that has been compared to cabbage, turnips, celery and even cucumbers.

PLANTING GUIDE

What to plant Seeds or transplants.

Starting indoors Easy to start seeds indoors or in a frame.

Site preparation Enrich the soil as for cabbage (see pages 170–71).

When From spring to mid-summer in succession.

Spacing 15cm (6in) apart; rows 30–90cm (12–36in) apart.

Intensive spacing 10–15cm (4–6in) apart in a staggered double row.

How much *Seeds* Sow about 30–60cm (12–24in) of double row per person, or 0.9–1.5m (3–5ft) of standard row. *Plants* Grow about 6 to 10 plants per person.

BEST OF THE BUNCH

'Busta' Deep purple variety that is slow to become woody, with a sweet flavour.
'Early White Vienna' Compact plants; light green skin and white flesh globes; slow to bolt.
'Kolibri' Purple globes with white flesh; tolerates heat.

Sowing and planting

Soil Plant a cover crop and turn it into the soil a few weeks before planting. Or work a 5-cm (2-in) layer of compost into the soil before you begin planting. Apply lime if necessary to raise the soil pH to guard against club root.

When to plant Sow seeds where they are to grow from mid-spring until mid- to late summer, sowing in succession every two or three weeks. Sow small amounts at a time because the plants will become tough and woody if they are not eaten young.

For early crops, raise seeds under cover in early spring and transplant in mid- to late spring. Transplants are prone to bolting, so sow in modules or individual pots to avoid root disturbance, and plant out when the seedlings are small, about 5cm (2in) high. Choose bolt-resistant varieties for early crops.

Care

Kohlrabi tastes best when it has been grown quickly, so make sure the plants never run short of water and keep weeds under control. For directly sown crops, thin the seedlings as early as possible to avoid unecessary root disturbance. In poor soils, an application of a high-nitrogen liquid fertiliser will boost growth.

Harvesting

Harvest kohlrabi before the globes swell beyond 7.5cm (3in) in diameter or they may become woody. Cut the plants 2.5cm (1in) below the globe. Kohlrabi leaves are also good to eat; you can cook them as you would other greens.

If you discover that a globe has turned tough, peel away the outer layers. The centre may still be tender and have good flavour. Lift the remaining plants in early winter.

Storing You can store kohlrabi globes in a cool place for up to three months, or for up to three weeks in the refrigerator if wrapped in plastic.

Harvest kohlrabi globes while they are young and still tender.

Oriental greens

These exotic cabbage family members are not difficult to grow – most of them will thrive in British gardens. Whether you eat them in salads or lightly cooked, they will bring a touch of Eastern magic to your dinner table.

PLANTING GUIDE

What to plant Direct sowing for most types. Transplants or seeds for Chinese cabbage.

Site preparation Enrich the soil with plenty of compost before planting. Add lime if soil is acidic.

When Depends on the type of Oriental green, but for most types sow from mid- to late summer.

Spacing Depends on the type.

How much to plant Per person, 5 to 10 plants.

Quick Tip

The name game

Oriental greens have many different names, both in English and Asian languages. If you're not sure which seeds to order in garden centres or catalogues, ask a salesperson for advice or call the company's customer service line.

Sowing and planting

Soil These crops like rich conditions and don't do well in acidic soil. Work a 5-cm (2-in) layer of compost into the soil and keep the soil moist – Oriental greens will tolerate heat better when they grow in consistently moist soil. If you make succession sowings, add another 5-cm (2-in) layer of compost before sowing or planting each new crop.

When to plant Most Oriental greens are short-day plants – if sown before the longest day they are likely to bolt to seed instead of producing a good crop of leaves. Midsummer is the peak season for sowing. Plants often bolt if transplanted, so directly sow them where they are to grow.

Bolt-resistant varieties are available if you want to try earlier sowings. Sow in modules or individual pots under cover in mid-spring and keep the seedlings at a steady temperature of 18-21°C (65-70°F) – a cold spell also induces bolting. Harden off gradually and plant out with the minimum of root disturbance. After transplanting, keep the soil moist at all times, as dry conditions also encourage bolting.

Salad crops You can also sow Oriental greens as salad crops. Use the cut-and-come-again technique to harvest the leaves when young and fresh, as some become unpleasantly hot and spicy for eating raw if they become too large – their texture may also become rather coarse.

Sowing seeds For Chinese broccoli, sow seeds 5–10cm (2–4in) apart in rows about 30cm (12in) apart; thin to 15–20cm (6–8in) apart.

For pak choi, sow seeds a few inches apart and thin them to 15–38cm (6–15in) apart, depending on whether you plan to harvest young leaves or mature plants.

To grow mizuna, sow seeds 5cm (2in) apart in rows 45cm (18in) apart. Thin the plants 25–30cm (10–12in) apart. You can also plant mizuna intensively by spacing them 15cm (6in) on centres.

Grow choy sum with 10cm (4in) between the plants.

Care

These plants need frequent watering, so keep the top few inches of the soil moist at all times. Oriental greens won't need fertiliser applications in fertile soil. Keep the plants free from weeds. Although they can suffer many of the normal cabbage-family pest and disease problems (see page 171), they are usually trouble free – but they are prone to slug damage.

Harvesting

Cut Chinese cabbage when the heads are large enough to use and feel firm and well-hearted. Use a knife to cut the plants an inch or so above ground level; the remaining stump may produce a further crop of leafy greens.

When the stems of Chinese broccoli reach about 12.5mm (½in) in diameter, cut them 7.5cm (3in) above ground level.

For pak choi, harvest individual leaves from these plants for as long as they survive in the ground or let them form heads like Chinese cabbage.

You can harvest the young leaves of mizuna as soon as three weeks after the seedlings appear.

After the flower buds open on choy sum, use a sharp knife to cut the plant at the base.

Storing Chinese cabbages will last about two to three months in humid, cool storage. If temperatures drop

To harvest just a few leaves of mizuna, you can use the cut-and-come-again technique.

below 10°C (50°F), the heads will also keep well in place in the garden.

Chinese broccoli, pak choi, mizuna and choy sum don't store well, so prepare them as soon as possible after harvesting. The stems of Chinese broccoli will still taste good even if the flower buds open before harvest.

Choy sum usually has green leaves and stems, but some have attractive red-purple stems.

AN ORIENTAL CONTAINER GARDEN

If you've never tried eating Oriental greens, you may want to experiment with these crops on a small scale. One way to do that is to plant just a few specimens of each in pots or a planter on a sunny terrace or patio. Oriental-themed pottery would be an appropriate choice, but use whatever you have available. A 30-cm (12-in) pot is the right size for a Chinese cabbage or Chinese broccoli plant. All containers should have adequate drainage holes.

Prepare the potting compost as you would for any other container vegetables (see pages 44–45). Transplant crops or sow seeds into the containers at the same time you would plant them in the garden.

If you have a planter you can interplant Chinese cabbage, Chinese broccoli, mizuna and tatsoi, placing the taller crops at the back. Their contrasting leaf colours and unusual shapes will be an attention-getter, and you can educate both yourself and your friends about these unusual crops. For an extra-special touch, insert a trellis at the back of the planter and sow mangetout at the base. Your Oriental container garden will supply the basis for wonderful stir-fries.

Temperature alert
Hot, dry weather accelerates the tendency to bolt to seed. Keep the plants well watered during dry spells.

Types of Oriental greens

Among the types of Oriental greens are Chinese cabbage, choy sum, pak choi, Chinese broccoli and mizuna. Oriental vegetables may be found under a variety of different names in seed catalogues – so be careful that you don't order the same thing from two different sources.

◀ **Pak choi**

This crop is also known as bok choy. The leaves are succulent and are especially suited for stir-fries. They are very attractive with their contrasting midribs.

▲ **Chinese cabbage**

Chinese cabbages are also called celery cabbage, michihli, napa and pe tsai. You can use them as you would regular cabbage in stir-fries, salads or for cole slaw.

▶ **Mizuna**

This attractive plant produces feathery green leaves with white midribs. It's so pretty you may want to include it in a flower garden for its looks alone. The leaves have a mild flavour and are good added to a mesclun mix. In cooking, mizuna pairs well with root vegetables, or try it stir-fried with ginger and soya sauce.

TYPES OF ORIENTAL GREENS

▶ Choy sum

This crop is also known as choi sum and Chinese flowering cabbage. You can harvest when first flower buds begin to open. Use the flower shoots and young leaves in salads or stir-fries.

▶ Chinese broccoli

Chinese broccoli, also known as Chinese kale, gai lohn and gaai lohn, doesn't form large heads. The tender young stems, along with flower buds and leaves, are a tasty addition to stir-fries. Some varieties are quick to mature.

◀ Tatsoi

Tatsoi is a variety of pak choi and is also called flat cabbage or rosette pak choi. As these names suggest, it forms a flattened rosette, with small round dark green leaves at the end of slender stems. Tatsoi is easy to grow and withstands cold temperatures well to -9.5°C (15°F).

10 Root and stem crops

Root crops hail from a range of plant families, but they all share the need for the sheltering environment of the soil as they produce succulent storage roots and tubers. Some of our favourite vegetable crops are root crops, including carrots, radishes and potatoes. A few of these crops, including turnips and beets, also offer a bonus of tender leaves that are delicious when cooked. Some other crops such as celery and Florence fennel are grown primarily for their bounty of fleshy, crisp stems.

Freshly dug potatoes are full of goodness extracted from the soil.

Potatoes

You can grow your own potatoes from small tubers or pieces of tubers known as seed potatoes. From these, you can enjoy an astounding selection of delicious potato varieties that are not normally found in the shops.

Sowing and planting

Soil Potatoes thrive in rich, fertile soil. To avoid scab, a type of disease, the soil pH should be 5.0–6.5, so do not apply lime to the area in which potatoes are to be grown.

Chitting seed potatoes Potato tubers are swollen stems, not roots. The potato 'eyes' are buds, which sprout to form stems and leaves when the tubers are planted. For the earliest crops and to give the tubers a good start, these shoots are encouraged to start into growth before planting, a process known as chitting.

Stand the seed potatoes in shallow trays with the rose end (the end with the largest number of eyes) upwards, and set them in a cool but frost-free, light place to sprout. Keeping them in light ensures the shoots will be sturdy.

Planting You can plant the seed potatoes without chitting, but the crop will be later and not so heavy.

Red potatoes are just one of the more interesting types of potato to grow.

PLANTING GUIDE

What to plant Seed potatoes.

Starting indoors Pre-sprouting (chitting) is helpful.

Site preparation Check soil pH.

When *Early varieties* Early to mid-spring. *Maincrop varieties* Mid- to late spring.

Spacing *Early varieties* 20–35cm (8–14in) apart, with 30–45cm (12–18in) between rows. *Maincrop varieties* Allow 75–90cm (30–36in) between rows.

Intensive spacing 45cm (18in) apart on centres.

How much Per person, 4.5m (15ft) of row or a 1.2x2.4-m (4x8-ft) bed.

Quick Tip

Smart shopping

Supermarket potatoes may have been treated with chemicals that inhibit sprouting and will not be certified disease free. Buy seed potatoes only at garden centres in late winter or from mail-order suppliers.

 PROBLEM SOLVER

Brown spots and white mould appear on foliage. Potato blight fungus will attack potatoes during warm, humid conditions. Brown flecks first appear on the leaves and stems and become larger; later a white velvety coating will appear. The haulms will yellow and die. It is important to remove the affected topgrowth immediately to prevent spores spreading to the tubers. For future plantings, plant only certified disease-free seed potatoes and resistant cultivars. As a preventive measure, use a copper-based fungicide.

Stunted plants with puckered or yellow leaves. Potatoes are prone to virus diseases. For future plantings, cover the plants with horticultural fleece to keep virus-spreading aphids off.

Corky patches on tubers. Caused by scab. The potatoes are still edible, but cut away and discard the corky areas. For future crops, test the soil pH and adjust it to 5.5; choose resistant cultivars.

Holes eaten in tubers. Soil-living slugs can cause serious problems on maincrop varieties, particularly on heavy soils and in wet seasons; wireworms also tunnel in potatoes. Harvesting the crops as soon as they are ready will help to limit the damage. For slugs, you can try biological control with parasitic nematodes (see page 99).

Sometimes the seed potatoes are cut to provide more plants, but is best to plant them whole to avoid disease.

Make a trench 7.5–10cm (3–4in) deep and wide, set the seed potatoes in it and fill the trench to cover the tops of the potatoes with 2.5cm (1in) of soil. Or make individual holes.

Plant the earliest varieties in early to mid-spring if you have a light soil that warms up quickly. Plant maincrop potatoes in mid- to late spring.

Care

Earthing up If tubers are exposed to light they develop a green colour, making them bitter and poisonous. Earth up the plants, using a draw hoe to pull soil up round the bases of the stems. If a frost is forecast in early spring, pull the soil up to cover the tops of the shoots. Otherwise, earth up when the plants are 15–23cm (6–9in) tall; repeat once or twice in the season.

Or grow the potatoes under sturdy black plastic spread over the area after planting, with the edges buried in the soil. As the shoots grow they make bumps under the plastic; use a sharp knife to cut slits at each bump to let the

Air-dry unwashed tubers for a few hours after harvesting, then brush off any soil.

topgrowth through. You won't need to weed, but slugs can be a problem.

Water potatoes in dry spells once the tubers reach the size of marbles. Give sufficient water to moisten the soil several inches deep.

Harvesting

For early varieties harvest as 'new' potatoes as soon as they are large enough – often when the plants come into flower. Scrape some soil away to check their size before digging. Allow maincrop potatoes to grow until early autumn. Remove the yellowed topgrowth (the haulm) as it dies down, and leave the potatoes in the soil for another week or two. On a dry day lift them with a fork and allow them to dry on the soil surface for a few hours.

Storing Use new potatoes as soon as possible after harvest. For maincrops, use any damaged tubers, and store the rest in sacks (not plastic) or covered boxes at 4.5–10°C (40–50°F). Keep them dark at all times.

BEST OF THE BUNCH

'Pink Fir Apple' Thin, knobbly tubers; good flavour and waxy texture.
'Rocket' A fast-maturing type for the earliest potatoes, with white skins and pure white flesh. Heavy yield.
'Pentland Javelin' A disease-resistant 'first early'; does well in all soil types.
'Desiree' Rosy-skinned potato with well-flavoured, creamy yellow flesh.
'Sante' Large, smooth tubers, creamy flesh; noted for disease and pest resistance.

Types of potatoes

Instead of the typical white potatoes available year-round at the supermarket, why not plant something a little different? There's a whole range of types of potato available, with fine flavours and textures that lift potatoes into the gourmet class.

◀ Russet potatoes

Russets have a distinctive reddish brown russetting of the skin and light, fluffy-textured flesh when cooked. Russet varieties are more popular in the USA than in Britain, but 'Golden Wonder' is a well-established variety with red skin and light yellow flesh, and 'Record' is a yellow-skinned type. Both are maincrop varieties.

▶ Yellow potatoes

'Yukon Gold' has a rich golden skin and fluffy yellow flesh, while the older 'Bintje' has floury flesh of good flavour. These smooth-skinned yellow potatoes are excellent for baking, boiling, mashing, frying, steaming and in potato salad.

▲ Heirloom varieties

'Pink Fir Apple' is an old variety, still popular because of its distinctive flavour and firm, waxy texture – the ultimate salad potato. The long, thin and often knobbly tubers are washed and boiled in their skins. 'Ratte' has a similar long, finger shape but tubers are more regular and easier to prepare. They have a fine flavour. Other unusual heirloom types are available, including ones with deep purple-blue skins or with blue or burgundy-red flesh.

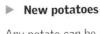 **New potatoes**

Any potato can be a new
potato if you harvest it early.
Wait for your plants to start
blooming. Once flowering is
well under way, try reaching
into the soil with your hand
to fish out some tubers to
see if they are large enough
to eat. If you don't want
to harvest the whoe crop,
only take a few from each
of your plants, and allow the
rest to mature. New potatoes
have delicate skin, so don't
scrub them. Wash and cook
them gently.

Red potatoes

Red potatoes usually have
firm flesh and thin skin. The
thin skin is generally easier to
peel than that of other types
of potatoes. 'Desiree' is one of
the best-known varieties, with
rosy pink skin, yellow flesh
and a rich flavour. 'Maxine'
has white flesh.

 **White potatoes**

White potatoes include some
of our most useful, all-purpose
varieties. 'Epicure' and 'British
Queen' are both old varieties
known for their floury texture
and good flavour, while 'Arran
Pilot' and 'Foremost' are
among the earliest of new
potatoes. 'Valor' is a more
recent introduction, with
some resistance to blight.

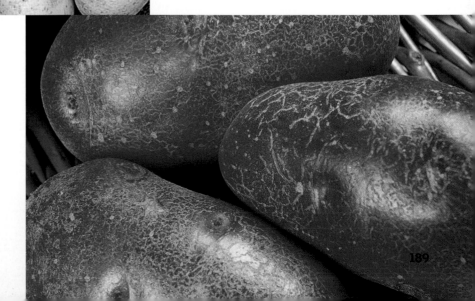

Sweet potatoes

Here's a crop for adventurous gardeners! The sweet potato is a native of much warmer climates than ours, but with a good season and a bit of luck you can still produce a worthwhile crop in your own garden.

Sowing and planting

Sweet potatoes will need warm conditions to thrive, so you should grow them outside only in the milder areas of the country. You can obtain a much better crop by growing the plants in a polythene tunnel or inside a greenhouse.

The ideal soil is slightly acid, light and free draining, but rich and fertile. For plants growing outdoors, make a raised bed and cover it with black plastic mulch for several weeks before planting to help warm the soil.

Obtaining plants Sweet potatoes are not related to normal potatoes, but are members of the morning glory family. They are grown from 'slips' – sprouted shoots that are removed from the tubers and rooted. Slips are sometimes available from mail-order suppliers; however, they may not be easy to obtain.

Grow your own slips If you cannot find a supplier of slips, try growing your own from supermarket-bought sweet potato tubers. Bury half the tuber in a pot of moist sand or seed compost, put a plastic propagator top on the pot and keep it in a warm position. Shoots should develop on the top of the tuber, and when these are 5cm (2in) long you can remove them and place them in a jar of water or in moist compost to form roots.

Planting slips Slips ordered via mail order may look wilted or even dead when they arrive, but they should recover quickly after planting. Plant as soon as they arrive, usually in late spring or early summer, cutting planting slits in the black plastic if you are using it. Plant the slips deeply, so that just the tops are above the soil. Cover the young plants with cloches or horticultural fleece to provide them with extra warmth.

Care

Watering, feeding and supporting

Keep the soil moist at all times while the plants are getting established, and

BEST OF THE BUNCH

Note: Sweet potatoes are not readily available in Britain although they can be found from specialist mail-order suppliers. You may need to start sweet potatoes from your own slips.

'Beauregard' Pale purple skin and deep orange flesh. Fast maturing with high yields; resists splitting.
'T65' Vigorous, early, high-yielding variety that is a good choice for cooler conditions. It has reddish skin with creamy-white flesh.

PLANTING GUIDE

What to plant Certified disease-free slips.

Starting indoors Start your own slips indoors.

Site preparation Raised beds covered with black plastic.

When Late spring or early summer, when soil is at least 18°C (65°F).

Spacing Plant 30–45cm (12–18in) apart in rows 90cm (36in) apart; or grow 3 slips per mound, 90cm (36in) apart.

How much Two to four plants per person.

Temperature alert
Grow sweet potatoes under cover, or use black plastic to warm the soil and fleece to protect plants from chilly conditions.

give regular applications of a balanced liquid fertiliser.

As the vines grow, train them up supports. When trained upwards the plants put their energy into producing one batch of larger tubers. Continue to water in dry weather, but reduce the amount of watering in late summer.

Harvesting

Harvest crops grown outside before the first frost, digging the tubers up carefully. For crops grown in frost-free conditions under cover, wait until the top growth starts to die down.

'Cure' the tubers in a warm place (30°C/85°F) for 7 to 10 days to develop the sweetness. The tubers are an ideal accompaniment to turkey and pork. You can bake them for an hour wrapped in foil, or boil in water and mash them (with the skins removed).

Storing After curing, store the sweet potatoes at 13–15.5°C (55–60°F).

PROBLEM SOLVER

Small tubers form. If planted too close together, sweet potatoes produce more but smaller tubers – for future crops, space plants further apart. Otherwise, the plants were not supported and were allowed to trail on the soil, which encourages them to root and produce lots of little groups of small tubers. For a harvest of large tubers, make sure the plants have sufficient support to keep them off the ground.

Tubers split. Providing too much water during the late summer days as the tubers mature is often responsible for causing the tubers to split. Make sure you reduce the amount of water provided to the plants during this period.

Heat-loving sweet potatoes, a member of the bindweed family (and a cousin of the morning glory), thrives where summers are long and hot.

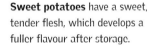

Sweet potatoes have a sweet, tender flesh, which develops a fuller flavour after storage.

Quick Tip

Not the same
Sweet potato is sometimes referred to in the USA as yam (*Dioscorea batatas*) However, this is a different climber that you can grow up a sturdy wigwam of canes. It produces a large, edible, floury root in fertile soils. You can use it like potato.

Carrots

With well-worked soil, proper thinning and regular watering, you can enjoy crunchy carrots with flavours that are far more sweet and satisfying than any carrot you can purchase at the supermarket.

Sowing and planting

Soil Loose, even soil without clods or stones is essential for long, straight carrots. If you have only 5cm (2in) of loose, stone-free soil, select round varieties such as 'Parmex'. If you have heavy soil make a raised bed (see pages 22–23). If you add compost to the soil, make sure it is very well rotted to avoid forked roots.

When to sow For spring crops sow in mid-autumn or late winter under cloches, in a frame or in a greenhouse. For summer crops sow outside from early to mid-spring onwards, sowing at two-week intervals for a continual supply of tender young roots. Make the last sowings in midsummer. You can leave some of the spring and summer-sown crops in the ground for autumn and winter use.

Sowing seeds Make sure you water the area thoroughly before you sow seeds. It can be difficult to sow tiny carrot seeds thinly, but with practise and patience, you should be able to sow seeds about 1.25cm (½in) apart. Sow the seeds in shallow drills, spreading the seeds lightly by hand if necessary. Alternatively, you can use a seed sower, available from mail-order catalogues and garden centres.

Carrot seeds germinate slowly and wash away easily. Sow the seeds 6mm (¼in) deep and cover them with compost or vermiculite to avoid a cap forming on the soil.

Sow a crop for winter harvest in a block with rows spaced closer together; it's easier to insulate a block than a long row (see *Storing*, opposite).

Thinning The seeds will germinate in two to three weeks. Handling the

Roll about a dozen seeds between your thumb and finger to sow seeds thinly.

When seedlings reach 5cm (2in) tall, use nail scissors to clip extra seedlings.

PLANTING GUIDE

What to plant Seeds.

Site preparation Prepare the soil the season before sowing; for a heavy soil, prepare a raised bed.

When Sow seeds from early spring to midsummer outdoors for a summer crop, or mid-autumn to late winter under cover for a spring crop.

Spacing Allow 15–30cm (6–12in) between rows; for a winter harvest, space rows 10–12.5cm (4–5in) apart.

How much Per person, 20 to 40 carrots (1.8–3.6m/6–12ft of row per person) per sowing for fresh eating.

Temperature alert
Hot spells can cause split roots and bitterness. You can grow carrots when temperatures are below 29°C (85°F), but 15.5–18°C (60–65°F) is ideal.

foliage of carrots releases a scent that will attract carrot root fly, so thinning needs to be done carefully. Do the job in the evening, to give the flies the minimum length of time to find the crop; using nail scissors to clip off excess seedlings releases less scent than pulling them. Sowing the seed very thinly in the first place will reduce the amount of thinning necessary.

For summer varieties that are pulled young, thin the plants to 2.5–5cm (1–2in) apart. Thin winter varieties so the plants are 8–10cm (3–4in) apart.

If your plants come up poorly and leave gaps, make sure you reseed the gaps. Otherwise, you'll be inviting weed problems.

Care

Watering If there is no rain after sowing, water the seeded rows daily. Apply the water gently, or open a trench in the space between two rows and add water slowly to the trench. To prevent weeds from sprouting in the trench, you can fill it with shredded leaves.

After carrots are established, reduce watering, but don't let the soil dry out completely. If it does, restore soil moisture gradually – with moderate watering for several days rather than one drenching – or the roots will split and their flavour may be ruined.

Quick Tip

Interplanting

Plant parsnips with your carrots so you can harvest some of both crops each time you raid your in-ground winter supply. To prevent the larger parsnips from casting shadows on the carrots, make sure you leave plenty of space between the two.

Carrots are available in many shapes, including round golf ball-sized carrots and finger-sized types known as fingerlings.

Mulching Make sure you weed carrot rows frequently when the seedlings are small. After the last thinning, mulch the area completely with hay or shredded leaves, pulling mulch close to block the sunlight. This will prevent the carrots from developing green shoulders.

Harvesting

At the expected time of maturity, check the size of the carrot roots every few days by poking your finger into the soil around them. Pull out individual carrots by hand as desired when they reach the right size. To harvest several roots at once, insert a garden fork beside the row to loosen the soil.

Storing In general, store carrots in cool conditions and high humidity. Carrots will rot in cold, wet soil, but you can store an autumn crop in a well-drained garden bed into winter by applying a thick insulating mulch of straw or leaves in cold areas.

Alternatively, harvest the whole crop in early winter and store in boxes of just-moist soil or sand in a cool garage or shed, or in a root clamp (see page 117). Roots stored in the soil are prone to damage by carrot fly larvae.

PROBLEM SOLVER

Roots split. This is caused by heavy rainfall or watering after a spell of dry weather – the roots cannot cope with the sudden uptake of water. Split roots can be eaten but will not store. Keep carrots watered regularly in dry spells.

Tunnels in roots. To help prevent carrot fly maggots from ruining the roots, sow thinly to reduce the need for thinning. Avoid bruising the foliage of plants as this releases a scent that attracts flies. In areas that have bad attacks, cover the crop with horticultural fleece.

Forked roots. Caused by adding fresh manure or compost to the soil before sowing, or by stony soil. Add organic compost to the soil the season before root crops are grown. Dig the area for carrots deeply and remove stones.

Yellow, red-tinged leaves. This is often the first sign of a carrot fly attack, but it can also be caused by viral disease, which will reduce the size of the crop. Keep aphids, which spread the virus, under control. Grow carrots away from willow trees, a host for the aphid.

BEST OF THE BUNCH

'Amsterdam Forcing' Very early maturing, with a good colour and sweet flavour.
'Parmex' Round baby carrot; smooth skin does not need peeling; grows to only 2.5–5cm (1–2in) long.
'Resistafly' Early, Nantes-type carrot with resistance to carrot fly damage. Good colour and flavour.
'Touchon' Good for fresh eating and in-ground storage; grows to 15–20cm (6–8in) long.

Beetroot

The sweet, colourful roots of beetroot are a tasty treat at any time of year, and beet leaves are one of the best cooked greens. If you hanker after your own supply of pickled beets, you'll be pleased to learn that beetroot is easy to grow in most gardens.

Sowing and planting

Soil Dig the soil deeply and work it well to break it down to a fine tilth. Remove stones and break down clods that could interfere with root growth, particularly if you are growing the long-rooted varieties.

Like other roots, beetroot grows best in soil that has had manure or compost added the previous season. A light, free-draining soil is preferable.

Choosing beetroot Beetroot is usually deep red or purple, though there are also golden, white and red-and-white varieties. There are two main types of beetroot. Most popular are the globe varieties, which are perfectly round or slightly flattened; these can be harvested as 'baby beets' or you can allow them to become larger, to about tennis-ball size.

There are also long or cylindrical varieties that have longer, barrel-shaped or tapered roots. These are ideal for slicing.

When to sow For early crops, sow seeds in a frame or under cloches in early spring, but be sure to choose a bolt-resistant variety for early sowings.

You can also sow seeds in modules in a frost-free greenhouse in late winter. Sow two or three seeds per module and plant them out in mid-

spring to produce baby beets. You can either thin the seedlings carefully with nail scissors, or plant them unthinned. Take care not to disturb the roots when transplanting as this will result in the plants bolting.

Sow the main crop of beetroot from mid- to late spring through to midsummer, making small sowings every three weeks for a succession of young roots.

Beet leaves also make a good addition to salad mixes – you can sow seeds for this purpose in short rows from spring onwards.

Sowing and thinning Each knobbly beet 'seed' is not really a seed, but is a dried fruit that contains several tiny true seeds. Presoak these seeds for 12 hours before sowing to help speed germination. Seedlings will sprout in clumps. Use small scissors to snip off unwanted seedlings at ground level.

Monogerm varieties are also available: these generally produce only one seedling per seed so less thinning out is necessary.

Care

In cold areas early summer crops will grow faster when covered with cloches or horticultural fleece. These are suitable for providing protection from chilling winds.

PLANTING GUIDE

What to plant Seeds or transplants.

Starting indoors Sow seeds in modules in late winter for transplanting in spring.

Site preparation Dig the soil deeply; remove stones and clods.

When Make successional sowings from early spring to midsummer.

Spacing About 8 to 10 seeds per 30cm (12in), with the rows 45cm (18in) apart; thin the seedlings to about 10–15cm (4–6in) apart.

Intensive spacing Broadcast seeds lightly over a 38–45-cm (15–18-in)-wide bed.

How much Per person, a row 1.5–3m (5–10ft) long or a 1x1.5-m (3x5-ft) bed.

Temperature alert
Hot, dry conditions can cause woody roots. Keep beetroot watered regularly.

When direct-sowing during the summer, keep the soil constantly moist or germination will be poor.

Preventing weeds To prevent weed competition and to conserve moisture, make sure you water your stand of beetroot seedlings well and then put down a layer of mulch between the rows at least 10cm (4in) deep. If slugs are a problem in your garden, wait until the plants are a few inches tall before mulching.

If weeds spring up round your beetroot, pull them carefully by hand rather than using tools. Tools may nick the developing roots and leave them open to disease organisms.

Harvesting

Cut young beetroot greens for salads beginning about one month after sowing. Rinse the greens repeatedly in a sink full of cold water before use to remove any grit.

For baby beetroot, try lifting some roots about 40 days after sowing. Full-sized beetroot should be ready to pick two to three weeks later. Roots that are ping-pong to golf-ball size will have optimal flavour.

Storing Store beetroot greens in plastic bags for up to 10 days in the refrigerator. Freshly harvested beetroot generally lasts in plastic bags in the refrigerator for up to three weeks. Twist the leaves off – do not cut them or the roots will bleed, which spoils the odour and flavour.

For long-term beetroot storage, you can pack the roots in containers of moist sand or peat and keep them in a cool shed or garage (4.5–10°C/ 40–50°F is ideal). Sort the roots by size before packing – small beets won't last as long as large roots.

You can also store beetroot in a clamp (see pages 116–17) or in boxes of soil or sand.

Quick Tip

Salad treat

Use the first thinnings for salads. A continued gradual harvest will allow the remaining roots to enlarge.

A versatile vegetable, both the root and the leaves of beetroot are edible.

clamp (see pages 116–17)

PROBLEM SOLVER

Black spots or brown hearts on roots. Caused by lack of boron. Cut away the discolored parts; the rest is edible. If soil is chalky or has recently been limed, add boron by raking in about 7.5ml per sq m (1½tsp per sq yd) of borax or feeding plants with calcified seaweed.

Holes in leaves. Ragged holes may be caused by slugs. Use slug traps as deterrents, or spread a band of sharp sand, crushed eggshells or diatomaceous earth round the plants.

Tunnels in leaves. Leaf-miner larvae leave tunnels and blisters, which can stunt the growth of young plants. Destroy the infested leaves.

Brown spots on leaves. Fungal leaf spot can cause these symptoms. Pick and destroy diseased leaves. Plants are not usually badly affected.

Young plants go to seed. Bolting is due to exposure to temperatures below 10°C (50°F) or lack of moisture. Adjust planting times to avoid cold exposure; use mulch and/or an irrigation system for consistent soil moisture. Choose bolt-resistant varieties.

BEST OF THE BUNCH

'Boltardy' Good for early sowings – it is resistance to bolting. Deep red, medium sized, globe-shaped roots.

'Burpee's Golden' Sweet, non-staining golden flesh; large and tasty greens for salads or cooking.

'Chioggia' Roots reveal rings of red and white when sliced; sweet; use greens in place of spinach.

'Cylindra' Long, dark red roots good for making pickled beets.

'Red Ace' Fast-growing and resistant to leaf spot. Tasty greens; sweet roots.

Radishes

Most vegetables grow slowly and steadily, but radishes (a member of the cabbage family) race to the finish line – they are ready to pick as soon as three weeks from sowing. Radishes have zesty colour and flavour that add appeal to any meal.

Sowing and planting

In loose, moist soil, radish seeds will germinate almost overnight. Begin sowing seeds in early spring and make a new sowing every 10 days right through the summer.

You can sow small patches of radishes in nooks and crannies among other crops such as between cabbage-family transplants. You will be able to harvest the radishes before the other crops grow enough to shade them.

Care

In hot, dry weather radishes can be disappointing – heat and drought toughen the roots and make them unpleasantly woody and hot flavoured. Make sure you keep young plants well watered at all times during dry spells.

Harvesting

Pull radishes when they have grown up to 2.5cm (1in) across (except winter radishes, see box, left). Don't let the roots grow larger, or they'll become woody, have a sharp taste and may crack. Pick the roots all at once while their quality is prime.

Storing Cut off the plant tops and refrigerate the roots.

PROBLEM SOLVER

Small holes in leaves. Flea beetles are particularly attracted to radishes but plants are not usually badly affected. Keep the seedlings well watered and weed free to help them grow strongly. You can grow the crop under horticultural fleece to protect it.

Tunnels in roots with maggots present. Prevent damage from cabbage root fly by covering the crop with horticultural fleece.

BEST OF THE BUNCH

'Cherry Belle' A variety with round, scarlet red roots.
'French Breakfast' Elongated radishes; crisp, mild flavour.
'Scarlet Globe' Round, scarlet roots with crisp, mild-flavoured flesh.

Whether elongated or round, radishes are enjoyable in salads and other dishes.

PLANTING GUIDE

What to plant Seeds.

Site preparation No special preparation needed.

When As soon as soil can be worked in spring; successional sowings throughout the season.

Spacing 2.5cm (1in) apart in rows 15cm (6in) apart; thin 5–10cm (2–4in) apart.

Intensive spacing 5cm (2in) apart on centres.

How much Per person, 60–90cm (24–36in) of row per planting.

WINTER RADISHES

Summer varieties of radish are by far the most popular, but there are also winter varieties, sometimes known as daikons. They have large roots with black or red skins, and a spicy, hot flavour. Sow winter radishes in midsummer and thin seedlings to 15–23cm (6–9in) apart in rows 30–38cm (12–15in) apart. They will be ready for harvesting from mid-autumn.

Parsnips

The sweet nutty flavour of these roots improves after frost, making them a star of the autumn and winter garden. Parsnips have a reputation for being hard to grow, but that's only to get the plants established – otherwise, they are trouble free.

Sowing and planting

Soil To prepare the planting area, dig the soil about 45cm (18in) deep, removing all stones and clods. Ideally, grow parsnips in soil that has been manured the previous season. If you need to enrich the soil, use a very well-rotted compost, spreading a 7.5–12.5cm (3–5in) layer and thoroughly mixing it into the soil.

To cut down on labour, dig a trench or individual planting holes. For a trench, loosen the soil and dig a 45-cm (18-in)-deep trench. Fill it with well-rotted compost mixed with soil, open a drill and sow the seeds.

To make planting holes 15cm (6in) apart, use a crowbar to open holes a few inches across and 45cm (18in) deep. Fill each hole with compost mixed with soil. Open a small hole in the compost with a dibber. Sow several seeds at each spot.

Establishing seedlings Make sure you always use fresh parsnip seeds as old ones do not germinate well. Cover the seeds with sand or vermiculite to prevent capping.

Care

Side-dress with compost or a balanced organic fertiliser once in the growing season. When the seedlings are a few inches tall, apply a mulch of chopped leaves to conserve moisture and suppress weeds.

Harvesting

Young roots are more tender than large roots, but flavour is usually best after a frost. Use a garden fork to loosen the soil around the roots before pulling out the plants.

Storing Parsnips store well in the garden. In cold areas apply mulch 15–30cm (6–12in) thick over the bed to insulate them; dig roots as needed in autumn and winter. Lift some roots and store in damp sand for use when the soil is frozen. Harvest all the roots before they start into growth again in the spring, or they will become flabby.

PROBLEM SOLVER

Sunken brown areas on tops of roots. Parsnip canker is a fungal disease that thrives in wet, acid soils; ensure the soil is free draining and lime if needed. Cut away cankered areas and use the rest of the root straight away. Choose resistant varieties.

Tunnels in roots, maggots present. Carrot fly can attack parsnips; use horticultural fleece to cover the crops.

PLANTING GUIDE

What to plant Seeds.

Site preparation Work the soil deeply and enrich it with compost.

When Early to late spring, depending on the climate.

Spacing Sow the seeds thickly with 45–60cm (18–24in) between the rows; thin the seedlings to about 10–15cm (4–6in) apart.

Intensive spacing 15cm (6in) on centres.

How much Up to 30 plants per person.

BEST OF THE BUNCH

'Avonresister' Fairly short roots wtih good canker resistance.
'Harris Model' Long, slim roots with few side roots.

Temperature alert
Avoid sowing parsnip seeds too early. In most areas mid- to late spring sowings will give the best results.

Turnips and swedes

The large, sweet roots of home-grown swede are truly a fantastic winter vegetable, while turnips can be grown almost all year round – and they even provide the bonus of a spring crop of tasty greens.

Sowing and planting

Soil Dig the soil well to 15cm (6in) deep, breaking up any clods and removing stones. Like other root vegetables, swedes and turnips prefer soil that has had compost or manure added the previous season.

If you need to add organic matter before sowing, make sure it is well rotted and thoroughly incorporated into the soil. Add lime if necessary to bring the pH to around 6.5 (see pages 32–33).

Sowing turnips Turnip seeds are readily available from garden centres and mail-order suppliers. You can have an early crop by sowing seeds of a suitable fast-maturing variety under cloches in late winter; this sowing will be ready to harvest in early summer.

You can sow seeds of summer varieties in the open between mid-spring and early summer for crops throughout the summer and into early autumn.

Sow maincrop turnip varieties midsummer for an autumn and winter harvest of roots. You can make another sowing of maincrop varieties in mid- to late summer to provide a crop of leafy greens known as turnip tops for picking in early spring – one of the first crops to make an appearance after the winter.

Sowing swedes Sow swedes in late spring and early summer. They will need a long growing season to reach their full size, but smaller roots will be ready to harvest from early autumn onwards.

Care

Summer turnips need to grow quickly and require plenty of moisture in order to produce crisp, tender, well-flavoured flesh. Thin the seedlings out in stages – you can use the first thinnings as salad leaves.

Dry conditions, especially during hot weather, will produce tough, harsh-tasting roots. Water regularly –

PLANTING GUIDE

What to plant Seeds.

Site preparation Work soil well.

When *Turnips* Under cover in late winter, or mid-spring to mid-summer. *Swedes* Late spring and early summer.

Spacing Sow 5cm (2in) apart, in rows 45cm (18in) apart. Final spacing if growing turnips for roots is 10–15cm (4–6in); final spacing for swedes, 20cm (8in).

How much *Turnips* 1.5m (5ft) of row per person for storage; less for fresh eating. *Swedes* 2.4m (8ft) of row per person for storage.

Temperature alert
Cool conditions and frost bring out the best in swedes and turnips, but lift a few roots before cold weather freezes them into the ground.

BEST OF THE BUNCH

Swede 'Best of All' Purple-topped variety with mild-flavoured, golden flesh. Very reliable.

Swede 'Marian' Variety with globe-shaped, purple-topped roots of excellent flavour. It has some resistance to mildew and club root.

Turnip 'Purple Top Milan' A variety with white, flat-topped roots with a purple crown. Good for early sowings; matures quickly.

Turnip 'Snowball' A round, white variety with a mild flavour.

Turnip 'Tokyo Cross' A spring variety that provides tasty greens; harvest roots 5–15cm (2–6in) across.

otherwise heavy rain or watering after a long dry spell can cause the roots to split.

Once the seedlings are established, you can mulch the rows for weed control and to help keep the soil cool and moist.

Swedes also like a steady supply of moisture during the growing season. You should thin the plants out in stages until they are at their final spacing.

Harvesting

Baby turnips about the size of golf balls are tasty when eaten raw in salads, rather like radishes; they can also be cooked. You can start harvesting these young roots as early as five or six weeks from sowing. Pull every other plant in the row, leaving alternate roots to grow to around tennis-ball size – these are good for boiling sliced or diced.

Maincrop turnips will grow larger, and you can harvest them from mid-autumn onwards. Unlike summer turnips, they will need peeling when they are prepared for cooking.

You can harvest turnip tops in early spring, as soon as the leaves reach 10–15cm (4–6in) tall. If you cut off all the leaves with a knife, the roots should resprout to provide two or three cuts.

Harvest swedes as soon as the roots are large enough. They are usually thought to be sweeter after a frost.

Storing Summer turnip roots will last in the refrigerator for up to two weeks in plastic bags, but they are best eaten fresh. You can refrigerate turnip tops for a few days, too, but they're best cooked as soon as possible after harvest.

Maincrop turnips and swedes can remain in the ground throughout the winter in all but very cold, wet areas. If it is more convenient, they can be lifted in late autumn or early winter and stored in boxes of sand or a clamp (see pages 116–17).

PROBLEM SOLVER

Tunnels in roots. Due to cabbage root fly; damage is generally worst early in the season. Cover spring crops tightly with horticultural fleece.

Swollen, distorted roots; wilting leaves. Club root is the cause. Practise a crop-rotation plan. Add lime to raise soil pH. Remove and destroy infected plant materials.

Small holes in leaves. Caused by flea beetles; prevent future problems by covering the planting area with horticultural fleece.

Turnips are cabbage-family crops and are susceptible to some of the same problems. See page 171 for additional problems and solutions.

Harvest swedes in the autumn for use throughout the winter.

Quick Tip

Getting your greens

For more turnip greens from thinnings, sow the seeds closer than the standard 5cm (2in). For only greens, allow 2.5–10cm (1–4in) for final spacing between plants.

Celery

Garden-grown celery has a delightful flavour that you'll never find in celery from the shop. Old-fashioned trench celery is hardy and has fine flavour and texture, but self-blanching types with tight heads and green stringless varieties are easier to grow.

Sowing and planting

Soil Dig in a 3.75-cm (1½-in) layer of compost 10cm (4in) deep.

When to plant Sow celery seeds in mid-spring in a heated propagator or greenhouse, keeping the temperature above 10°C (50°F). After hardening off, set out young plants after all risk of frost has passed. Seedlings need a constant temperature, careful pricking out with minimum root disturbance and no check to growth at any time – so many gardeners buy in young plants in late spring and early summer.

Care

Plant self-blanching celery in a block rather than rows, to help the centres of the plants remain blanched. Set them out at 23cm (9in) centres. Plant green celery 25–30cm (10–12in) apart in rows 30–38cm (12–15in) apart.

Grow trench celery in a 30-cm (12-in)-deep trench that is gradually filled with soil as the plants grow, or grow it on level ground and blanch the stems by tying brown paper or corrugated cardboard round the heads. Blanching makes the stems tender and string free.

Keep the soil thoroughly moist at all times, and feed with a high-nitrogen fertiliser every three or four weeks.

PLANTING GUIDE

What to plant Seeds or transplants.

Starting indoors After soaking seeds in compost tea for six hours, sow seeds in early spring at 18–21°C (65–70°F); keep moist. Harden off plants, then transplant.

Site preparation Enrich soil.

When Set out transplants after danger of frost has passed.

Spacing Set transplants about 25–30cm (10–12in) apart in rows 30–38cm (12–15in) apart.

Intensive spacing 23cm (9in) apart on centres.

How much Six plants per person.

Temperature alert
If seedlings are exposed to temperatures below 10°C (50°F) for more than a day, the plants are liable to bolt later.

PROBLEM SOLVER

Holes in stalks. Hand-pick slugs. Spread diatomaceous earth, crushed eggshells or sharp sand round plants. Set out traps.

Rotted stalks. Destroy plants infected by fungi or bacteria. Use a crop-rotation plan. Water soil, not stems; allow air circulation.

Misshapen leaves with sticky coating. Wash aphids off plants with jet of water. Spray plants with insecticidal soap.

Young plants form seed stalks. Bolting occurs when plants are exposed to low temperatures. Protect plants with cloches.

Harvesting

Cut self-blanching and green types at the base before the first frost. Harvest trench celery in mid-winter.

Storing Store celery in plastic bags in the crisper or salad drawer in the refrigerator for a week or more.

BEST OF THE BUNCH

'Utah 52–70' Long stems with tender texture. Vigorous plant; resists bolting.
'Golden Self Blanching' Early variety with crisp, tender stems.

Celeriac

Sow some celeriac this year and enjoy its mild celery flavour with nutty overtones in your cooking without the hassle of growing celery. Celeriac and celery are closely related, but celeriac produces skimpier tops and a fat, fleshy stem base.

Sowing and planting

Work in 5cm (2in) of compost over the area to be planted – it will help the soil to retain moisture. Test the soil (see pages 32–33); the best pH range is 6.0 to 6.5.

Sow seeds in early spring or set out transplants in late spring. You should water in transplants with a balanced liquid fertiliser.

Care

Celeriac doesn't tolerate heat well. You should provide lots of water and mulch to keep the soil cool.

During summer, you can pull back some soil from the crowns; then with your thumb rub off the side shoots. This will make the roots smoother and easier to peel after harvesting.

Harvesting

Smaller 'roots' may have better texture and quality than large ones. You can try harvesting celeriac when the 'roots' are 7.5–12.5cm (3–5in) across. Cut off the leaves and compost them, or add the leafstalks and leaves to soup stock in place of celery stalks and leaves. Scrub the celeriac well. Tender roots may be enjoyable for eating raw, especially grated. Peel away the tough outer parts before cooking celeriac.

PLANTING GUIDE

What to plant Seeds or transplants.

Starting indoors Sow seeds in early spring.

Site preparation Add compost and test the soil pH.

When Set out transplants when daytime temperatures consistently exceed 13°C (55°F).

Spacing Set transplants or thin the seedlings 20 25cm (8–10in) apart in rows 60cm (24in) apart.

Intensive spacing 30cm (12in) apart on centres.

How much Up to 10 plants per person if you plan to store over the winter.

Temperature alert
Plant out celeriac in late spring so that young plants have a chance to get established before the hot weather arrives.

PROBLEM SOLVER

Tunnels in leaves. Celery leaf miners feed internally in leaves. Snip off leaves that show tunnels and destroy them. If leaf miners are a serious problem in your area, cover the crop with horticultural fleece to prevent adults laying eggs.

Storing In most places you can overwinter celeriac in the garden if you cover the 'roots' with mulch. In cold regions you should dig the crop in autumn and store it in boxes packed in damp sand in a cool shed or garage (see pages 116 17).

You should avoid storing celeriac near vegetables with strong flavours such as onions, because it may pick up their flavours.

BEST OF THE BUNCH

'Giant Prague' Pleasant flavour. Uniform smooth roots will grow to about 10cm (4in) in diameter.
'Diamant' A vigorous grower that also resists pithiness. Stores well.

Salsify and scorzonera

Expand your root-crop repertoire with two crops that have a reputation for having an unusual taste. Salsify and scorzonera (or black salsify) resemble slim carrots – however, their flavour is reminiscent of oysters.

Sowing and planting

Soil Salsify and scorzonera roots are long and slender. For best results dig the soil well at least 30cm (12in) deep and remove any stones. Avoid adding fresh nitrogen sources such as manure, which may cause forked roots. Work a 2.5-cm (1-in) layer of finished compost into the soil.

Establishing seedlings Use fresh seeds and sow thickly. The seeds may take up to three weeks to germinate. Never let the seedbed dry out during this period.

Once the seedlings appear, water the bed well and gently pull out excess seedlings or cut them off at ground level.

Care

These crops don't need much special care and almost never suffer from pest problems. When they are young, remove any weeds but be careful not to mistake the grasslike foliage of the crops for weeds. Water as needed to keep the soil moist.

Harvesting

Try clipping some scorzonera foliage to add to green salads, leaving enough at the base to allow regrowth.

While you can harvest them as soon as they reach full size, keep in mind that their flavour will improve after exposure to frost. The roots will grow up to 2.5cm (1in) in diameter – some varieties even larger – and 20–30cm (8–12in) in length. Because the roots can be very long, you will need to dig deeply to get them out. Be specially careful with digging up scorzonera – it is brittle and can easily snap.

You should cook the roots before peeling them or you'll lose their delicate flavour. After peeling, serve the cooked roots with melted butter and lemon, or you can add them to soups or stews.

Storing The roots will store well in the ground. Mulch them thoroughly with a deep layer of chopped leaves or straw in very cold areas.

If you dig a full crop, store the roots in damp sand (see pages 116–17). The roots will last only about a week in the refrigerator in plastic bags.

PLANTING GUIDE

What to plant Seeds.

Site preparation Work the soil deeply and remove any stones. Work in well-rotted compost.

When Early to mid-spring.

Spacing Sow the seeds thickly with 38–45cm (15–18in) between the rows; thin the seedlings to about 10–15cm (4–6in) apart.

Intensive spacing 15cm (6in) on centres.

How much Up to 3m (10ft) of row per person.

Scorzonera roots have black skin. Salsify roots (above) are whitish with side roots.

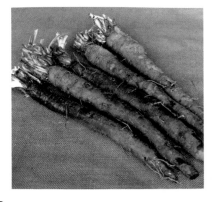

BEST OF THE BUNCH

Salsify 'Mammoth Sandwich Island'
Variety with roots that grow to 3.75cm (1½in) in diameter.

Scorzonera 'Russian Giant' Long, thick, black-skinned tasty roots.

Florence fennel

With its feathery, liquorice-scented foliage and attractive form, Florence fennel is a great addition to a flower garden. The harvest of crunchy 'bulbs' (swollen stem bases) is delicious raw in salads or appetisers and irresistible braised or grilled.

Sowing and planting

Florence fennel can be a difficult crop to grow in Britain – it can easily bolt to seed if the conditions are not exactly right. It likes a rich, fertile soil which has had plenty of organic matter added.

When Sow the seeds directly where they are to grow in midsummer. However, time the sowing carefully. If you sow them too early, when the days are lengthening, the plants will often bolt, though some varieties are bolt resistant.

If you want to try an early sowing, choose a bolt resistant variety and sow under cover in a steady temperature of 10°C (50°F) or above. Sow the seeds in modules to minimise root disturbance on transplanting. Fennel likes a long growing season in order to form good bulbs, so an early start can often give good results.

Care

For the best yields, you should water the plants regularly and feed them by watering with a balanced liquid fertiliser every three weeks.

When the bulbs are about the size of an egg, push the soil up around them to blanch them; this will make the bulbs more tender.

PROBLEM SOLVER

Plants bolt without forming swollen stems. Disturbing the roots can cause bolting, so apply mulch to control weeds instead of cultivating round the plants. Sow seeds instead of transplanting.

Harvesting

Florence fennel bulbs can grow to a large size, but smaller bulbs are better for eating. If the plants do not form good bulbs, you can still use the stems and leaves for flavouring. Ideally, harvest bulbs when they grow to 7.5–12.5cm (3–5in) across.

Storing You can wrap Florence fennel bulbs in plastic and store them in the refrigerator for two to three days after cutting.

To harvest Florence fennel cut off the bulbs at soil level using a sharp knife.

PLANTING GUIDE

What to plant Seeds or transplants.

Site preparation No special preparation needed but prefers a rich, fertile soil.

When Sow seeds or set out transplants in midsummer.

Spacing Set transplants about 25–30cm (10–12in) apart on centres; thin seedlings to the same spacing.

How much Up to five plants per person per planting.

Quick Tip

Extra shoots
When cutting the bulbs, leave a small stump in the ground. This should produce a forest of feathery, aniseed-scented shoots, which can be used in salads and for flavouring cooked dishes.

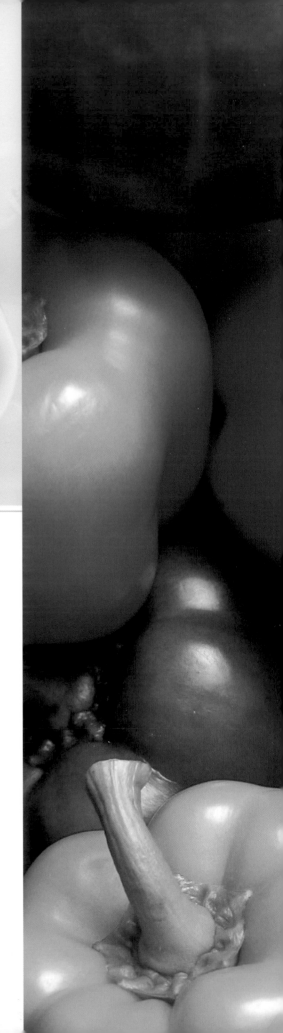

11 Tomatoes and other heat lovers

Tomatoes and peppers are favourite vegetables for most home gardeners. These flavourful fruits are ideal for fresh eating, cooking and preserving. Aubergine is now gaining popularity as more gardeners are discovering how delicious it tastes grilled or combined with other ingredients for starters and sauces. Tomatillo, a prolific tomato relative, deserves a try in every salsa-lover's garden. Okra rounds out this group of heat-loving crops. Although it prefers very warm conditions, you can grow in most regions by choosing early yielding varieties.

Sweet bell peppers are versatile staples of Italian and Mexican cuisine.

Tomatoes

The temptation of tomatoes has lured many a gardener to plant just a few too many plants. It's difficult to rein in your enthusiasm for garden-fresh tomatoes, especially when such a wide range of types is available.

PLANTING GUIDE

What to plant Transplants.

Starting indoors Sow seeds in early to mid-spring.

Site preparation Loosen soil; add organic matter. Or under cover prepare pots, growing bags or greenhouse border.

When Plant outside after danger of spring frost is past; 12 to 14 weeks before first autumn frost.

Spacing Set plants 60–120cm (24–48in) apart, depending on the type of tomato.

How much Two to four plants per person; one or two cherry tomato plants per household.

Temperature alert
Tomatoes may not set fruits in temperatures above 32°C (90°F) or below 13°C (55°F). Fruit set should resume when the weather changes.

Sowing and planting

Soil Loosen the soil 25cm (10in) deep, then work a 5–7.5cm (2–3in) layer of compost into the top several inches of soil. To warm up the soil faster for outdoor crops, shape the soil into a raised bed 15cm (6in) high.

When you dig planting holes, add compost to the removed soil. Create a mixture that's half soil and half compost for refilling the holes.

Choosing what to grow Consider what you want from the plants: an early harvest, large fruits, best flavour, disease resistance or an extended harvest period – no single variety provides all of these qualities. The variety you choose will also depend on whether you are growing it outside or in the greenhouse. If you have space, grow several varieties with different characteristics.

Tomato plants are determinate, indeterminate or semi-determinate. Determinate types are bushy, growing 90cm (36in) tall. Their side branches are short, and each side branch forms a flower cluster at the branch tip at about the same time. The fruits form and ripen in two to three weeks.

Indeterminate plants produce lots of sideshoots from the main stem, and each sideshoot expands into a rambling branch. The branches flower and set fruits as long as conditions are good.

Semi-determinate plants have characteristics of both types. They produce some sideshoots that end in a flower cluster, and some that ramble. These plants stop growing when 0.9–1.5m (3–5ft) tall.

Indeterminate varieties (also called vine or cordon tomatoes) are usually grown under cover, in a greenhouse or tunnel. Sideshoots that grow from the leaf axils are pinched out (see page 208) and the single stems trained up a support. Flower clusters grow from the main stem. Determinate or bush tomatoes are usually – though not always – grown outside.

Tomato varieties are also classified as early-season, mid-season or late-season producers.

Sowing and planting Sow seeds in a heated greenhouse or propagator. For the earliest greenhouse crops, ready for picking in early summer, sow in mid- to late winter, but as the night-time temperature must not be allowed to drop below 10°C (50°F), this could involve high heating costs in some areas. Most gardeners sow seeds in early to mid-spring for midsummer crops.

Do not sow seeds for outdoor crops earlier than eight weeks before the average last frost date for your area. If the seeds are sown too early, the plants will be ready for planting out before it is safe to do so, and will suffer a check to their development while waiting for conditions outdoors to warm up.

As soon as the seedlings emerge, ensure they receive plenty of light. Prick them out into individual pots as soon as they are large enough to handle and grow them on steadily. They are ready for planting out in their cropping positions when they are about 20cm (8in) tall. You can plant out tomatoes in late spring or early summer, when all danger of frost has passed.

Growing under cover The heaviest and most reliable crops come from plants grown to maturity under cover, in a greenhouse or polytunnel. There is a much wider choice of varieties available for protected cropping than for growing outdoors.

You can grow tomatoes under cover in growing bags, pots or directly in the greenhouse border – remember they will need frequent watering. Use a 23-cm (9-in) pot for each plant, filled with a good quality potting compost, or set two plants to a growing bag. Puncture a few holes in the base of the growing bag to allow drainage, and cut cross-shaped slits in the top for planting.

Mix some water-retaining granules with the compost to help cut down the frequency of watering needed.

Training The most suitable types for greenhouse growing are cordon or indeterminate varieties; bush tomatoes take up too much space and are difficult to care for in confined spaces. Remove the sideshoots of cordon varieties (see page 208) and train the plants up stakes, or strings attached to the greenhouse roof (see page 79). Once the plants reach the roof, or set six or seven clusters of fruits, pinch out the growing tips to divert the plants' energies into ripening the fruits.

Transplanting to the garden

Whether you raise your own transplants or buy them at a garden centre, be sure to properly harden them off before transplanting. The day before transplanting, water them with fish emulsion or compost tea. If the transplants are tall and rangy, remove the first couple of true leaves and lay the bare stretch of stem on an angle in a shallow trench.

1 Gently slide the plant out of its pot, supporting the stem of the plant between your thumb and forefinger.

2 Set the plant deeply, so that the first true leaf is just above soil level.

3 Refill the planting hole. Shape a small depression round the plant to capture and hold water, and water the plant well.

Growing outdoors In Britain only try growing outdoor tomatoes in reasonably mild, sheltered gardens. Choose a variety recommended for outdoor growing – greenhouse varieties are not suitable. Cover the planting area with sturdy black plastic to warm and dry the soil for planting. Put the plastic in place the preceding autumn, and leave it there throughout the growing season – you need to cut slits into it for planting the tomatoes.

Staking and training Using stakes, trellises or cages to train outdoor tomato plants will provide several benefits. The plants will have fewer disease problems because the fruits won't rest on the ground and air can circulate better through the foliage. The fruits will also be easier to reach for harvesting. You'll need to maintain the plants more often to train them, so you'll be more likely to spot potential pest and disease problems early, when you can still take effective steps to control them.

Make sure you install the method of support at the same time you set transplants in the garden. Otherwise,

you may damage the plant roots, or the plants may grow large enough to flop over before you get round to setting up the supports.

You can train plants on single vertical stakes or on a wigwam made of four long bamboo poles – one plant per pole. Stakes work for determinate or indeterminate plants, but prune indeterminate plants so they don't overgrow the support.

Determinate plants also do well when supported by a horizontal wire framework. Set out hoops as you would for a protective plastic tunnel, but make the tunnels out of wire mesh fence or concrete reinforcing wire. The plants will grow up through the wire grid, which will support them.

Another method is to surround each plant with a sturdy cage made out of wire-mesh fencing and sturdy wooden stakes. Use fencing with mesh at least 12.5cm (5in) square.

Care

Removing sideshoots You'll need to prune indeterminate tomatoes to train them to a support. Unpruned

plants develop dense foliage that blocks air circulation and leads to disease. The extra leafy growth is also made at the expense of fruits, and unpruned plants also eventally become so large and heavy that they'll topple their supports.

Semi-determinate plants will benefit from light pruning. Wait until the plants form a first flower cluster, then remove all but one or two sideshoots below that flower cluster. Do not prune the sideshoots immediately below the cluster.

Don't prune determinate (bush) plants. They produce the heaviest crops when all the sideshoots are allowed to remain.

Watering In general, a tomato plant needs 11–19 liters (20–33pt) of water per week. However, outdoors, soil type, relative humidity, rainfall and mulch affect the rate at which soil dries out. Check soil moisture regularly, and when you do water, moisten the soil 20cm (8in) deep. Early in the season, watering with heated water (26.5°C/80°F) will help to warm the soil.

For outdoor crops, after the soil is thoroughly warm, you can apply a mulch of straw, plastic or paper. Mulching will help conserve soil moisture and prevent disease spores from splashing up from the soil on to the plants.

Plants grown under cover will need frequent watering to keep the soil evenly moist.

Fertilising Don't overfertilise the plants, especially with nitrogen, or they may produce excessive leaves at the expense of fruits. Plants growing outside in rich, fertile soil may not need fertiliser, but if you're concerned about soil fertility, or the plants are growing in containers,

Pound an 1.8-m (6-ft) stake into the ground at least 15cm (6in) away from a newly planted transplant.

Fasten the stems to the stake using soft cloth strips or plant ties. As the plant grow, add strips or ties every 30cm (12in).

Remove sideshoots when they're 7.5–10cm (3–4in) long. Bend them to the side with your fingers to break them off the plant.

Use your fingers to pinch out the growing points of tomato vines when they reach the top of a trellis.

feeding can begin once the first fruits have started to form. Use a high-potash fertiliser, applying it according to the pack instructions.

Harvesting

Gardeners who plant for an early harvest may start harvesting ripe tomatoes as early as May or June, but July and August are more usual. Tomatoes ripen from the inside out. Once the skin colour changes from green to the mature colour, the fruits are fully ripe. Ripe fruits can drop from the plants, so inspect the ground around your plants when you harvest. Many heirloom varieties are prone to cracking. To prevent this, harvest them two days before they are ripe and let them finish ripening indoors.

Extending the harvest outdoors

At the end of the season, before the first frosts, prune the roots of outdoor plants that are still carrying unripe tomatoes. Use a spade to slice down into the soil in a circle around the plant, 30cm (12in) away from the base of the stem. This cuts the roots, triggering the plant to ripen its fruits more quickly. If a light frost is forecast, cover the plants with horticultural fleece, sheets, sacking or large cardboard boxes in the late afternoon, removing the cover the next morning once temperatures rise above freezing. This can allow the remaining fruits to ripen on the plant.

Once harder frosts are likely, cut an entire plant at the base, take it indoors to a garage or shed and hang it upside down. The fruits will ripen slowly. Alternatively, pick all the fruits when the season ends. Use green fruits for pickling or cooking. Fruits that are at least three-quarters of their mature size and have started to change colour will ripen if stored in the right conditions.

Storing Ripe tomatoes won't last long, and refrigeration ruins their flavour. Use them quickly or store them. To ripen underripe tomatoes off the vine, place them in a paper bag or a dark cupboard at 18–21°C (65–70°F). Leave them in a single layer – don't stack them.

If you have a large quantity of underripe tomatoes, spread them out on a shelf in a cool larder, shed or garage. Cover them with layers of newspaper. Check them frequently, and remove any fruits that are ready to use, as well as any that start to rot.

PROBLEM SOLVER

Brown or black spots on leaves on outdoor plants. Suspect potato blight, especially on outdoor crops in warm, wet weather. The disease progresses rapidly; with spots and streaks spreading to the stems and to the fruits, which rot. Spray plants with a copper-based fungicide every 7 to 10 days as a protective measure in humid summers.

Brown spots on leaves on greenhouse plants. On greenhouse plants, blight (see above) is less common. However, brown spots on the leaf surface with mould growth below may be caused by tomato leaf mould disease. Destroy infected leaves and thin the foliage to improve air circulation. Increase greenhouse ventilation.

Distorted growth, wilting plants. Spray plants infested by aphids or whiteflies with insecticidal soap.

Mottled, crinkled leaves. Mosaic virus is spread by aphids. Destroy the infected plants. Use fleece at planting time outdoors. Keep tobacco away from plants.

Grey mould (botrytis). This starts on a dead or dying portion of the plant, producing a grey, furry mould, which quickly spreads to healthy parts. It is worst late in the season and in greenhouses, as it thrives in cool, humid conditions. Remove dead and damaged leaves and fallen fruits promptly, and increase ventilation in greenhouses. Avoid splashing water late in the season.

Brown or black area on bottom of fruits. Blossom end rot occurs if there is not enough calcium in developing fruits, which occurs when the soil dries out. Unaffected parts of fruits may still be edible. Check soil moisture regularly and mulch to maintain even soil moisture.

Large holes in fruits. Slugs and snails eat tomatoes close to ground level. Keep fruits off the ground. Remove the pests.

Types of tomatoes

From tiny currant tomatoes to oversized beefsteaks, you'll want to grow some of every kind of tomato. However, keep in mind that fresh tomatoes won't keep for long, and a large tomato vine can be amazingly prolific.

▶ **Salad tomatoes**

The bread and butter of the tomato world, salad – or slicing – tomatoes are round and juicy with a rich taste. Most of these tomatoes are red, but orange and yellow varieties are also available. You can choose between determinate or indeterminate plant varieties. Some types are early-season plants, but most of them are mid-season types. A wide range of varieties is available.

▲ **Paste tomatoes**

Pear-shaped paste tomatoes have thick walls and small seed cavities, and they are ideal for making tomato sauce or paste. 'Roma' and 'San Marzano' are popular varieties: others are available from specialist suppliers.

◀ **Beefsteak tomatoes**

The giants of the tomato world, beefsteaks produce fruits that can weigh 0.9kg (2lb) or more each. The fruits are wider than deep, and the flesh is juicy. Classic varieties include 'Marmande' and 'Big Boy'. 'Brandywine' is a popular heirloom type.

▲ **Cherry tomatoes**

A single indeterminate plant produces hundreds of fruits in clusters, and they may be red, orange, golden or white. The fruits are usually sweet and juicy. Currant tomatoes produce fruits the size of currants. 'Supersweet 100', 'Tiny Tim' and 'Sweet Million' are the best-known varieties.

▼ Heirloom tomatoes

For a feast of unusual colours, shapes and flavours, try some heirloom tomato varieties. The names often give a clue to their flavour or appearance: 'Cherokee Purple' tomatoes are dark pink and purple when ripe and have a rich flavour, while 'Green Zebra' will bear small, yellow-green fruits with green stripes when ripe. Heirloom tomato plants may be either indeterminate or semi-determinate.

▲ Pear, plum and grape tomatoes

These plants produce clusters of small, pear-shaped or elongated tomatoes that have a meaty texture and sweet flavour. The plants are indeterminate. The fruits may be red, yellow or orange. Many types are low in acid.

▶ Patio tomatoes

Ideal for containers, these compact determinate tomato plants bear small, salad-type tomatoes. One patio tomato plant will generally produce 30 to 40 egg-size tomatoes. Some types also grow well in hanging baskets.

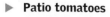

Tomatillos

Green tomatoes, the recommended substitute for tomatillos, are no comparison to the delightfully tart flavour of tomatillos. This bushy plant produces small tomato-like fruits with firm flesh, but they need warm, sheltered conditions.

BEST OF THE BUNCH

'Verde Pueblo' Large, yellow-green fruits with a thin, non-bitter skin.
'Purple' Small to medium-sized, deep purple fruits with a sharper flavour than green varieties.
'Grand Maje' Large, sweet green fruits with good disease resistance.

Sowing and planting

Soil Make sure you loosen the soil well. For each transplant make a planting hole, add a spadeful of compost and mix it lightly.

Starting seeds indoors Sow seeds in a heated greenhouse or propagator in early to mid-spring – the temperature needs to be at least 15.5°C (60°F).

You can prick the seedlings out into individual 9-cm (3½-in) pots as soon as they are large enough to handle easily. By moving the seedlings to individual pots, you'll provide their roots with plenty of room to expand.

Planting outdoors In all but mild, sheltered areas, you'll have to grow the plants in a greenhouse or polytunnel for good crops. However, if your garden does meet these conditions, you can set transplants outside in early summer when all risk of frost has passed. Tomatillos are not self-fertile, so you will need to plant at least two transplants.

Protecting plants from cold Cover the soil with black plastic two weeks before planting to help warm the soil and promote strong growth. You should also cover the plants with horticultural fleece to protect them from chilly air temperatures for the first few weeks after planting.

Care

Although tomatillo plants generally are problem free, they are susceptible to the same pests and diseases as tomatoes. If your tomatillos develop a problem, turn to pages 208–209 to find the solutions.

Watering Don't overwhelm your tomatillos with water. Water them deeply once a week if conditions are dry. You can mulch the soil to help retain moisture as well as suppress weeds.

Fertilizing You can feed tomatillos with a balanced organic fertiliser or liquid feed when the plants start to bloom. You should avoid overfertilising the plants, or they may produce a lot of lush foliage but no fruits.

Staking Tomatillo plants are bushy but can grow up to 1.2m (4ft) tall. Without support, the fruiting branches may end up sprawled on the ground, which makes harvesting difficult. To ensure an easy harvest, corral each plant inside a wire cage or tie the plants to canes.

Harvesting

To determine when to harvest the fruits, watch for the papery husks to change from green to tan or pale gold. Once the husks change colour, you can pick some of the fruits and taste them. Green fruits will be tarter than those left on the plants until they turn yellow. The papery 'lantern' will split open and reveal the fruits when ripe.

It will be easier to remove the husks and the sticky coating on the fruits if you set the fruits in a bowl of warm water for one minute.

Frost will kill tomatillo plants, so be sure to strip off all the fruits at the end of the season.

Storing Tomatillos will keep for one week at room temperature. The ideal storage conditions are 4.5–10°C (40–50°F) and high

humidity. However, tomatillos can be stored in the refrigerator, too. Leave the husks intact and put the fruits in paper bags (not plastic); they will keep in the refrigerator for up to one month. Tomatillos freeze well: remove the husks, wash the fruits and freeze them whole in plastic bags.

Tomatillo fruits are packaged inside delicate, paper-thin husks, resembling Chinese lanterns.

Peppers

Peppers make a great crop for patio containers – modern varieties cope well with cool climates. The plants can be decorative as well as useful, especially the smaller chilli pepper types, with their plentiful, colourful fruits.

Sowing and planting

Soil Peppers need moderately rich soil. Side-dress plants with compost or balanced fertiliser every three weeks. Don't use a high-nitrogen fertiliser, otherwise your plants will produce leaves, not fruits.

Planting outdoors Cover the planting area with black plastic a few weeks before planting. Cut slits in the plastic for planting and set the plants in a double- or triple-row block rather than a single row. Leave the plastic mulch in place all season to warm the soil, conserve moisture and prevent weeds. Covering transplants with horticultural fleece at planting time can supply extra warmth and protection from wind. For patio growing, set each plant in a 23-cm (9-in) pot of compost.

Growing under cover In cold, exposed gardens grow peppers in a greenhouse or polythene tunnel. Plant them in tubs, growing bags or the greenhouse border like tomato plants (see pages 206–9).

Care

Watering and feeding Keep the soil evenly moist at all times, especially when fruits are setting. Peppers under cover and in containers need daily watering. Plants growing in fertile soil in the open garden may not need extra feeding, but give plants growing in poorer soil or containers regular feeds of a high-potash fertiliser.

Staking When peppers are staked, the branches can't break under the weight of a prolific crop. It also

Some types of hot peppers need to ripen to their full colour before they are ready for picking.

PLANTING GUIDE

What to plant Transplants only.

Starting indoors Sow seeds in a heated greenhouse or propagator in early to mid-spring

Preparing the site Warm soil; remove soil cover seven days before planting.

When to plant After all danger of frost has passed.

Spacing Plant in blocks, setting plants 60cm (24in) apart.

How much to plant *Bell peppers* Three plants per person; more if you plan to freeze some. *Hot peppers* Two plants per household; more if you cook a lot of spicy food.

Quick Tip

Frozen food

When you need some frozen, chopped bell pepper for cooking, remove it from the freezer and use a spoon or fork to separate chunks of the fruit from the mass of frozen flesh. Reseal and return the pepper to the freezer.

PROBLEM SOLVER

Misshapen, mottled leaves. Viruses are usually the culprit, and there is no cure. Plants may grow out of the problem. To prevent it choose virus-resistant types.

Poor fruit set. Peppers set fruits at 18–29°C (65–85°F). If your plants aren't forming fruits, it's probably too cold. Wait a week or two. When the weather changes, the fruits will probably start to set again.

Dark patches on fruit. Lack of calcium causes blackened areas on the bottom, called blossom end rot. You can't undo this problem; however, you can still eat undamaged parts of the fruits. To prevent it from occurring again, water frequently because a lack of moisture disrupts the calcium supply within the plant.

Dry, speckled or bronzed leaves, with webbing. Red spider mites love greenhouse-grown peppers. Discourage them by spraying plants with a fine mist of water every day to increase the humidity. Once plants are attacked, consider using a biological control.

Red bell peppers achieve their full sweetness when the fruits are a rich red. However, you can harvest them when green.

keeps the fruits off the soil, reducing the danger of them rotting and being attacked by slugs and snails.

Harvesting

With bell peppers, leaving fruits on the plant suppresses further fruit production. So start the harvest early by picking some fruits while they are green, although they won't be as sweet as fully ripe fruits. Continue picking as needed while the fruits change from green to their mature colour. Be sure to let some fruits reach full ripeness because they'll have the sweetest flavour. Fruits that are just starting to change colour will continue to ripen off the plant.

Cut peppers off the vine with secateurs or a sharp knife. If you try to pull off a fruit by hand, you might break off most of a branch along with the fruit.

Wear gloves and glasses when harvesting hot peppers to protect yourself from the burning effects of capsaicin – the substance that gives hot peppers their heat.

Storing Peppers will keep in the refrigerator for up to two weeks. When frost threatens at the end of the season, pick all the remaining fruits. You can chop them into chunks and freeze them in plastic bags.

Types of peppers

Variety does add spice when it comes to peppers. One way of dividing peppers is by flavour: sweet or hot. Beyond that, there's an amazing range of colours, shapes and hotness from specialist suppliers. A pepper's degree of heat is rated in Scoville heat units. Mild peppers have a low score; very hot peppers, a high score.

▼ Bell peppers

With a sweet flavour and crisp texture, bell peppers are excellent when eaten fresh in salads, cooked in casseroles and sauces, baked for stuffing or roasted. These mild peppers rate 0 Scoville heat units. Bell peppers are about 7.5cm (3in) wide and 10cm (4in) long. Most bell peppers start out green, and you can harvest them at the green stage. However, for full sweetness and flavour, allow some to ripen to their mature colour, which may be bright red, orange, yellow or purple.

▶ Cayenne peppers

You can pick long and slim cayenne peppers when green or fully ripe. Their mature colour may be red, yellow or purple, and their heat-unit rating ranges from 30,000 to 60,000. Cayenne peppers are popular for making salsa and for use in Cajun cooking.

▲ Poblano peppers

These heart-shaped, thick-walled peppers can be stuffed and are often used to flavour chilli. The 10-cm (4-in)-long fruits are dark green to red when mature. These Mexican favourites are slightly hot, with a rating of 1,000 to 1,500 heat units. When dried, they are called ancho peppers.

▼ Thai peppers

These small peppers have an intensely hot flavour, and their Scoville rating is 150,000. They may remain green when mature or turn bright red. They are used often in Asian cuisine. These bushy plants are also attractive as ornamental plants.

▼ Habanero peppers

These orange peppers are hot, hot, hot! Their Scoville rating is 200,000 heat units and higher. The peppers ripen from green to gold to orange. Handle these peppers with extreme care – make sure you avoid getting the juice on your skin or in your eyes.

▲ Banana peppers

Named for their shape, banana peppers are a good choice for frying. The fruits grow up to 15cm (6in) long and turn yellow, orange or red when ripe. Banana peppers have a Scoville rating of 100 to 500, and these mild peppers are suitable for eating fresh in salads and sandwiches.

Aubergines

Also known as eggplant, aubergines will produce a beautiful harvest of fruits in an array of sizes, shapes and colours. In all but the warmest gardens, you will need to grown them under protection to produce a good crop.

Sowing and planting

Soil Aubergines need fertile, well-drained soil. Work a 2.5-cm (1-in) layer of compost into the top several inches of soil when planting outside or in the greenhouse border, or use good-quality potting compost for containers.

Starting seeds Sow seeds in a heated greenhouse or propagator in early to mid-spring. Seeds take one to two weeks to germinate and sprout irregularly. After the first true leaves appear, transplant seedlings carefully into 10-cm (4-in) pots.

Planting outside Choose the sunniest, most sheltered spot available and prewarm the soil by covering it with black plastic before planting. Set the plants out in late spring or early summer and cover them with horticultural fleece or cloches until they become established. You can also encircle the plants with rocks or bricks after planting – they will absorb heat during the day and release it at night.

You can also grow aubergines in containers on a patio or in a sunny area. The compost in the containers will warm up rapidly, and you can move them to a more protected spot whenever a cold spell threatens.

Growing under cover Aubergines are most reliable when grown in a greenhouse or polythene tunnel. They like similar conditions to tomatoes and peppers.

Care

Watering and feeding Keep the compost moist at all times; regularly water plants growing under cover or in containers. Aubergines like a humid atmosphere, so spray them frequently with a fine mist of water, especially under cover.

Start feeding with a high-potash liquid fertiliser once the first fruits have set, applying it every 10 to 14 days or according to the instructions

BEST OF THE BUNCH

'Black Beauty' Heirloom purple variety producing medium-sized fruits; holds well after harvest.

'Fairy Tale' Purple-and-white striped fruits with few seeds. This variety is a good producer.

'Moneymaker' Long, slender, purple fruits; early cropping variety that is heavy yielding.

'Pingtung Long' Asian-type aubergine with long, narrow lavender fruits; compact plants that tolerate humidity and heat well.

'Rosa Bianca' Round, rosy pink fruits with white streaks; mild flavour, good for stuffing.

PLANTING GUIDE

What to plant Transplants.

Starting indoors Provide bottom heat for germinating seeds; the optimal temperature is 26.5°C (80°F).

Site preparation Add compost to improve soil fertility; in mild, sheltered areas, warm the soil by covering it with black plastic two to three weeks before planting outdoors.

When Set out transplants two to six weeks after the last spring frost date.

Spacing Allow 45–60cm (18–24in) between transplants.

How much Two to three plants per person.

Temperature alert
Only sheltered gardens in the mildest areas of Britain are suitable for growing aubergines outdoors.

on the pack. Don't overfeed or the result may be lush foliage at the expense of the fruits.

Staking When plants are 25–30cm (10–12in) tall, pinch out the growing tips to encourage bushy growth. Use a sturdy stake to keep the plants upright or they will sprawl, and the fruits may become misshapen.

Encouraging large fruits Once the first fruits have set, remove all fruits except the largest in each cluster, and allow four to six fruits to develop per plant. Leave more fruits on the plant for mini aubergines.

Harvesting

Cut the fruits as soon as they are a suitable size; check the seed packets to see how large the fruits are likely to grow, as they will probably be smaller than those you are used to seeing in the shops. The fruits should be firm, with shiny skins; aubergines with dull skin may be bitter and woody. The plants often bear sharp spines on the stems, so wear long sleeves and gloves to harvest. Cut the stems with a knife, leaving 2.5cm (1in) of stem attached to the fruits.

Storing Aubergines are not easy to store, and refrigerators are usually colder than the ideal temperature. If possible, store aubergines between 4.5–10°C (40–50°F) and in high humidity. Even in these conditions, aubergines will last 10 days at most.

You can grow dwarf, bushy aubergines in a container – this is an ideal option for a sunny patio.

PROBLEM SOLVER

Speckled, dry leaves, often with webbing; stunted growth. Red spider mites are a common pest of aubergines, especially under cover, and also attack outdoor plants in hot, dry summers. The tiny red mites can sometimes be seen scuttling about on the undersides of the leaves or running along the strands of webbing that stretch between leaves at the tops of the plants – you may need a magnifying glass to spot them. Red spider mites thrive in dry conditions, so keep a humid atmosphere round plants by spraying them regularly with a fine mist of water, especially in greenhouses. Once plants are attacked it is difficult to control the mites, but under cover you can use a biological control.

Sticky foliage with small, white, mothlike insects. Whitefly will attack plants under cover and weaken them; the sticky deposit they exude also encourages the growth of black sooty mould on leaves and fruits. They will fly up in a cloud whenever the plants are touched. They are difficult to control with insecticides, but a biological control is available. Yellow sticky traps hung in the greenhouse will also trap large numbers of the insects, particularly if the plants are frequently shaken gently to get the whitefly on the wing.

Small green insects clustered at the tips of shoots. Aphids weaken plants by sucking sap, and help to spread viral diseases. Use an insecticide such as insecticidal soap as soon as they are seen.

Grey, furry mould on leaves, stems or fruits. Botrytis (grey mould disease) thrives in cool, damp conditions, so is most common at the end of the season, as the weather cools down. It starts on damaged or dead tissue and spreads to healthy parts. Remove dead or dying foliage and plant debris promptly, and keep a good air circulation round the plants. Keep greenhouses ventilated.

Okra

A favourite of Indian cuisine, okra pods, or ladies' fingers, are a good source of vitamins, minerals and fibre. You will need to grow the plants under cover in all but the mildest, most sheltered gardens.

Sowing and planting

Soil Okra grows best in fertile soil that is barely acid, neutral or slightly alkaline. Because okra prefers somewhat dry soil, don't overdo adding organic matter. Too much soil nitrogen will promote foliage growth at the expense of pod formation. Before planting, loosen the soil to 30cm (12in) deep to promote strong, deep root growth.

Cover the soil tightly with black plastic to speed soil warming. Check the soil temperature before planting; okra will languish when planted in soil that is cooler than 21°C (70°F).

Sowing and planting tips Okra seeds have a hard outer coat. To crack the outer coat and speed germination, place the seeds in a freezer overnight or soak them in water for 24 hours before sowing.

Sow the seeds in a temperature of 18–29°C (65–85°F); do not let it drop below 15.5°C (60°F). Prick the seedlings out into individual pots when they are large enough to handle, and keep the temperature high – okra prefers temperatures of 26.5°C (80°F) or more. Set young plants in their cropping positions when they are about 15cm (6in) tall. Handle the seedlings with great care when transplanting. They are brittle

and the roots don't readjust easily if they are disturbed.

Set the plants out in a very warm, sheltered position if growing outside – they are suitable for growing in pots on a sunny patio. Okra will do best in a greenhouse or polytunnel, planted in pots, growing bags or (preferably) directly in the greenhouse border. Space plants 30–60cm (12–24in) apart and provide them with a stake for support. They like same growing conditions as tomatoes and peppers.

Care

Okra is generally trouble-free. As insurance against disease problems when grown outside plant in raised beds to ensure good drainage.

Watering Okra is more drought tolerant than most other vegetable crops but, for best results, keep the soil evenly moist. Mulch with chopped leaves to help keep soil moisture even, but be sure the soil is thoroughly warm and the plants are at least 15cm (6in) tall before mulching.

Fertilising Feed okra like tomatoes, using a high-potash liquid fertiliser every 7 to 10 days once flowering has begun.

PLANTING GUIDE

What to plant Transplants.

Starting indoors Sow seeds in a heated greenhouse or propagator in early to mid-spring.

Site preparation Loosen the soil and add some organic matter, but not too much nitrogen. Warm up the soil by covering it with black plastic before planting out.

When Set transplants out in early summer.

Spacing Set the transplants 30–60cm (12–24in) apart.

How much One to four plants per person for fresh eating; more for freezing.

Temperature alert
Okra loves hot conditions, so for a reliable crop in Britain, grow it under cover.

Harvesting

Once the pods start to form, you should check the plants frequently. Pick the pods when they grow 5–10cm (2–4in) long – larger pods will be woody and unappealing. Use secateurs to cut through the thick stems.

Most varieties bear spines that can cause skin irritation. You should protect your skin by wearing long sleeves, long trousers and gloves when harvesting. Even spineless types may have a few spines.

Okra pods contain a thick, sticky, mucilaginous substance, which can be used to thicken soups and stews (such as gumbo). Some people don't like the slimy texture – you will need to try it and see.

Storing It is best to eat okra pods when freshly picked, but they will keep in the refrigerator for up to three days. You can store a large harvest by freezing the pods.

Attractive flowers make a welcoming appearance before the arrival of the fruits.

PROBLEM SOLVER

Stunted growth, poor or no crop. Okra needs a very hot summer to give a good crop outdoors in Britain, and even when grown under cover the results can be disappointing. Try growing okra for a challenge, but keep your expectations realistic – unless there is a prolonged heatwave, yields won't be high.

BEST OF THE BUNCH

'Clemson Spineless' High yielding; produces spineless pods on bushy plants.
'Pure Luck' An early, high-yielding F1 hybrid variety; slender, spineless pods.
'Red Burgundy' Red stems and pods on bushy plants; the pods will turn green when cooked.

Quick Tip

Floral treat

Okra is related to hibiscus, and its large creamy white or red flowers resemble hibiscus blossoms. These bushy plants with showy blooms will look right at home in your flower garden.

12 Vine crops

From the fleeting pleasure of fresh melons to the
reliable keeping quality of winter squash, vine crops
offer gardeners plenty of reward. By growing early-
maturing varieties, even gardeners in Britain's chilly
climate can grow melons and pumpkins. Cucumbers
and summer squash will grow in any garden if they
are protected from troublesome insects.

Planting in the proper conditions and keeping
plants healthy will also avoid disease problems. So
set aside as much space as you can for vine crops –
but if you grow them vertically on a support, they
will need less space and be easier to harvest, too.

Vine crops require a
considerable amount of
garden space, rich soil and
warm, sunny weather.

Cucumbers

The long, smooth, slender cucumbers we are most familiar with need to be grown in the protection of a greenhouse, but stubbier, rough-skinned ridge cucumbers are simple to grow outside – and many people think they have a better flavour too.

PLANTING GUIDE

What to plant Seeds or transplants.

Starting indoors Sow the seeds in a heated greenhouse or propagator in early to mid-spring.

Site preparation Add organic matter to improve the fertility and moisture-holding capacity of the soil.

When After danger of frost has past.

Spacing Thin the seedlings or set the transplants 30cm (12in) apart. Or sow six to eight seeds per mound, with 0.9–1.2m (3–4ft) between the mounds; thin to three plants per mound.

How much *Slicing varieties* One plant per person for fresh eating. *Pickling varieties* About 10 plants.

Sowing and planting

Soil Work a 5-cm (2-in) layer of compost and into the top several inches of soil. Cover the planting area with black plastic for two to three weeks before planting to warm the soil.

Growing outdoor cucumbers

Start seeds in a heated greenhouse, frame or propagator in early to mid-spring. Seedlings don't transplant easily, so use 5- or 10-cm (2- or 4-in) peat pots to avoid root disturbance when raising plants for transplanting.

In sheltered positions in mild areas, you can sow seeds outside in their growing positions in mid- to late spring. These plants like a warm, sunny, sheltered position. You can also grow them to maturity in a frame.

Sow three seeds per peat pot or planting position. When the seedlings emerge, pinch off the weakest, leaving the strongest one to grow on.

Harden off transplants thoroughly and set them out in late spring or early summer. Protect the transplants with cloches or fleece until they are established. If you grow the plants in a frame, gradually increase the amount of ventilation given.

Growing greenhouse cucumbers

Sow seeds indoors in peat pots in the same way as for outdoor cucumbers.

Plant out in late spring or early summer in the greenhouse border or in pots or growing bags, like tomatoes.

Care

Watering Proper watering is needed for good fruit development. A drip irrigation system maintains even soil moisture without wetting the foliage, which is important to avoid diseases.

Supporting cucumbers For outdoor plants, use posts and heavy netting or wire for a vertical or A-frame support. Or use wire-mesh fencing to make a tunnel over the row, and train the vines along the top of it. For greenhouse cucumbers, see pages 80–81.

Pollination Outdoor cucumbers must have female flowers pollinated by a male to set fruits. But stop greenhouse cucumbers from pollinating, or bitter, misshapen fruits will result. Grow all-female varieties, and remove any rogue male flowers that appear.

Quick Tip

Finding a male
When hand-pollinating a cucumber (or squash) flower, it doesn't matter if the male flower is from the same plant or another one.

Harvesting

The best time to harvest cucumbers is in the morning, while the fruits are still relatively cool. Make sure that you don't let the fruits become too large, otherwise they may become bitter or pithy.

You can pick outdoor cucumber types as pickling cucumbers when they grow to 7.5–10cm (3–4in) long (5cm/2in for gherkins) or 15–20cm (6–8in) for slicing. Harvest greenhouse varieties when they are about 25–30cm (10–12in) long.

If you miss harvesting a cucumber and it grows too big, remove it from the vine anyway; otherwise, it will suppress production of more fruits.

Storing Plunge cucumbers into cold water to chill them; then store them loosely in plastic bags in the refrigerator for up to three days. For the best pickle quality, make pickles with freshly picked fruits.

BEST OF THE BUNCH

'Burpless Tasty Green' F1 hybrid ridge cucumber with dark green skin and sweet taste. Resistant to powdery mildew.
'Calypso' Medium-green fruits; tolerates diseases well.
'Carmen' An 'all-female' variety. High yielding; excellent disease resistance.
'Crystal Apple' Small, globe-shaped, yellow fruits; very sweet flavour, best picked young. Outdoor variety.
'Femspot' F1 hybrid greenhouse cucumber with long, tasty fruits. Resistant to disease. 'All-female' variety.
'Lemon' Heirloom variety; lemon yellow, round fruits with sweet flavour.
'Marketmore 76' Tolerates powdery mildew, mosaic and other diseases; slender dark green slicing variety.
'Salad Bush' Disease tolerant; smooth-skinned slicing variety. Good for containers.

Outdoor cucumber flowers must be pollinated to set fruit. To hand-pollinate remove a male flower (one without a swelling behind the bloom), strip off the petals and press its centre into the centre of the female flowers (see page 227).

PROBLEM SOLVER

Poor growth; speckled foliage with webbing. Red spider mite is a common cucumber pest on those grown in greenhouses. These mites like dry conditions, so increasing the humidity in the greenhouse is the best way to prevent attacks.

Pale, translucent spots appear on foliage and spread to fruits. Anthracnose can be a serious disease of greenhouse cucumbers. Destroy the infected fruits and treat the plants with sulphur. Make sure you improve ventilation in the greenhouse to prevent this disease on future crops.

Powdery coating on leaves. Spray the plants with fungicide when powdery mildew appears. Destroy all infected plant material. For future plantings, make sure you train the plants on supports to improve air circulation. Choose resistant varieties.

Mottled leaves and bitter fruits. You should suspect cucumber mosaic virus. Destroy all infected plants. For future crops, plant resistant varieties.

The fruits are oddly shaped. Those growing on outdoor types can be due to poor pollination. Make sure you hand-pollinate. For those growing on greenhouse types, pollination can cause oddly shaped fruits. In this case you should grow all-female varieties. If you do grow varieties that include male flowers, inspect the plants and remove the male flowers before they have a chance to pollinate the female flowers. Another cause of oddly shaped fruits for both outdoor and greenhouse cucumbers is inconsistent watering during fruit development. Water the plants regularly.

Outdoor plants don't set fruit. Male flowers appear before female flowers, so female flowers may not be present yet. If they are wet, weather or lack of bees hindered pollination. Hand-pollinate.

Courgettes and marrows

These summer vegetables belong to a group known as summer squashes, which includes lots of varieties in a range of shapes and colours. They all have thin, tender skin and mild flesh. The fruits enlarge rapidly, and picking them encourages production.

Sowing and planting

Soil Mix a 2.5-cm (1-in) layer of compost into the soil if you want to plant transplants in rows. If sowing seeds in mounds, add several shovelfuls of compost to each mound.

Sowing seeds Sow seeds in slightly raised planting mounds. Sow six to eight seeds a few inches apart in a ring. Sow the flat seeds on edge, to reduce the chances of them rotting in the soil. Thin each mound to the two or three strongest plants.

Speeding up the season Summer squashes will do best in a warm, sheltered spot in the garden. To get them off to a good start, cover the soil tightly with black plastic for two to three weeks before planting to help warm the soil. In addition, cover the plants with a plastic tunnel or horticultural fleece after planting.

Starting transplants inside gives you a head start towards an early harvest, too. Squash seedlings don't transplant easily and the roots need space to expand, so use 7.5- or 10-cm (3- or 4-in) peat pots. Sow three seeds per pot, and when the seedlings emerge cut off the weakest seedlings, leaving only the strongest one in each pot.

Make sure you thoroughly harden off plants raised inside before setting them out in the open garden. A frame is useful to start the hardening off process; gradually increase the ventilation of the frame until you can leave the frame lights off altogether.

Care

Mulching Mulching helps conserve soil moisture, which in return will help produce larger crops of better–

BEST OF THE BUNCH

'Black Beauty' Classic courgette with dark green fruits that has an open growth habit.

'Eight Ball' Dark green, round courgette.

'Gold Rush' Golden yellow squash with creamy flavour; vigorous grower.

'Kojac' Virtually spineless stems; a high yield of dark green fruits.

'Peter Pan' Green, bushy scallop squash; good raw or cooked. Best when harvested at 10cm (4in) or under.

'Ronde de Nice' Round, milky green courgette; harvest as baby fruits or at size of a tennis ball.

'Spineless Beauty' Medium-green courgette; spineless.

'Sunburst' Bright yellow scallop squash with a blotch of green at each end; early bearing; firm but tender fruits, even when fully mature.

'Venus' Very compact plants, ideal for small gardens or containers. Glossy, deep green fruits.

'Zephyr' Straight-neck squash with slender, yellow fruits tipped with pale green. Good flavour and texture.

Quick Tip

A question of size

Marrows are the same as courgettes but allowed to grow larger. Traditionally, marrow varieties are striped green and white, while courgettes area all-green. If you wish you can let courgette varieties develop into marrows – the flavour is the same.

quality fruit. Do not apply the mulch right up to the neck of the plant, as this can encourage the main stem to rot, leading to the collapse of the plant – leave a clear area just around the stem. Keep large fruits off the ground by placing them on dry straw, tiles or pieces of wood; this helps to prevent rotting due to contact with damp soil, and also keeps slugs and snails at bay.

Fertilising When fruits appear, apply a balanced organic fertiliser or a liquid feed with a high-potash fertiliser, following the pack directions.

Hand-pollinating Hand-pollinating can improve fruit set in cool or cloudy weather. First, identify the male and female flowers. Female flowers have a small swelling at the base below the blossom.

You can use a cotton swab or artist's paintbrush to collect pollen from male flowers and transfer it to female flowers. Alternatively, pick a male flower, pull off the petals and rub the pollen, which looks like yellow grain, directly on the stigma – the central structure in the female flower. A single male flower has enough pollen to pollinate several female flowers. In warm, sunny weather there are usually enough pollinating insects to do the job for you.

Harvesting

When the fruits appear, check summer squash (especially courgette) daily. Fruit quality declines if the fruits become oversized. Small fruits are tender and have excellent flavour. Use a sharp knife to cut the squash from the plants, leaving about 2.5cm (1in) of stem attached. For courgettes, 7.5–15cm (3–6in) long is ideal. Harvest scallop squash when 7.5cm (3in) across. You can allow scallop squash to mature, with a hard rind, and harvest them like winter squash (see page 229).

Most summer squash plants have hairy or spiny stems and leaves. To avoid skin irritation, wear long sleeves and gloves when harvesting.

Storing Store the squashes unwashed in plastic bags for up to four to five days in the refrigerator.

Smooth, spineless varieties are just one of the many types to choose. Also look for virus-resistant varieties or parthenocarpic types – these can set fruits without pollination.

PROBLEM SOLVER

Leaves mottled yellow and are distorted. Cucumber mosaic virus attacks squash plants, causing severely stunted growth and poor crops; the fruits can be mottled and distorted as well as the leaves. Destroy all infected plants. Keep aphids under control – they spread the virus.

Leaves with a powdery white coating. Powdery mildew is worst in hot, dry summers; bad attacks can stunt the plants and reduce crops. Remove badly affected leaves and ensure the soil is kept moist at all times. Spray the plants with a suitable fungicide. Do not confuse the normal silver leaf patterning on some varieties with mildew.

Fruits are oddly shaped. This can be the result of inconsistent watering during fruit development or poor pollination. Water regularly and hand-pollinate.

Plants don't set fruits. Male flowers will appear before female flowers, so female flowers may not be present yet. If they are, wet weather or lack of bees may have hindered pollination. Hand-pollinate.

Fruits have pitted skins. The fruits have been exposed to temperatures that have dropped below 4.5°C (40°F) for several days. At the end of the season, use horticultural fleece, or harvest the fruits when a cold spell is predicted.

Small fruits turn mouldy. Fruits may rot if the plants have been overfertilised with nitrogen. Try hand-pollinating and cut back on fertilising.

Leathery area at blossom end of fruits. Squash suffer from blossom end rot due to a lack of calcium in the developing fruits when it doesn't get enough water. Mulch the soil to conserve moisture and water regularly.

Pumpkins and winter squash

It would take a mighty big garden to grow just one of each popular type of pumpkin and winter squash. These bountiful and delicious squashes are available in a truly amazing variety of shapes, forms and colours.

PLANTING GUIDE

What to plant Seeds or transplants.

Starting indoors Sow seeds three weeks before the last spring frost.

Site preparation Add compost and cover with black plastic to speed soil heating.

When Mid-spring to late summer.

Spacing Sow mounds or plant transplants of bush and compact varieties 0.6–1.2m (2–4ft) apart in rows about 1.5–1.8m (5–6ft) apart. Sow mounds or plant transplants of large varieties 1.8m (6ft) apart.

How much As many vines as space will allow; most vines produce four to five fruits.

Quick Tip

Edible flowers
The flowers of both summer and winter squashes are edible. Pick the male flowers just as they start to open; use a paintbrush to remove any pollen beetles. Dip the flowers in batter and deep fry them, or stuff with a rice or meat filling.

Sowing and planting

Soil Winter squash and pumpkins are usually planted on mounds, but their vines and roots spread widely. To ensure fertility and moisture-holding capacity, spread a 5-cm (2-in) layer of compost over the entire planting area and work it into the soil.

These crops will also do well planted directly in a mature compost heap, as long as the vines can sprawl in full sun.

Two weeks before you sow seeds or set out transplants, wet down the planting area thoroughly and cover it tightly with black plastic to speed soil warming. Pumpkins and winter squashes like an open, sunny and protected position – they will not grow well in cold, exposed gardens.

When Winter squash and pumpkins won't grow well until soil temperature is 15.5°C (60°F). To ensure the warm soil and air conditions that these plants like, hold off planting until two to four weeks after the last spring frost. You can obtain a better crop with transplants rather than direct-seeding. (See pages 226–227 for raising summer squash transplants.)

Mound planting Form mounds for sowing seeds or setting transplants. If you've spread black plastic over the planting area, use a knife to cut a circular hole 30–60cm (12–24in) across for each mound. Mix about 18 litres (half-bushel) of compost into the soil for each mound, and shape a low raised mound 30–60cm (12–24in) across.

Sow five or six seeds per mound or set two transplants per mound. When you thin seedlings, leave the two strongest plants per mound.

Most winter squash and pumpkin varieties are trailing types and spread very widely, so they will need lots of space. You can train the shoots round in a circle to keep the plants more compact. Alternatively, if space is limited bush varieties are available, though the seeds of these types are not so readily available.

Care

Watering Pumpkins need lots of water or the fruits won't develop to full size. As a general rule of thumb, supply 9–13 litres (2–3gal) of water per mound each week if it doesn't rain. Or dig a test hole to monitor the soil moisture. When you water, you should soak the soil up to about 30cm (12in) deep.

Once the vines begin to elongate, the spreading foliage will shade the soil and slow down moisture loss. Withholding water as the fruits near maturity will hasten ripening.

Feeding You should either mulch the plants with compost or apply a balanced organic fertiliser when the first blossoms begin to appear.

Pinching and thinning If the squash and pumpkins are planted closer than the standard recommendations, you can control their growth by pinching the growing tips after the first several fruits have set. Although the fruits may not turn out as sweet as would otherwise be – there won't be as many leaves to supply sugars to them – this is a better choice than facing the chaos of rampant squash vines taking over your garden. Plus, crowded vines are more prone to disease problems.

If a vine sets too many fruits, the fruits will compete for sugars and nutrients, and as a result all of the fruits will suffer and be small at maturity. If you want larger fruits, especially for jack-o'-lantern–type pumpkins, you will need to remove some of the developing fruits from each vine.

Harvesting

When winter squash and pumpkins are ripe, the rind turns slightly dull. The rind should be tough enough to withstand light pressure from a fingernail. For best keeping quality, harvest winter squash and pumpkins before the first frost, ideally before temperatures drop below 4.5°C (40°F). Cut the fruits off the vines, leaving about 5cm (2in) of stem attached to the fruits. Handle them carefully: if the stem breaks off, there will be an entry point for decay organisms.

Storing

Cure squash at 29–32°C (85–90°F) for several days to promote hardening of the rind; then move the fruits to a cool area. Temperatures of 10–15.5°C (50–60°F) and humidity of 50 to 75 per cent are ideal. Some types last for four months in these conditions. Before moving squash to storage, wipe the rind with a 10 per cent bleach solution to improve its keeping quality.

PROBLEM SOLVER

Powdery coating on leaves. This condition is caused by powdery mildew. Spray the plants with a fungicide when it appears. Destroy all infected material, and for future crops try choosing resistant types. To prevent powdery mildew, you should ensure the soil is kept moist at all times.

Leaves mottled yellow and distorted. Cucumber mosaic virus attacks squash plants, causing severely stunted growth and poor crops; the fruits can be mottled and distorted as well as the leaves. There is no treatment available. You'll need to destroy all infected plants by burning them. For future crops, keep aphids under control – they are responsible for spreading the virus.

Plants don't set fruits. Male flowers will appear before female flowers, so the female flowers may not be present yet. If they are, wet weather or lack of bees may have hindered pollination. Hand-pollinate to ensure pollination.

Fruits start to rot on the undersides. Keep the developing fruits off damp soil by raising them on dry straw, tiles or pieces of wood. Remember that the fruits of many pumpkin varieties grow very large, and these will require plenty of sturdy support to keep them off the ground completely.

Fruits rot when kept in store. Make sure squashes and pumpkins are properly ripened and cured before storage. Do not store fruits that are damaged, and always keep the temperature and humidity at the correct levels.

Small vines can bear four to five small fruits. Medium-size pumpkins and large squashes can handle three or four fruits per vine. For large pumpkins, leave two to three fruits per vine.

Types of winter squash

The huge range of sizes, colours and shapes of winter squashes (*Cucurbita pepo*, *C. moschata* and *C. maxima*) available can be a revelation to many gardeners. The sweet-flavoured, tasty fruits are worth growing for their ornamental value alone.

▼ Butternut squash

This favourite moschata-type of winter squash is a reliable producer and has good keeping quality. Butternut squashes have elongated or hourglass-shaped fruits, which are orange or tan. The yellow flesh is mealy and sweet. There are many cultivars to choose from, including the classic variety 'Waltham'.

▲ Acorn squash

One of the smallest types of winter squash, acorn squash can have green, gold or white rinds. These ribbed fruits are a pepo type, and their flavour is more nutty and not as sweet as some other types of squashes. 'Table Ace' is early bearing and has dark skin, while 'Cream of the Crop' has a creamy white rind.

◄ Delicata squash

Green stripes on white skin make this oblong fruit a beauty. This winter pepo squash is good for baking and stuffing. It's also called sweet potato squash and has dry flesh. A bush variety, 'Bush Delicata', is available.

◄ Hubbard squash

Perhaps the least attractive winter squash, hubbards are large, lumpy, blue-grey squashes with pointed ends. However, these maxima-type squashes offer thick, dry, sweet flesh and impressive yields, often more than 4.5kg (10lb) apiece. 'Blue Ballet' is a more compact plant that bears fruits half the size of regular Hubbard squash.

▲ Kabocha squash

These large maxima-type squashes can be dark green or bright orange. Orange varieties such as 'Sunshine' resemble squat pumpkins with very thick stems. The flesh is sweet and delicate.

► Spaghetti squash

Named for its stringy flesh, this winter pepo squash has oblong, yellow fruits. When cooked, the flesh separates into strands. Many people use spaghetti squashes such as 'Vegetable Spaghetti' as a pasta substitute. Its delicate flavour comes forward when you prepare it with cinnamon or a light curry seasoning.

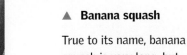

▲ Banana squash

True to its name, banana squash is very long, but unlike bananas,it sports a grey-green or pinkish rind. This is a winter maxima-type squash, and it is good for making pies, baking and pureeing. These squashes can grow more than 60cm (24in) long in the right conditions.

Types of pumpkin

Pumpkins are a type of winter squash, but unlike other winter squashes, they do not develop a fully hard rind. Small-space gardeners can grow mini pumpkins. Gardeners with room for sprawling vines can grow jack-o'-lanterns – and giant pumpkins.

▶ **Giant or jumbo pumpkin**

Monstrous maxima-type pumpkins can grow to an amazing size (the British record is more than 408kg/900lb) if you give them special care and feeding. 'Atlantic Giant' is one of the best-known prize-winning varieties.

◀ **Jack-o'-lantern**

These classic, smooth-skinned, round pumpkins are pepo-type pumpkins. They range in size from 0.9kg to 11kg (2lb to 24lb). Many of the small varieties such as 'Small Sugar' are good for making pies. Intermediate and large varieties are popular for carving or painting. 'Connecticut Field' is probably the best-known large variety.

▶ **Mini-pumpkin**

'Jack Be Little' is one of the most popular of these tiny flattened pumpkins, which are usually about 10cm (4in) across. The vines are short, and each vine produces up to a dozen single-serving pumpkins. These small pepo-type pumpkins are fun to decorate or eat.

▶ **White pumpkin**

These unusual pumpkins have become popular as seasonal decorations and for painting. 'Lumina' and other varieties are maxima-type pumpkins; 'Baby Boo' is a white-skinned, pepo-type pumpkin. The vines need excellent care because the skin colour dulls when the plants are stressed.

Melons

Most melons grow on sprawling vines and need lots of space, and all melons need warm weather to grow and ripen fruits. Choose early ripening varieties and give the plants protection from cold for the best chance of success.

Sowing and planting

Soil Grow melons outdoors only in the mildest areas of Britain. Even then you will need a good summer for worthwhile results. Choose the most sheltered, sunniest spot in the garden and spread a 5-cm (2-in) layer of compost over the planting area, working it well into the soil. Make a raised bed to ensure the soil warms up well. Moisten the soil and cover it tightly with black plastic.

For the best results, cover outdoor plants with cloches, or grow them in a frame, polytunnel or greenhouse.

Starting seeds in containers Use 10-cm (4-in) peat pots or plastic pots. Plant two seeds per pot and cut off the weaker one after the first true leaf appears. Handle the seedlings carefully when transplanting to avoid damaging the lanky stems or prolific roots.

Planting transplants Cut 60-cm (24-in)-diameter holes through the plastic and create raised mounds for transplants. After planting, cover plants with cloches.

Or set the plants in the greenhouse border or in large pots or growing bags, and train the growth up wires or twine. Melons will grow well set in the centre of a frame. Train the shoots out to the corners.

Care

Watering and feeding Don't let the plants suffer moisture stress. Drip irrigation is ideal for melons. However, you should hold off watering in the final week before the expected harvest. This will help concentrate the sugars in the fruits to produce sweeter, more flavourful melons. Also, excess watering can cause melons to split.

BEST OF THE BUNCH

'Ambrosia' Produces fruits with peach- or salmon-coloured flesh that have an excellent flavour and aroma; it tolerates powdery mildew.

'Fastbreak' Early bearing plants that produce fruits weighing 2.25kg (5lb); the netted fruits have a very sweet, golden flesh.

'Galia' Good for growing in a frame or under cover. Vigorous and early with very sweet, flavourful fruits.

'Passport' Hybrid honeydew melon with sweet flesh that ripens quickly. Good disease resistance.

'Sweetheart' Very popular Charentais type, with medium-sized fruits having sweet, pale orange flesh. Good flavour; will do well outdoors as well as in a greenhouse.

'Yellow Baby' Watermelon with yellow, almost seedless flesh. Very sweet flavour. More tolerant of cool conditions than most watermelons.

PLANTING GUIDE

What to plant Transplants.

Starting indoors Sow seeds indoors in mid-spring.

Site preparation Add organic matter to increase moisture-holding capacity. For the best results, make a raised bed and cover it with black plastic to warm the soil.

When After all danger of frost is past; wait until soil is 21°C (70°F).

Spacing *For cantaloupe* Set transplants about 1.2–1.8m (4–6ft) apart. *For watermelons* Set transplants about 1.5–2.1m (5–7ft) apart.

How much As many vines as space in your garden allows. Most types produce three to five fruits per vine.

Temperature alert
Melons won't develop a nice flavour unless they ripen in warm conditions. Choose fast-growing varieties and start the crop early.

Add a high-potash liquid fertiliser to the water once flowering starts.

Training and supporting Melons are carried on sideshoots or laterals. Pinch out the growing tips of young plants when they produce four leaves and train the shoots that are produced along horizontal supports. Pinch out the tips of these sideshoots when they have five or six leaves and they will then produce fruit-bearing laterals. In a frame, under cloches or in the open, leave the shoots to sprawl over the ground rather than trained up wires.

When the flowers appear, fertilise them by hand to ensure pollination (see page 227). Wait until plenty of flowers are open before pollinating – once the first fruits set on a plant it tends to inhibit the formation of any more melons, so you should pollinate several flowers at the same time for the best results.

Melon fruits are heavy, and on plants trained up wires they will need supporting or they will pull the vines down. Once the fruits reach about tennis-ball size, provide slings made from mesh bags or old nylon tights, tied securely to the support structure.

For vines that are growing at ground level, keep the fruits off the soil by placing each fruit on a board, brick or flat rock.

Harvesting

As the expected harvest date nears, check the fruits regularly for signs of ripeness. The tendril by the stem where a fruit is attached to the vine dries up at about the time of ripening, although this may happen up to a week before the melon is ripe. Inspect the fruits around the stalk; as fruits ripen, small cracks appear in this area. Probably the best test is to sniff the blossom end of the fruits. Ripe fruits give off a pleasant, sweet aroma.

Storing Use melons as soon as possible. Underripe fruits may ripen a little off the vine if left at room temperature. Uncut melons last for one to two weeks at a cool room temperature. Refrigerated cut pieces of melon will keep for a few days.

PROBLEM SOLVER

Powdery coating on leaves. Spray the plants with a fungicide when powdery mildew symptoms first appear, and improve air circulation round the plants. Remove and destroy infected plant material. For future crops, try choosing resistant varieties.

Poor growth; speckled foliage with webbing. Red spider mite is a common pest of melons grown in greenhouses. Increase the humidity to prevent attacks (the mites prefer dry conditions), and use a biological control.

Sticky foliage with small, white, mothlike insects. Although greenhouse whitefly is difficult to control with insecticides, there is a biological control available. Yellow sticky traps hung in the greenhouse will also trap large numbers of the creatures, particularly if you gently shake the plants to get the whitefly on the wing – a cloud of them will appear.

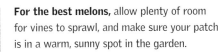

For the best melons, allow plenty of room for vines to sprawl, and make sure your patch is in a warm, sunny spot in the garden.

Quick Tip

Quality control

Limit each plant to three to five fruits, depending on the variety and the ultimate fruit size. Allowing more fruits to remain on the vine is likely to produce disappointing results, with small fruits that do not ripen satisfactorily. Thin fruits when they are golf-ball sized or less.

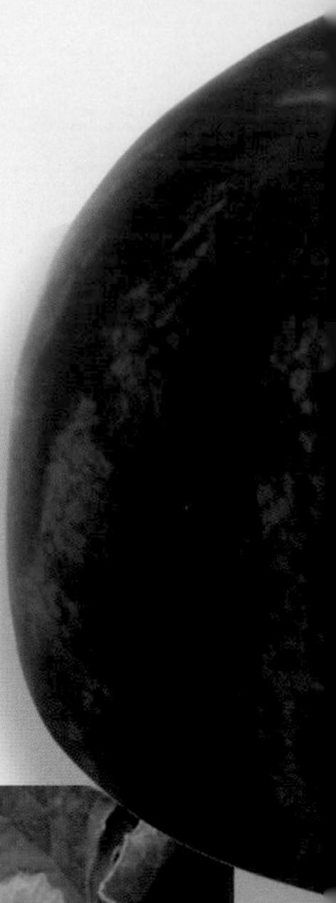

Types of melons

There are several types of melon available, many of which are suitable only for growing in the greenhouse in Britain. If you live in a mild, sunny area, you can try some of the more exotic types, but you will need to find a specialist seed supplier.

▶ **Muskmelon**

Cantaloupe melons contain some of the most reliable varieties for the British climate. The skins are pale green and often have prominent ribs. Charentais melons are a type of cantaloupe, with juicy, aromatic, orange flesh. In sheltered gardens you can often grow varieties such as 'Sweetheart' outside.

Most varieties identified as cantaloupes in American seed catalogues are really muskmelons. These melons usually give off a musky aroma, and they have netted skins and orange flesh (but there are green- and white-fleshed muskmelons too).

◀ **Crenshaw melon**

Crenshaws have smooth, dark green skin that lightens to yellowish green as it ripens. The flesh is salmon or pinkish orange and has a rich, sweet flavour. They are not commonly grown in Britain, and you will need to find a specialist seed supplier.

▼ Honeydew melon

Honeydew melons have smooth skin and green or white flesh. (Varieties with orange flesh are available, too.) While honeydews don't have a strong fragrance even when ripe, their flesh is wonderfully sweet and refreshing. Seeds are available from specialist seed suppliers.

▲ Watermelon

Most watermelons need a much warmer climate than the climate found in Britain to do well. However, there are one or two varieties that you can grow in a greenhouse or polytunnel in the milder areas of the country. They will not reach the large sizes that you are used to seeing in supermarkets. Although crimson-fleshed varieties are most familiar, there are also yellow-fleshed types such as 'Yellow Baby' – a good variety for cooler conditions. Botanically speaking, watermelons are *Citrullus lanatus*, while other melons are *Cucumis melo*.

13 Corn

'Boil the water before you pick' is a saying from sweet-corn growers who enjoy the experience of eating sweet corn as soon as possible after it has been harvested. They know that the sugars in the corn start to turn to starch as soon as the cobs are removed from the plant, reducing its flavour.

Every vegetable gardener should try growing sweet corn at least once. Although your crop may not produce 100 per cent perfect ears, the experience of eating freshly grown sweet corn is not to be missed. Just for fun, you may want to consider trying a patch of popcorn, too.

Yellow kernels of sweet corn are at their sweetest at the moment the cob is picked. Home-grown sweet corn will always be sweeter than shop-bought corn.

Sweet corn

The joy of eating fresh corn repays the effort it takes to grow this crop well. Sweet corn has many requirements, but with proper preparation and well-chosen varieties, a successful harvest can be yours – even if you live in a cool climate.

Sowing and planting

Soil The ideal preparation for corn is to plant a nitrogen-fixing green manure such as alfalfa or clover the preceding autumn (see pages 36–37). Leave the crop in place through winter, and dig it into the soil two weeks before you plan to plant.

If you have poor soil fertility or you're planning to plant intensively, spread 5cm (2in) of compost over the planting area. Add a nitrogen-rich supplement such as blood, fish and bone, sprinkling a light coating over the compost. Work the compost and supplement into the top several inches of soil. Shape the planting area into a raised bed to speed soil warming and ensure good drainage.

Choosing what to grow Sweet corn varieties are available with 'regular' sweetness (called sugary varieties), sugar-enhanced or super-sweet. Sugar-enhanced types have the same amount of sweetness as regular varieties, but keep their sweetness longer after picking. Supersweet varieties are two to four times sweeter than standard varieties. They keep their sweetness and crispness better when frozen than other types do. However, supersweet seedlings are less vigorous and more cold sensitive than standard varieties. Also, you must isolate supersweet varieties from other corn plantings that tassel at the same time, because if super-sweet ears are pollinated by non-supersweet varieties, the ears will not develop properly. To isolate a supersweet planting, make sure you plant it at least 120m (400ft) away from fields of maize or other sweet corn.

Some varieties are known as 'tendersweet'. These have a very thin, tender skin on the kernels. They also retain their sweetness well.

Most sweet-corn varieties have golden or creamy yellow kernels, but some varieties have different-coloured kernels in the same cob such as 'Indian Summer' or 'Honey Bantam'.

Starting seeds indoors In cool areas you can get an earlier start by sowing seeds in peat pots or individual plastic pots. Two weeks after the seeds germinate, move the pots to a frame or protected outdoor area to harden off for one week. Transplant the plants carefully to avoid disturbing the roots.

If you use plastic pots, soak them thoroughly so the root ball slips easily out of them. With peat pots, peel away the top rim of the pot so that it can't be left exposed and wick moisture away from the roots.

Sowing seeds outside In mild areas you can sow seeds directly in the

PLANTING GUIDE

What to plant Seeds or transplants.

Starting indoors Sow seeds in a heated greenhouse or propagator in mid-spring.

Site preparation Add compost and nitrogen supplement; make raised beds.

When After danger of frost is past.

Spacing Sow the seeds about 7.5–10cm (3–4in) apart, with 90cm (36in) between rows. Thin the seedlings or set transplants about 25cm (10in) apart, but up to 60cm (24in) apart for tall varieties.

Intensive spacing Sow the seeds 7.5–10cm (3–4in) apart in double rows 30cm (12in) apart; allow 90cm (36in) between double rows; thin seedlings or set transplants 30cm (12in) apart. Do not choose tall varieties.

How much For fresh eating and freezing, about 30 plants per person.

The spiky male flowers, or tassels, stand above the female flowers with silks – both on the same plant.

garden, which helps to avoid the check to growth that occurs when transplanting. Cover the raised bed with black plastic or cloches several weeks before sowing to help warm the soil. The ideal germination temperature range is 21–29°C (70–85°F). Sow three seeds per station and thin the seedlings to the strongest one shortly after they emerge.

Block planting No matter whether you sow the seeds directly or set out transplants, always set up small corn plantings as a block consisting of at least four rows, instead of growing the plants in single rows. Sweet corn is unusual in that it is pollinated by wind, not by insects, and planting in a block will help to ensure a good pollination.

Sweet corn is a grass with separate male and female flowers, and both of these occur on the same plant. The male flowers appear at the tip of the plant, in spiky, upright 'tassels'. The female flowers arise from the leaf axils, and can be seen as pale green or yellow 'silks' – like long, silky threads. Imperfect pollination will lead to gappy cobs, with kernels missing where the silks have not been properly pollinated.

Care

Watering If plants are water-stressed plant growth will come to a standstill, even if the plants appear vigorous. Using drip irrigation is best because it's an easy way to deliver water evenly throughout the stand, even when the stalks are tall. Check the soil moisture and water when the top 5cm (2in) have dried out. When you water, soak the soil at least 15cm (6in) deep. Mulching the soil with organic mulch will help conserve moisture.

If you don't have a drip irrigation system, make drills between your rows of corn as shallow 'irrigation ditches'. When you need to water, direct the water into these ditches and let it soak into the surrounding soil; you won't have to direct the water at the foliage or directly at the base of the plants (which could destabilise them).

BEST OF THE BUNCH

'Champ' An F1 hybrid producing large, golden cobs. Tolerant of cool weather.
'Honey Bantam' Early, sweet variety with attractive bicolour kernels of deep gold and pale creamy yellow.
'Indian Summer' Bicolour supersweet hybrid with yellow, white and purplish-red kernels; grows 2.1m (7ft) tall.
'Mini Pop' Not a popcorn type, but a hybrid variety specially bred for harvesting as mini corn. Pick the cobs when they are about 5cm (2in) long, before the kernels begin to swell, and cook them whole.
'Northern Xtra-Sweet' Yellow super-sweet hybrid; grows 1.5m (5ft) tall.
'Red Strawberry' A novelty corn with berry-shaped 5-cm (2-in)-long cobs bearing tiny red kernels. The whole cob can be 'popped' in a microwave.
'Swift' Very sweet, early, extra tender variety, good for cooler conditions.

Temperature alert
Corn seeds tend to rot in cold soil, so wait until the soil is warm before planting them; the soil should be at least 18°C (65°F).

POPCORN

Home-grown popcorn is a healthy snack, and a fun project to try with children. Plant popcorn as you would regular sweet corn. Because you don't need to harvest before the weather turns cold, you can plant popcorn in a garden bed after you harvest early broccoli or lettuce. As few as six ears of corn can produce 5.5 litres (9½pt) of popcorn, but remember that you need to plant a small block to ensure good pollination.

You should care for your popcorn plants as you would sweet corn. The difference comes at harvest time. Instead of picking the ears when the silks dry up, leave them on the plants until all the stalks have turned dry and brown; then snap off the ears, pull down the husks and put the ears in a warm, dry place to cure. Putting the ears in mesh onion bags and hanging them to cure works well. Curing generally takes four to five weeks.

The goal is to get the moisture level in the ears in the right range for successful popping. To tell when your popcorn is dry enough, select an ear, use your thumbs to remove the kernels from the husk and try popping them. If the kernels won't pop allow the ears to continue to cure for another week; then try the popping test again. Once you've had success with a test popping, remove the rest of the kernels and put in sealed jars; store them in a cool, dry spot. The kernels should retain good popping quality for several years.

Grow popcorn to provide a tasty – and healthy – snack. Try popping short-cob varieties in a suitable container in a microwave oven.

Unfurling, bright green leaves above the female silks soak up the sun, producing plenty of sugar to pump into succulent ears of tender kernels of corn.

Stalk management When the plants reach about 30cm (12in) tall, you should use a hoe to earth up extra soil around their stalks. This will make the plants better able to withstand any strong gusts of wind.

Do not remove any suckers (the small side stalks). They will not harm the plants or reduce yields; however, removing them could injure the stalks and leave them open to invasion by disease organisms.

When the stalks are 30–45cm (12–18in) tall, you can feed them with a balanced fertiliser, and repeat the feeding when the tassels appear.

Ensuring pollination To help good pollination on a windless day, shake the cornstalks when the tassels are shedding pollen. This will help to distribute the pollen to the silks.

Alternatively, shake the tassels over an opened envelope to collect the pollen. Carefully sprinkle the pollen on to the silks.

Quick Tip

Corny border

You can prepare a bed for sweet corn along a sunny boundary line of your property. It will provide a summertime privacy screen and a delicious harvest. Alternate sweet corn with sunflowers from year to year as a mini crop-rotation plan.

Harvesting

Ears of corn will be ready to pick when the silks turn brown and dry up. To test for ripeness you can pierce the kernels of an ear – if it's ripe a milky liquid should leak out. (However, for supersweet types, the liquid stays clear even when the ears are ripe.) Generally, ears will ripen at the same time in a single planting, so check your corn patch daily once the silks start to turn brown.

Remove the ears by twisting them down, away from the stalks. After the harvest is complete, remove any crop debris from the garden so pests cannot use it to overwinter.

Storing It's best to eat sweet corn as soon as possible after picking, or quickly blanch and freeze it. You can freeze the kernels on the cob or stripped off. Supersweet varieties hold their sweetness better than other types when frozen.

PROBLEM SOLVER

Seedlings fail to appear. Sweet corn will not germinate in cold, wet soil, so adjust the sowing time. Mice and voles may dig up and eat the seeds; cover the newly sown area with fleece or use traps.

Soft, white swellings on cobs or stems. These burst open and reveal a dense mass of dark powder. Sweet corn smut is unmistakable. It usually occurs only in hot summers but is becoming more common. Smut is a fungus disease that cannot be treated; remove the swellings as soon as they are noticed, before they burst open to release the spores. Burn all diseased parts, and the crop debris after harvest. After an infected crop, do not grow sweet corn in the same place for five years.

Striped or frayed, twisted leaves and stunted plants. Fruit flies sometimes attack the plants in early summer. The larvae feed on the growing points of plants, causing stunted growth and poor crops, or even killing the plants. Healthy transplants are less likely to be damaged than plants from seeds sown outdoors. Give the plants good growing conditions to reduce the impact of attacks.

Nearly ripe cobs broken or bitten off. Badgers in rural gardens like sweet corn. The sheaths covering the corn cobs are often shredded by the badgers' claws, causing distinctive damage. Secure fencing round the garden, or at least the sweet-corn area, to keep them at bay, though they are strong and persistent animals, which are protected by law.

Gaps in ripe cobs. Poor pollination results in kernels failing to form, which only becomes evident after harvest. Plant sweet corn in a block rather than a single row. (See *Ensuring pollination*, left.)

Sturdy stalks of sweet corn will tower over the other occupants of the vegetable garden.

14 Perennial and annual herbs

Every garden needs herbs, but if you don't have room for a separate herb garden, don't fret! Perennial herbs such as sage, thyme, marjoram, oregano and rosemary have lovely form, foliage and flowers that will make delightful edgings or accents in a flower garden. You can tuck annual herbs such as summer savory, dill and basil in and round your vegetables.

Herbs are generally undemanding and rarely suffer pest and disease problems. Many may even repel pests, and several produce flowers that attract beneficial insects to your garden.

Feathery fronds of fennel
take centre stage
alongside sage and mint
in this herb garden.

Mint

Peppermint (*Mentha piperita*) and spearmint (*M. spicata*) are popular types of mint, a highly fragrant perennial herb. However, you can also choose from a wide variety of flavoured mints, including orange mint, apple mint and pineapple mint.

PLANTING GUIDE

What to plant Rooted cuttings, divisions or potted plants.

Site preparation Sink a root barrier into the soil before planting.

When Divisions in autumn; rooted cuttings or potted plants when they are available.

Spacing About 30–45cm (12-18in) between plants.

How much One plant of each type you want to grow.

Sowing and planting

Soil Mints like moist, well-drained soil. To prepare for planting, dig a hole at least 30cm (12in) in diameter and 30cm (12in) deep.

This perennial herb can quickly spread and engulf a garden bed, so you will need to control it by sinking a root barrier into the soil before planting. You can use a clay drainage tile or a plastic bucket with the bottom cut out. Position the barrier into your planting hole, but leave 5–7.5cm (2–3in) sticking up above the soil level. Fill the container with the removed soil, and plant the mint inside the barrier.

You can start your mint planting with divisions or rooted cuttings from another plant. Alternatively, purchase mint from your local garden centre. Even if it is a small plant, mint establishes quickly and provides plenty of tender leaves for harvesting.

Care

Pruning Mints are hardy and fast-growing plants, and they respond well to frequent cutting. Always pay particular attention to shoots at the edge of the clump. If these are allowed to grow unchecked, they may spill over the side of the root barrier and root into the soil outside.

Dividing You should dig your mint clumps every few years and divide them, replanting small sections and leaving them room to spread. Be careful how you dispose of the excess plant material. Discarded mint can easily take root in a compost heap.

Mints occasionally suffer from rust, a fungus disease, but otherwise it is usually trouble-free.

Growing indoors You can grow a pot of mint indoors in winter. Root cuttings to start your mint plant. Potted mints don't need as much sun as some other indoor herbs, but good air circulation is crucial.

The plants will try to spread and may become pot-bound. To prevent this unpot the mint regularly, divide it and repot. Pinch the stems frequently so they don't become rangy.

Harvesting

Cut the sprigs frequently, beginning shortly after new growth emerges in spring. Shear the plants after they flower so they will produce new growth by autumn.

Storing Tie bunches of mint stems loosely and hang them to dry in a warm, airy spot. Store whole leaves in airtight containers. You can freeze leaves in well-sealed plastic bags.

Quick Tip

Aromatic choice
Visit a herb garden or garden centre specialising in herbs to see and smell a variety of mints so you can choose your favourites for your own garden. Foliage colour, shape and fragrance vary among the species.

Oregano

The intense aroma and unmistakable flavour of true oregano are invaluable for seasoning tomato-based dishes, roasted meat and vegetables. Oregano (*Origanum vulgare*) is a member of the marjoram family.

Sowing and planting

Soil Oregano needs both excellent drainage and good air circulation to thrive; moderate fertility is sufficient. Choose a site in full sun.

Greek oregano (*Origanum vulgare* subspecies *hirtum*) is a variety with a warm, spicy flavour, native to the Greek mountains.

Care

Watering If soil conditions are too wet, oregano will be subject to rot and fungal diseases. You should allow the top inch of the soil to dry out between waterings.

Pruning Snip the stems frequently to encourage branching and delay flowering. If desired you can cut all the stems to within 5cm (2in) of ground level in August to encourage fresh growth.

Dividing Over time, the plants will spread moderately by sending out runners. If you want to increase your planting of oregano, dig up and divide the plants in the autumn, or take stem cuttings in spring or autumn.

Winter care Oregano may survive the winter in pots placed on a sunny window sill with good air circulation.

You can use rooted stem cuttings to start oregano indoors.

Harvesting

Begin harvesting lightly as soon as the plants are about 15cm (6in) tall. The plants will flower in early summer. The best time to harvest leaves for drying is when the flower buds have set but are not yet open.

Storing Oregano is best used fresh. If you harvest it in the morning for use later that day, wash and refrigerate the stems or store the stems in a jar of water on your kitchen work surface.

To dry oregano hang bunches of stems in a warm, dry place. Don't strip the leaves from the stems. They will last longer if you store whole stems in glass containers in a dark place. Remove the leaves from the stems just before using.

PROBLEM SOLVER

Plants rot at the base. The soil is too damp and conditions are too cold. Choose a planting position in full sun and mix sharp sand into the soil to improve drainage.

PLANTING GUIDE

What to plant Potted plants; rooted cuttings, divisions.

Site preparation No special preparation needed.

When Potted plants in spring; divisions in autumn.

Spacing Set the plants 30cm (12in) apart.

How much One or two plants per person.

Quick Tip

Telltale scent

'Oregano' is applied to a range of plants, but some have nearly no aroma or flavour. At the garden centre, rub the leaves of any plant labelled oregano and inhale to check for scent. Greek oregano is the classic culinary oregano.

Thyme

English thyme (*Thymus vulgaris*), also called French thyme and common thyme, forms a low bushy mound with pink to purple flowers in midsummer. Thyme's sharp woodsy flavour and peppery aroma make it a favourite for meat and poultry dishes.

PLANTING GUIDE

What to plant Potted plants, rooted cuttings or seeds.

Site preparation No special preparation needed.

When Spring or summer.

Spacing Set plants 20–30cm (8–12in) apart.

How much One or two plants for culinary use; as desired in ornamental plantings.

Quick Tip

Other thymes
You can grow citrus thymes (*T. x citriodorus* and *T. pulegioides*) for culinary use, but their flavours are not as consistent as English thyme. Other species of thyme are used as low ground covers along pathways and in ornamental beds.

Sowing and planting

Soil A garden bed needs no special preparation before planting thyme, which grows fine in average soil. However, thyme must have good drainage, so plant it in a raised bed if possible. Thyme does best in full sun, but it will tolerate partial shade.

Care

Although it's a member of the mint family, thyme is not an aggressive grower. It is usually trouble-free, thriving even in dry conditions once it is established.

Replanting Over time, thyme plants become woody and scraggly. It's best to dig out plants every two years or so and replant new ones. Buy potted plants from a garden centre, or start your own by rooting cuttings from the original plants. Take cuttings in spring or early summer before plants bloom. Stick the cuttings in moist sand to root. Or dig and divide established plants in spring. Replant the most vigorous divisions and add the rest to your compost heap.

Winter care English thyme is reasonably hardy, but in cool areas use an airy mulch such as pine branches to help it overwinter.

It's possible to grow thyme indoors on a sunny windowsill during the winter. The best choice for this is lemon thyme (*T. x citriodorus*). Plant it in a pot or hanging basket or as a filler in a window-box planting. Feed potted thyme plants with a balanced liquid fertiliser twice a month.

Harvesting

Cut leafy stems as needed during the growing season. In early summer just before the plant blooms, make a full harvest by shearing the plant 5cm (2in) above ground level. The plant will resprout and can be cut again in the same manner in late summer.

Storing When you make a full harvest, gather stems in a bunch and put them in a paper bag, tip end down. Hang them to dry in a warm, airy place. Strip dried leaves from the stems. Store the leaves in an airtight container.

PROBLEM SOLVER

Straggly plants with dead centres. Thymes will generally deteriorate as they age so you wll need to divide or replace the plants every two or three years.

Sage

While not as showy as ornamental sages, culinary sage (*Salvia officinalis*) has beautiful grey-green, purplish or variegated foliage. Cooks treasure sage's pungent flavour as a seasoning for pork, stuffing, soup, egg dishes and sausage.

Sowing and planting

Soil Sage will need a position in full sun. It thrives in light, well-drained soil. Avoid heavy soil, or the plants may become diseased.

To start sage from seeds, sow them in containers indoors in early spring. When they grow to about 7.5cm (3in) high, harden them off, then transplant outdoors.

Varieties with grey-green leaves are the hardiest types. Variegated sages may suffer in cold, exposed gardens. In reasonably mild areas sage will be evergreen, but in cold gardens it will lose most of its leaves in winter.

Care

Watering Water the plants regularly only until they become established. Afterwards, sage prefers dry conditions and needs water only during drought.

Pruning After the first year cut sage plants back by one-half to two-thirds, after new growth begins to appear in the spring – this encourages tender growth. Fertilise at the same time, too.

Sage becomes straggly after three or four years. Take some cuttings each year in late spring and root them to renew your supply. You can also take cuttings in autumn to root for growing indoors in the winter.

Winter care In areas that are too cold for sage to overwinter safely, grow it in a container. When the season ends, move the container to a cool, protected spot and allow the plant to go dormant. Take it back outdoors the following spring.

Try growing a pot of sage on a sunny window sill indoors for a supply of fresh leaves in the winter. Compact varieties are best for indoor growing. If flowers form clip them off right away; if seeds form the plant may die.

Harvesting

Potted plants will be ready for harvest in the first year. If you have started plants from seeds, pinch the stem tips periodically to encourage branching; begin harvesting in the second year.

Cut the stems in early summer just before they bloom, taking 15–20cm (6–8in) of growth. You should harvest the plants only once in the first year. In subsequent years, you can harvest two or three times as regrowth allows.

Storing To dry sage tie stems in bunches and hang them in a warm place with good air circulation. Sage can become mouldy in the drying process. As you remove dried leaves from the stems, inspect them; discard any that are mouldy. You can also freeze fresh sage (see pages 118–19).

PLANTING GUIDE

What to plant Seeds, potted plants or rooted cuttings. Some varieties may not come true to type from seeds.

Site preparation No special soil preparation needed.

When Seedlings and potted plants in spring; rooted cuttings in summer.

Spacing Plant 45–60cm (18–24in) apart.

How much Start with two plants; increase your supply as needed by rooting cuttings.

BEST OF THE BUNCH

Note: These are attractive plants, but they are not as flavourful as culinary sage.
'Berggarten' Compact growth; reaches 30cm (12in) tall; blue-grey leaves.
'Tricolor' Broad leaves with green centres edged in purple or white.

Rosemary

A beautiful evergreen shrub, rosemary (*Rosemarinus officinalis*) has narrow, leathery leaves that are useful for seasoning meats, bean dishes, roast potatoes and in baking. Some varieties grow up to 180cm (6ft) tall in areas where they are hardy.

Sowing and planting

Soil Light, well-drained soil with full sun is best for rosemary. It will not overwinter successfully in cold, exposed areas.

Care

Watering Once established in the garden, water rosemary only during droughts. In most cases rosemary won't need any feeding. If plants are not thriving, dress with compost. If that helps, dress once every other year.

Cuttings Propagate rosemary by taking cuttings or by layering. Take 15-cm (6-in) cuttings from stem tips in late spring. After the cuttings root, plant them directly in the garden.

Gardeners in cold areas can take cuttings in late summer, root them and pot them for overwintering inside.

Growing rosemary indoors To succeed indoors, rosemary needs at least 4 hours of direct sun or 12 hours of artificial light daily. Plants do best with cool nights (about 13°C/55°F).

Rosemary doesn't like constantly moist soil conditions; however, if it dries out to the point of wilting, it probably won't recover. You should monitor the soil moisture of potted rosemary often. When the soil is moderately dry, water it thoroughly. If the leaves turn brown, it is a sign that the plant has been overwatered.

Harvesting

Snip leaves as needed for fresh use. To harvest rosemary for drying, cut stems back to a few inches above the point when growth has become woody. Don't cut more than one-quarter of the plant's growth at a time.

Storing Hang cut branches to dry in an airy spot, or spread stems to dry on racks. Strip dried leaves from stems and store them in airtight containers.

PLANTING GUIDE

What to plant Potted plants; rooted cuttings.

Site preparation No special preparation needed.

When Late spring through to autumn.

Spacing As periennials, set the plants 1.2m (4ft) apart; as annuals, set the plants 30–60cm (12–24in) apart.

How much One or more plants, depending on how fast they will normally grow.

BEST OF THE BUNCH

'Miss Jessopp's Upright' Strong, upright growth decked with pale plue flowers in early summer.

Temperature alert Rosemary is a tender perennial. Most varieties won't survive outdoors where winter temperatures drop below -15°C (5°F).

SWEET BAY

A tender perennial, sweet bay (*Laurus nobilis*) won't survive the winter in cold, exposed gardens. Plant young potted bays outdoors in moderately rich soil in full sun or partial shade. Once established, they need little watering. Indoors, treat bay the same as rosemary.

You should harvest the leaves as you need them or for drying. To dry bay leaves put them between two flat boards with weights on top for two weeks so that they dry flat. Store them in airtight containers.

French tarragon

The anise-flavored leaves of the shrubby perennial French tarragon (*Artemisia dracunculus*) help create memorable sauces, dressings and flavoured vinegars. Use this strongly flavoured herb sparingly, and add it to a dish towards the end of cooking.

PLANTING GUIDE

What to plant Potted plants or rooted cuttings.

Site preparation No special preparation needed.

When Spring or autumn.

Spacing Set 45–60cm (18–24in) apart.

How much One plant; increase your supply from cuttings or by division as needed.

Sowing and planting

Soil French tarragon will grow well in average soil in full sun or partial shade. However, excellent drainage is essential or the plant may rot. It may take two years for a plant to become fully established, so harvest lightly during the first year of growth.

French tarragon is a slightly tender plant, and it may not survive the winter in a cold, exposed garden. As an insurance policy, you can take cuttings in summer and pot them up to overwinter safely under cover. Russian tarragon is hardier than French tarragon and can be grown in colder areas. Grow it from seeds.

Care

Propagating This herb will need little special care. However, tarragon roots tangle and intertwine as they grow, and they will eventually choke themselves off. To keep your tarragon vigorous, dig and divide plants every two or three years.

You can also propagate tarragon from stem cuttings taken in late spring or summer. Snip 15-cm (6-in) lengths from the ends of stems, strip the lower leaves and stick the cuttings in a container of moist sand. Cuttings should root within four to six weeks and can be planted in the garden.

Cut the plants back in the autumn; the remaining foliage will die in the winter. You should mulch the roots in cold areas.

Harvesting

You can harvest small quantities of tarragon as needed. For established plants, cut all the stems when they reach about 25cm (10in) tall. Leave 5cm (2in) of growth intact at the base of the plants. The plants will resprout. You can make a second large harvest late in the season if you want.

Storing You can use tarragon fresh or freeze it (see pages 118–19). You can also dry tarragon, but it will probably lose some flavour during the drying process. Another way to preserve its flavour is by making tarragon vinegar (see page 123).

PROBLEM SOLVER

Powdery white coating on leaves. Powdery mildew is a fungal disease that is generally worse during cool, wet weather. Wait until the plants are dry; then thin their stems to help improve air circulation.

Quick Tip

Leaf alert
If you don't have a cold, exposed garden, be sure you buy the genuine French tarragon for the best flavour. Although Russian tarragon is hardier than the French type, it has an inferior flavour.

Marjoram

A type of oregano, the leaves of sweet marjoram (*Origanum majorana*) have a similar, but sweeter flavour. Marjoram is attractive in a flower garden or a hanging basket. The leaves are good for seasoning fish, meat, poultry and vegetable dishes.

PLANTING GUIDE

What to plant Transplants, rooted cuttings or potted plants.

Starting indoors Difficult because of low germination and slow growth.

Site preparation No special preparation needed.

When After last spring frost.

Spacing Allow 15–20cm (6–8in) between seedling clumps or plants.

How much One or two plants; several clumps of seedlings.

Quick Tip

Indoor success

Marjoram overwinters nicely as a potted plant on a sunny window sill. No matter where you garden, you can buy sweet marjoram once and, with proper management, enjoy it year after year.

Sowing and planting

Soil Sweet marjoram grows well in soil with low to moderate fertility, but it needs excellent drainage. Plant it in full sun and don't crowd the plants.

This plant is a tender perennial, grown as an annual or overwintered indoors. Pot marjoram (*Origanum onites*), a close relative, is hardier than sweet marjoram, but it does not have such a good flavour.

Raising transplants Raising your own sweet marjoram transplants can be challenging. Few of the seeds will germinate, and the tiny seedlings will grow slowly. You should sow the seeds about 8 to 12 weeks before the last expected spring frost date.

If you'd prefer an easier way to get started with marjoram, ask a friend for rooted cuttings, or buy a potted plant from a garden centre.

Care

Weeding and watering If you plant small transplants weed diligently until they become established. Weeds can easily choke the transplants.

Marjoram does not like constantly moist soil. Always allow the top inch of soil to dry out between waterings. However, if the plants start to wilt water them well.

Winter care After the first autumn frost, you should shear the sweet marjoram plants to 2.5cm (1in) tall. Dig them out of the garden and pot them to bring indoors.

An alternative to digging plants from the garden is to take cuttings in midsummer. The cuttings should root in about three weeks; plant the rooted cuttings in pots. Bring the pots indoors to overwinter. You can plant these new plants outdoors the following spring.

Harvesting

You can begin harvesting small sprigs of marjoram as required about six weeks after planting. You should trim the plants regularly to keep them from getting straggly.

Just before the flower buds form, shear the plant back to a few inches tall. In some areas plants may sprout enough new growth to provide a second harvest. Marjoram flowers are also edible.

Storing Dried marjoram retains its flavour well. Hang stems to dry in a warm, dark place. You can store it in airtight containers with the leaves still attached to stems. Strip the leaves from the stems as needed for use. You can also freeze marjoram leaves (see pages 118–19).

Chamomile

Delightful chamomile offers the choice of growing a perennial, an annual or both. Roman chamomile (*Chamaemelum nobile*) is a low-growing, spreading perennial; German chamomile (*Matricaria recutita*) grows as an upright annual.

<table>
<tr><td>

PLANTING GUIDE

What to plant *Roman chamomile* Potted plants or divisions. *German chamomile* Seeds.

Site preparation Prepare a fine seedbed for German chamomile.

When *Roman chamomile* In the spring. *German chamomile* In spring or autumn.

Spacing *Roman chamomile* Set the plants 30–45cm (12–18in) apart. *German chamomile* Thin the seedlings to about 15cm (6in) apart.

How much *Roman chamomile* Start with a few plants; increase by dividing. *German chamomile* Sow a 60x60-cm (24x24-in) area with seeds.

</td></tr>
</table>

Sowing and planting

Soil Roman chamomile generally does best in moist, humus-rich soil in full sun or light shade. You should spread a 12-mm (½-in) layer of compost over the soil and work it in before planting.

Sow German chamomile seeds in light, well-drained soil, in full sun. You should wait until soil temperatures are at least 13°C (55°F).

Care

Watering Water the plants to keep the soil moist; Roman chamomile will generally prefer slightly wetter conditions than German chamomile. Mulch the plants to suppress weeds.

Roman chamomile will spread to form a low-growing ground cover. Both plants are easy to grow and generally are pest-free.

Propagating To propagate Roman chamomile, you should divide the plants in spring and replant them 30–45cm (12–18in) apart.

German chamomile will self-sow if you leave a few flowers on the plant to dry and drop their seeds. However, don't leave too many flowers on the plants, or you may have so many seedlings that they will soon become a weed problem.

Harvesting

Cut chamomile flowers carefully when they are fully open. Pinch individual flowers off Roman chamomile; cut whole stems of German chamomile. Fresh flowers are edible and can be added to salad.

Storing You can spread the flowers on screens or sheets of paper to dry in a cool, airy place. Store dried flowers in sealed glass containers.

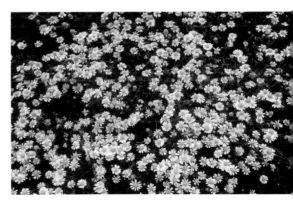

German chamomile (above) has a sweeter flavour than Roman chamomile (top left). The fragrant flowers are used as a tea.

Quick Tip

Fragrant lawn
Roman chamomile is used to make a lawn, and its sweet, fruity fragrance is released as you walk over it. Use the non-flowering variety 'Treneague' and keep the lawn area small – it is difficult to establish and keep free of weeds.

253

Parsley

Curly parsley (*Petroselinum crispum* var. *crispum*) is used as a garnish. Italian, or flat-leaved, parsley (*P. crispum* var. *neapolitanum*) has a tangy, sweet flavour. Parsley is a biennial, and it will grow well in a pot on a sunny window indoors, too.

Sowing and planting

Soil Rich, moist soil is best for parsley, in full sun or light shade. Loosen the soil; work 2.5cm (1in) of compost into the top several inches of soil.

Starting seeds To direct-sow seeds in the garden, try fluid sowing (see page 56). Or, before sowing seeds, soak them overnight in water or rinse them for a few hours in running water (put the seeds in a fine-mesh bag).

If starting seeds indoors keep the seed trays warm and cover them with damp newspaper or cling film. If the seeds don't germinate after two weeks, slip the tray into a plastic bag, seal it and put it in the freezer for two days. Transplant the seedlings when they are four to six weeks old; avoid damaging the taproot.

Sow the seeds from spring to late summer. Make successional sowings for a supply of vigorous plants. Mulch the plants with straw or protect with horticulatral fleece to overwinter for a spring harvest.

Care

Feed monthly with a balanced liquid fertiliser; keep the soil moist at all times.

Parsley flowers after two years. The flowers will attract a range of beneficial insects to the garden.

PROBLEM SOLVER

Stunted plants with reddish-orange leaves. Parsley is a member of the carrot family, and is subject to attack by carrot fly. Uproot and destroy affected plants. Do not grow carrots and parsley together.

Harvesting

Harvest the leaves when the plants are 15cm (6in) tall. Cut the stems about 2.5cm (1in) above the crown so the plants can produce more leaves.

Storing For short-term storage wash the leaves, blot dry and put them in a plastic bag in the refrigerator. To freeze leaves spread them on a baking sheet and put it in the freezer; place frozen leaves into freezer containers.

Curly parsley has frilly leaves that look pretty as an edging in a flower garden.

PLANTING GUIDE

What to plant Seeds or transplants.

Starting indoors Keep seeds warm (with soil temperature at 24°C/75°F) and moist.

Site preparation Loosen the soil to accommodate the taproot.

When Sow seeds outdoors when soil temperature is 10°C (50°F); sow indoors six to eight weeks before last spring frost.

Spacing Thin the seedlings to 7.5cm (3in) apart, then thin a second time to 20–25cm (8–10in) apart; allow about 20–25cm (8–10in) between the transplants.

How much Three to six plants per person.

BEST OF THE BUNCH

'Giant of Italy' Classic, flat-leaved variety with very tasty, large leaves.
'Moss Curled' An old favourite, this variety has very tightly curled, deep green foliage.

Coriander

Both the leaves and seeds of coriander (*Coriandum sativum*) are edible. The leaves, sometimes called cilantro, are cool and refreshing; the seeds have a citrus-like flavour. Both plant parts are desirable, and this is a popular herb worldwide.

PLANTING GUIDE

What to plant Seeds.

Site preparation Add organic matter to improve moisture-holding capacity.

When Sow seeds in spring and autumn; in cool areas sow in summertime, too.

Spacing Sow the seeds 5cm (2in) apart; thin the seedlings 15–20cm (6–8in) apart.

How much Up to 90cm (36in) of row per planting.

Planting

Soil Coriander grows well in average garden soil. Add some compost to increase moisture-holding capacity, but be sure the soil is well-drained.

If growing coriander for its seeds, choose an open, sunny position. Plants that are grown for their foliage will be happy in either a sunny or slightly shady spot.

Sowing Coriander prefers cool conditions. Sow the seeds in spring 2.5cm (1in) deep (presoak them if you want). Make successional sowings as desired every two weeks. When the weather turns hot, the plants will go to seed prematurely and offer a poor harvest of leaves. Successional sowings will ensure there are young plants coming on to replace them.

Care

Shield coriander plants over winter in a plastic tunnel. They may survive to produce an early spring harvest of leaves. Or try planting coriander in a pot to grow indoors on a sunny window sill or under lights.

Heat and long days will prompt the plants to form flower stalks. The flowers will attract beneficial insects, and if you leave some seed heads unharvested, the plants may self-sow.

Harvesting

You can begin clipping leaves when the plants are about 15cm (6in) tall. You should stop harvesting the leaves when newly sprouted leaves are feathery looking and the plants start to grow taller.

As the flower heads set seeds, the fresh seeds will smell and taste bad. However, when the seeds begin to dry out, the flavour and aroma are transformed. By the time seed heads are ready to harvest, the unpleasant smell should disappear. Cut coriander seed heads after they turn brown.

Storing Fresh coriander leaves are the most desirable. For short-term storage wash the leaves, pat them dry and store them in plastic bags for up to five days in the refrigerator.

To dry leaves put them loosely in a paper bag and place in a refrigerator for one month. The leaves will dry inside the bag, but remain fairly green and aromatic. You can also freeze the leaves (see pages 118–19).

You can dry the seed heads in a warm, airy place. Hang them upside down over a sheet, or hang them enclosed in paper bags to catch the seeds as they drop. If the seeds don't drop on their own, rub the seed heads gently between your palms. Store the seeds in airtight jars.

Dill

An annual herb, dill (*Anethum graveolens*) produces a stem clothed with lovely feathery leaves, and compact varieties are available, too. Use dill leaves in salads and fish and potato dishes. Dill seeds are a crucial ingredient in pickling spices.

PLANTING GUIDE

What to plant Seeds.

Site preparation Boost organic matter content of poor soil.

When Spring to midsummer.

Spacing Sow the seeds lightly in rows 25cm (10in) apart, or sow randomly in a patch of desired size; thin the seedlings to 25cm (10in) apart. However, space the rows 60cm (24in) apart if growing to harvest seed heads.

How much Up to 10 seeds per sowing in the garden; two to three seeds per pot.

BEST OF THE BUNCH

'**Fernleaf**' Compact; good for containers and in flower gardens.
'**Dukat**' Produces plentiful foliage before setting seeds; excellent foliage flavour; 25-cm (10-in) seed heads.
'**Mammoth**' Vigorous and matures to seed quickly.

Sowing and planting

Soil Dill prefers a rich, well-drained soil. Choose a site that is in full sun but sheltered from wind. If you are planting in a new garden that is sandy or low in fertility, spread a 2.5-cm (1-in) layer of compost on the planting area and work it into the soil. You should avoid planting dill in clay soil; the roots may rot.

Sowing Begin sowing seeds in early spring when the soil is dry enough to work. Sow small quantities and make repeat sowings at two- to three-week intervals to extend the foliage harvest (dill plants can go to seed quickly).

If you plant dill in pots, sow two pots and stagger planting dates by about two weeks. You can harvest leaves from one pot, then harvest from the other while the first one regrows.

After the first year, dill will usually self-sow. Seedlings are not easy to transplant, so sow *in situ* or use peat pots for minimal root disturbance.

Care

Dill likes moist conditions, so check the soil moisture regularly. If you have mulched round the plants, they will need less watering. If not mulched, dill may need watering twice a week in dry weather. Water at soil level to avoid wetting the foliage. Stake tall plants that seem at risk of falling or blowing over.

In containers pull out dill plants as soon as they begin to look fatigued. Afterwards, you can sow fresh seeds.

Harvesting

Dill is usually ready to harvest two months after sowing, but you can snip individual leaves earlier. Take your main harvest before the plants flower.

To harvest dill seeds, cut off the seed heads as soon as seeds turn light brown or start falling. Handle them gently to avoid knocking seeds loose. You should leave one seed head uncut so the plants will self-sow.

Storing Dill leaves remain fresh for a few days in the refrigerator. Stick the stems in a jar of water and cover the leafy tops with a plastic bag.

Hang leafy stems to dry in a cool shaded spot. Strip dry leaves from the stems and store in airtight containers.

Leaves wrapped in aluminium foil or resealable plastic bags will keep well in the freezer up to a month, or freeze in ice cubes (see pages 118–19).

Hang seed heads upside down in paper bags, or with a sheet spread below the heads to catch the seeds. Seeds separate easily from heads when dry; store them in airtight containers.

Fennel

The threadlike leaves of fennel (*Foeniculum vulgare*) have a liquorice flavour that enhances fish, cheese, eggs, beans, rice and other dishes. Gardeners also harvest the small, liquorice-flavoured seeds to use in cakes, biscuits and Asian cooking.

Sowing and planting

Soil Fennel prefers full sun, good drainage and soil with moderate to high humus. If your site is low in organic matter, spread 2.5–5cm (1–2in) of compost and work it into the soil before planting.

Fennel is a hardy perennial, but you can also grow it as an annual. Sow individual seeds lightly in the area where you want the plants to grow. Keep the seedbed moist, and thin the seedlings as needed.

Care

Fennel likes moist conditions, but don't keep the soil too wet or the plants may rot. Stake the plants when they reach about 45cm (18in) tall to protect them from flopping over when in flower.

Harvesting

You can start snipping leaf tips for fresh use when the plants grow to about 15cm (6in) tall. You should cut the leafy stems for freezing before the plants bloom.

If you plan to harvest the seeds, watch the seed heads carefully; you should harvest them as soon as the seed colour changes from green to brown. Make sure you handle the seed heads carefully – fennel will self-sow, and self-sown seedlings can become a weed problem. To avoid accidental sowing of seeds at harvest time, hold a paper bag open below a seed head and snip it so that the head drops directly into the bag.

Storing Store leafy stems in the refrigerator for up to a week with the stems in water and a plastic bag over the leaves.

Fennel foliage is not easy to dry; freezing in ice-cube trays is a better choice (see pages 118–19). Or store the leaves wrapped in aluminium foil or in small resealable plastic bags for about one month in the freezer.

For seed heads, place them in paper bags in a warm, dry place so that the seeds can dry completely. Store the seeds in airtight containers.

Florence fennel (see page 203) has an aniseed-flavoured foliage that can be used as a herb.

PLANTING GUIDE

What to plant Seeds.

Site preparation Add organic matter, if needed.

When Late spring or early summer.

Spacing Sow the seeds lightly over the planting area; thin the seedlings 25–30cm (10–12in) apart.

How much One to two plants for culinary use; as desired in ornamental gardens.

Quick Tip

Ornamental style

With its grand size, soft foliage and umbrella-shaped clusters of flowers, fennel is a wonderful choice for a background plant in an ornamental border. Bronze fennel, which has a coppery tinge to the foliage, is especially attractive.

Summer savory

The leaves of summer savory (*Satureja hortensis*) have a peppery taste akin to thyme. Summer savory is a great addition to egg dishes and soups, and it is also an excellent choice for flavouring stir-fries of mild vegetables such as summer squash.

Sowing and planting

Soil Summer savory will thrive in average, well-drained soil. However, it requires full sun.

Sowing Always sow fresh seeds, because the seeds lose their potency quickly. Scatter the seeds on top of the soil or in a shallow drill. Lightly cover them with fine soil or potting compost. If kept moist the seeds should germinate in less than a week.

Care

Summer savory is generally trouble-free, but keep the young plants moist until they are established. Be sure to thin seedlings to the recommended spacing, because crowded plants may develop disease.

Clearing up Summer savory is an annual and will die back at the end of the season. Uproot any remaining stems after they are killed by frost. If you allow the flowers to go to seed, summer savory may self-sow.

Harvesting

Cut sprigs from the plants as needed, beginning about six weeks after the seedlings emerge. Before summer savory flowers, make sure you harvest some of the leaves. You can make a large cutting before the plants bloom in midsummer. If you cut them about 7.5–10cm (3–4in) above the soil level, the stems will resprout.

Cutting the stems may delay flowering. However, once the plants bloom, they serve as a wonderfully fragrant filler for flower arrangements.

Storing You can hang bundles of stems to dry in an airy place. Strip the dry leaves from the stems and store them in airtight containers.

Cut sprigs of summer savory when the plants are at least 15cm (6in) long. They are often used to flavour bean dishes.

PLANTING GUIDE

What to plant Seeds.

Site preparation Prepare a fine seedbed.

When Sow the seeds in spring and early summer.

Spacing Sow the seeds lightly; thin the seedlings to 20–30cm (8–12in) apart.

How much Two or three plants for fresh use; plant more if planning to dry the leaves or for companion planting.

Quick Tip

Winter relative

Summer savory's cousin, winter savory (*Satureja montana*), is a low-growing, hardy, evergreen shrub. Its flavour is not as refined as that of summer savory, but it is still a useful herb that is available all year round.

Basil

Fresh basil (*Ocimum basilicum*) is a favourite herb for many gardeners. It is appreciated for its flavour and aroma, as a companion plant in the vegetable garden, and for its lovely foliage colours and forms in ornamental plantings.

Sowing and planting

Soil Basil needs rich, moist, well-drained soil. If the soil is sandy or low in organic matter, work a 2.5-cm (1–in) layer of compost into the soil.

Plant basil in full sun. In all but the warmest areas, you should sow seeds in a greenhouse or propagator for transplanting. If sowing in the garden, wait until the soil is 15.5°C (60°F).

Transplants Set out transplants in late spring or early summer. Basil does well in a container on a warm patio; you can also make sowings in summer to grow in pots on a sunny window sill indoors to extend the season into autumn and winter.

Care

Watering and feeding Keep the soil moist. When the soil is warm, mulch to conserve moisture. In midsummer apply a high-nitrogen organic fertiliser, or feed monthly with a liquid fertiliser.

If you're growing tall varieties on a windy site, stake plants to prevent them from blowing over.

Planting indoors For best results, use dwarf types and put them under supplementary light. Don't harvest too heavily, but pinch the stem tips often to prevent flowers from forming.

Harvesting

Begin pinching stem tips when plants are 15cm (6in) tall to promote leaf production. Every two weeks, cut stems just above a leaf node. Don't remove more than one-third of a plant's foliage at one time. If plants go to flower cut them back by one-third; they may resprout tender leaves.

Storing Store fresh, leafy stems in a jar of water (unrefrigerated) for up to one week; change the water daily.

You can freeze leaves in resealable plastic bags. Freeze them in a flat layer so you can break off pieces as needed.

PROBLEM SOLVER

Large holes in leaves. Slugs and snails have been enjoying night–time feedings at the expense of your plants. You should hand-pick and destroy them, or put out slug traps. As a deterrent, you can surround the plants with a band of sharp sand, crushed eggshells or diatomaceous earth.

Plants drop leaves or wilt suddenly. These symptoms generally occur in basil plants when they are either overwatered or underwatered. Make sure you monitor the soil moisture carefully at all times, especially during hot spells, and keep the soil just moist for the best results.

PLANTING GUIDE

What to plant Seeds; transplants.

Starting indoors Sow seeds four to six weeks before the last expected spring frost.

Site preparation Add compost to poor or sandy soils.

When After all danger of frost is past.

Spacing Set the plants or thin the seedlings to 30cm (12in) apart, dwarf types to 15–20cm (6–8in) apart.

How much Up to six plants per person – but dwarf types produce less than large-leaved types.

Temperature alert
Basil can't withstand frost, and even a spell of cool temperatures well above freezing can slow growth and stunt the plants.

Types of basil

Basil may have smooth, crinkled or ruffled leaves, and the foliage may be green or purple. Try mixing and matching the wide range of variations available to create a new twist for your favourite recipes.

▶ **Thai basil**

Thai basil has a delicate clove flavour and scent. It tends to be more compact than other basils, with thinner, smaller leaves. 'Siam Queen' is a popular variety.

▲ **Italian basil**

Classic varieties such as 'Genovese', 'Italian Large Leaf' and 'Lettuce Leaved' are widely grown for use in pesto and tomato-based sauces. Some varieties have smooth, green leaves; others have crinkly foliage. The flowers, which most gardeners discourage, are white. All basil flowers will attract bees.

▶ **Purple basil**

'Purple Ruffles', 'Red Rubin' and other purple varieties have gorgeous purple leaves, and their flowers are usually pink or lavender. Purple basils are attractive additions to flower gardens, and they add a beautiful accent to salads. In general, purple basils are not quite as vigorous as the green-leaved basils. Some have purple stems as well as purple foliage.

◄ **Dwarf basil**

These compact varieties can grow up to 30cm (12in) tall and have small leaves. The plants form a tight globe of foliage. Varieties such as 'Spicy Globe' and 'Fine Green' (also called 'Fino Verde') are good for tucking into small spaces, containers and window boxes. You can try dwarf basil as an edging plant for a flower bed.

► **Scented basils**

Scented basils include plants with cinnamon, lemon, lime, liquorice and other flavours infused with the taste and aroma of basil. Holy basil (*Ocimum sanctum*) has a strong camphor scent. Lemon basil (*O. x citriodorum*) has small leaves and grows to about 38cm (15in) tall.

15 Permanent plantings

Reserve a section of your garden for crops that need a permanent home. Asparagus and rhubarb are perennials that will resprout each spring, producing delicious stems for harvests that may span two decades or more. Although Jerusalem artichoke and horseradish are underground crops that can be planted each year in a new spot, most gardeners choose to give these crops a permanent home because it makes for easy replanting and keeps their potentially invasive nature under control.

Artichokes are beautiful perennials with decorative, silver-green foliage and shapely flower heads.

Asparagus

Succulent asparagus spears await gardeners who invest time and space in an asparagus patch. This long-lived perennial produces fernlike fronds after the harvest, providing an attractive backdrop when grown at the back of a bed.

Sowing and planting

The preceding autumn, test the soil pH; it should be between 6.5 and 7.5. Loosen the soil 30cm (12in) deep, and dig a 2.5–5-cm (1–2-in) layer of weed-free compost into the top several inches of soil.

Choose a spot with well-drained soil: on heavy soils make a raised bed to improve drainage. The site should be protected from wind to help prevent the tall fronds blowing over.

Seeds or crowns Asparagus plants started from seeds produce more than those planted as crowns. However, germination is difficult, and slow-growing seedlings are easily taken over by weeds. You'll have better success with crowns from mail-order suppliers or garden centres.

Planting crowns Shallow planting produces equal or better results than crowns planted 30cm (12in) deep. Soak the crowns in water or compost tea for 20 minutes before planting. Dig a trench, form mounds of soil (or mixed soil and compost) in it, then drape the crowns over the mound. Cover the crowns with a few inches of soil. As stalks poke up through the soil, add more soil, leaving the tips of the stalks exposed.

Spacing considerations You can fit a larger number of crowns in a wide trench by staggering two rows of crowns in it.

PLANTING GUIDE

What to plant One-year-old crowns (look for plump roots).

Site preparation Loosen the soil the preceding autumn; if the soil drains poorly, prepare a raised bed for planting.

When Plant the crowns in early spring.

Spacing Allow 45–60cm (18–24in) between crowns and 0.9–1.2m (3–4ft) between rows.

Intensive spacing Stagger two rows of crowns in a 60-cm (24-in)-wide trench; allow 60cm (24in) between crowns in the row.

How much Five crowns per person for fresh eating; double that if also freezing.

Temperature alert
Check the bed twice a day when it is hot – asparagus shoots that were too short to cut in the morning can be ready by late afternoon.

To plant asparagus crowns dig a shallow trench 10–20cm (4–8in) deep and at least 30cm (12in) wide.

Shape a small mound of soil, position the crowns, then spread their roots so that they radiate out in all directions; top with soil.

Care

Watering Drip irrigation is the best watering method for the first two years after planting the crowns. Make sure the bed receives 2.5cm (1in) of water a week during the summer. After that, an established stand is self-sufficient.

Mulch A mulch will suppress weeds and retain moisture. It also helps to ensure long, straight spears. Apply a 5-cm (2-in) layer of chopped leaves or finely shredded bark. Renew the mulch every autumn.

Weeding You should weed often while the stand becomes established. Hand-weeding is preferable because cultivating tools can damage the asparagus roots and the shoots just below the soil surface.

Asparagus produces separate male and female plants; male plants are the most desirable. The spears of male plants tend to be thicker, and the plants do not produce berries, which self-seed. Self-sown seedlings will never develop into worthwhile plants, so you should pull them out. Many suppliers sell "all-male" varieties.

Feeding Fertilise the stand in early spring and again after harvest ends to stimulate fern growth. Side-dress with compost or an organic fertiliser (analysis 4-5-4 or similar) at 0.9kg per 9.3sq m (2lb per 100sq ft).

Motherstalk method With this approach, allow one of the first spears from each crown to produce ferny foliage. The frond will feed the crown throughout harvest, which can lengthen the harvest period. Do not allow the plants to suffer moisture stress during harvest.

Cut off the stems with a thin, sharp knife just below ground level, but avoid damaging the emerging spears.

Autumn and winter care Once the harvest period is over, leave the fronds to grow and build up the roots. Continue to remove all weeds and self-sown seedlings. When the fronds turn yellow in late autumn, cut them down to about 2.5cm (1in). Apply a thick layer of well-rotted compost over the bed in late winter.

Harvesting

Wait until the crowns have been in the ground for two years before harvesting to allow strong plants to build up. Cutting spears earlier can weaken the plants and prevent them achieving their full potential. In the third year after planting, harvest before the bracts on the spear tips start to open, when the spears are about 15cm (6in) tall. Harvest every other day, or even twice daily in hot weather.

End cutting in mid-June to allow the ferns to develop and build up the plants' reserves for future years. Royal Ascot week is a useful reminder that it's time to end the harvest.

Storing After cutting the spears, cool them quickly. Asparagus is best the day of harvest, but you can refrigerate it for five days (see pages 114–15).

PROBLEM SOLVER

Chewed areas on spears, brown insect eggs on spears. Asparagus beetles chew on spears and foliage. The beetles are long and black, with orange markings on their backs. Hand-pick and destroy them (they often fall to the ground when the fronds are disturbed, making this a difficult job). Prevent beetles overwintering by destroying fern fronds as soon as they die back in autumn. Cover the bed with horticultural fleece to prevent beetles from reaching the spears early in spring.

Needles turn yellow. Asparagus rust can cause this problem. Look closely for red-brown spots on the leaves. Cut and destroy affected foliage. Plant your stand at a wide spacing to prevent diseases.

Fronds yellow and die back; roots covered with purple, feltlike mould. Violet root rot attacks asparagus plants; remove affected plants and all traces of their roots and the soil round them promptly; burn plant debris. Even so, the disease can spread to other plants in the bed; there is no treatment, so all affected plants must be destroyed. Make a new bed in clean soil elsewhere. Do not grow asparagus, celery or root crops in the affected area for four years.

BEST OF THE BUNCH

'Connover's Colossal' A well-established old favourite, still reliable even though not an all-male variety.
'Franklim' Large, good quality spears giving a heavy crop. All-male variety.
'Jersey Knight' An all-male cultivar with green spears that have purple spear tips. Vigorous grower that is disease resistant; it generally does well in heavy soil.
'Purple Passion' Not an all-male variety; however, it is a vigorous plant that produces large purple spears, which have a sweet flavour; the spears turn green when cooked.

Globe artichoke

Sculptured foliage, unusual flower stalks and attractive flowers make globe artichokes a fine candidate for an ornamental flower garden, as well as the vegetable garden. However, the unopened flower buds are appreciated by food lovers.

Sowing and planting

Loosen the soil to 30cm (12in) deep. Remove all perennial weeds (including roots). Spread a 15-cm (6-in) layer of compost and work it into the soil.

Planting offsets and container plants Spring planting is best, but you can plant whenever offsets or container plants are available at your local nurseries. Set the offsets with the crown just at soil level.

Starting seedlings The seeds will germinate best between 21–26.5°C (70–80°F). As the seedlings develop, cull out stunted or albino plants (artichoke seeds are not always uniform). After the first true leaves emerge, move the seedlings into individual 10-cm (4-in) pots and transplant them into their growing positions in early summer.

Growing artichokes as a annual crop This is an experimental method which has been tried in regions of the USA where plants can be provided with at least 90 frost-free growing days. Plants are raised from seed early in the year and then tricked into reacting as if they've lived through a winter, which helps them produce flower buds in one season. There are

two methods by which this can be done. One way is to refrigerate seeds for two weeks before sowing. An even more effective method is to place potted seedlings outdoors in a frame or other sheltered spot as soon as possible, when temperatures are still below 10°C (50°F) for part of each day, but to bring them back under cover if frost threatens. Transplant the seedlings to their cropping positions after all danger of frost is past.

Care

Watering Artichoke plants wilt dramatically when they're moisture-stressed. However, the foliage will recover after watering. Water well if dry spells occur during the active growth periods.

Feeding Make sure you feed both annual and perennial plantings monthly during their active growth, giving them a balanced liquid or organic fertiliser.

Care after harvest During the growing season keep the plants watered as necessary and free from weeds. In late autumn, when the leaves die back, you can either cut back the dead stems and foliage or leave them in place to provide a little winter protection for the plant.

PLANTING GUIDE

What to plant Seeds, offsets or container plants.

Starting indoors Start the seeds in early to mid-spring

Site preparation Work the soil to a depth of 30cm (12in), making sure you remove all weeds; add plenty of organic matter.

When Plant in spring and early summer.

Spacing Set the plants about 0.9–1.2m (3–4ft) apart.

How much Two to four plants per person.

Temperature alert
In most areas of Britain, artichoke plants need some protection to see them safely through the winter, especially young plants.

If the stems are removed, heap dry leaves, straw or other loose mulch over the crown to protect it.

Taking offsets In spring established plants will throw up several suckers, and you can remove these as offsets to grow on as new plants. Scrape the soil away from the base of the plant and cut the offset away with a sharp knife, keeeping as many roots intact as possible. Replant the offset firmly and keep it well watered until established.

Choose the heaviest-cropping plants to take the offsets from. For the best quality crops, replace artichoke plants after three or four years. Taking offsets each year will ensure you have a supply of new plants for replacements.

Harvesting

For the best crops from perennial plants, allow artichokes to build up their strength in the first year of planting by removing the flower buds that form as soon as you see them. From their second year, the heads will be produced between early and late summer.

Cut the flower buds when the scales are still tight and waxy, just as the tips of the scales at the base of the bud begin to lift. Use a sharp knife to cut through the stem 2.5–5cm (1–2in) below the bud. (The stems are edible, too.) Mature plants will grown several flower stalks a season, with a number of flower buds on each stalk.

If you allow buds to go to flower, you will inhibit production of more buds. However, if you like artichoke flowers for flower arrangements, for attracting bees and butterflies or simply for their beauty, you can grow one plant as your supply for flowers.

Storing Globe artichokes are best eaten right after picking, but you can store them in the refrigerator for up to two weeks.

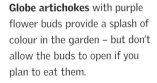

Globe artichokes with purple flower buds provide a splash of colour in the garden – but don't allow the buds to open if you plan to eat them.

PROBLEM SOLVER

Black or green insects on plants. These aphids spread viral diseases that can ruin your crop. Spray plants with a strong stream of water to wash them off. Spray seriously infested plants with insecticidal soap.

Young shoots eaten, with slimy trails. Slugs and snails may damage young shoots when they emerge in spring, especially in damp weather. Deter them with a band of sharp sand, crushed eggshell or diatomaceous earth round the plants, or use other control measures (see page 105).

Brown spots on buds; heads then shrivel and rot. This is petal blight, a fungus disease caused by botrytis. To prevent its spread, remove and destroy infected buds promptly, along with any other dead and dying plant material

---

BEST OF THE BUNCH

'Green Globe Improved' Heavy producer, best for perennial plantings.
'Violet de Provence' Similar to 'Green Globe Improved' but with attractive purple flower heads of a more elongated shape. Good flavour.
'Violetta' Rich purple buds; spineless plants; good for either annual or perennial plantings.

Horseradish

One horseradish root is all that's needed in most gardens to provide a satisfactory supply of this pungent ingredient for condiments and sauces. Choose a site for horseradish carefully. If it wanders uncontrolled you'll have a weed problem.

Sowing and planting

The preceding autumn dig an 45-cm (18-in)-deep hole for one plant. Add several litres (a few gallons) of compost or rotted manure to the bottom of the hole, then return the soil. Mark the prepared spot so you can find it in the spring.

Getting started You can order a root from a commercial source or buy it at a local garden centre. Or you can accept a root from a friend who already has horseradish. Choose a slender straight root that is about 20cm (8in) long.

Open the planting hole and set the root in place either vertically or on a 45-degree angle, narrow end down, with the root 5–7.5cm (2–3in) below soil level. Fill in the hole and water the planting well.

Care

Water early on if the soil is dry. Don't fertilise unless growth seems sluggish; avoid a high-nitrogen fertiliser. You should watch the adjacent beds to make sure stray plants do not emerge. Pest and disease problems are rare.

Keeping your stand going The easy way to perpetuate a horseradish stand is to allow a few side roots to remain in the soil when you harvest the main roots in late autumn. Or dig out all the roots and cut side roots from main roots. Replant the side roots immediately or store them in sand in a root cellar or in a plastic bag in the refrigerator. Replant the stored roots in early spring.

Replant horseradish in the same spot each year to reduce the chance of stray roots left in the soil sprouting round the garden. Alternatively, you can plant the root in a bottomless container sunk into the soil.

Harvesting

After a few fall frosts, dig up the main roots, which may be 5cm (2in) wide. Cut off the side roots. Keep or replant the side roots as needed; discard the rest (but not in a compost pile, where they can root). To extend harvest into winter, leave some main roots in place and mulch them well.

You can leave horseradish in the garden through winter and harvest in early spring. Avoid harvesting horseradish roots after shoot growth starts, because flavour will be poor when the plants are actively growing.

Storing Let the harvested roots dry for a few days. Store them in either the refrigerator or a root cellar; grate or grind roots as needed.

PLANTING GUIDE

What to plant Root cuttings.

Site preparation Work the soil at least 30cm (12in) deep and add organic matter.

When Early spring.

Spacing Set roots at least 30cm (12in) apart.

How much A single root may be all you need; don't overplant.

Temperature alert
Wait until there have been a few hard frosts before lifting horseradish roots. If harvested before a frost, they will not have developed their full, pungent flavour.

Jerusalem artichoke

Italian gardeners gave this North American member of the sunflower family the name *girasole* (sunflower), which led to the name Jerusalem artichoke. This crop produces tubers with a nutty flavour and crisp texture similar to water chestnuts.

Sowing and planting

Jerusalem artichokes grow best in rich sandy loam, but they can thrive in clay or sandy soils with sufficient organic matter. Spread a 5–15cm (2–6in) layer of compost and work it into the soil.

Jerusalem artichoke is an annual, but the tubers survive in the soil over winter and will come up year after year unless you remove every last tiny portion of root from the ground – they are extremely invasive.

Jerusalem artichokes are knobbly and rather difficult to clean; the variety 'Fuseau' is a smoother, more regular shape. There are one or two other named varieties available from specialist suppliers, but if you can't find them, you can grow plants perfectly well from tubers bought at the local greengrocers.

It's easiest to plant whole tubers. If you cut tubers into pieces, be sure each piece has at least one eye, and plant the pieces immediately after cutting. Set the tubers 7.5–10cm (3–4in) deep.

The plants are vigorous, so plant this crop in the same spot each year. It will be easier to see any 'escaped' sprouts and uproot them. Alternatively, you can dig a 15–30-cm (6–12-in)-deep trench round the planting and line it with a vertical root barrier made of metal or heavy plastic.

Care

Water the young plants until they're established, and mulch to conserve soil moisture. Once the plants are growing strongly, they will shade out weeds and be self-sufficient. In general, don't fertilise the plants or their growth may be too rampant. Pest and disease problems are rare.

Harvesting

After a frost dig through the patch, starting 0.9m (3ft) away from the base of the plants to ensure you don't miss far-flung tubers. Tubers have tender skin, so handle them gently.

Jerusalem artichokes are tasty baked, boiled, pickled or sliced raw in salads. You can put cut slices in a mild vinegar or lemon juice solution to prevent them from browning.

Jerusalem artichokes are known for causing flatulence, due to the inulin they contain. However, most people find that this side effect lessens when they eat artichokes regularly.

Storing Put the tubers into cold, moist storage straight away in a root cellar or in plastic bags in the refrigerator. Or leave the tubers in the soil and dig them as needed through the winter. In cold areas, mulch to prevent the bed from freezing solid.

PLANTING GUIDE

What to plant Tubers.

Site preparation Dig the soil several inches deep and add organic matter.

When From early to late spring.

Spacing Set the tubers about 60cm (24in) apart, leaving 0.9–1.2m (3–4ft) between the rows..

How much One plant can yield 0.9–4.5kg (2–10lb) of tubers, depending on the soil fertility, weather conditions and variety.

Quick Tip

Diabetic treat

The tubers contain inulin instead of starch. Inulin is a carbohydrate that breaks down into fructose during digestion, and fructose is a type of sugar that diabetics can metabolise.

Rhubarb

The tart stems of rhubarb must be cooked – however, they are delicious when added to sweetened sauces and desserts. The arching stems and large fanlike leaves add drama equally well to vegetable gardens or perennial flower beds.

Sowing and planting

Loosen the soil in the planting area about 25cm (10in) deep. Spread 7.5–10cm (3–4in) of compost or rotted manure over the area and work it into the soil. Alternatively, dig individual planting holes 30cm (12in) deep. Mix the removed soil from each hole with about 13.5 litres (3gal) of compost or well-rotted manure. Refill the hole with the mix.

Planting divisions You should set the divisions so that the buds are no more than 5cm (2in) below the soil surface. If you're concerned about wet soil conditions, create planting mounds raised about 15cm (6in) above the surrounding soil. Set the divisions in the mounds so that the buds are just below the soil surface.

Forcing rhubarb The delicate pink, exceptionally tender stems of forced rhubarb are a delicious winter treat. For the earliest crop, lift the crowns in late autumn and plant them in a large box, completely covering them with moist soil. Exclude all light by covering the boxes with black plastic or a similar material, and keep the crowns in a steady temperature of 7–13°C (45–55°F). They will start producing shoots in five or six weeks. For later crops, force crowns *in situ* in

the garden by covering them with a loose, dry mulch of straw or leaves, with an upturned bucket or a large clay pot to exclude light.

Care

After the stems emerge, lay 7.5–10cm (3–4in) of clean straw, compost or chopped leaves round the plants. When temperatures are over 26.5°C (80°F), keep rhubarb well watered but not soggy. Feed the plants in spring with compost and in midsummer with a balanced fertiliser.

Fall and winter care Clear away all stalks and leaves in autumn to prevent disease organisms from overwintering. After the soil freezes, cover the crowns with 5–7.5cm (2–3in) of straw mulch. Remove half the mulch in spring before new growth emerges.

Dividing The crowns may be ready to divide three years after planting. If plants aren't divided they may decline and die within 10 years. Divide in spring before growth starts or in autumn after growth stops. Thrust a shovel into the soil next to the base of the plant and lever out the crown. Break the crown up into fist-size pieces. Each piece should have at least one bud and one large root piece. Replant them as soon as possible.

PLANTING GUIDE

What to plant Divisions or seeds.

Starting indoors Start seeds indoors in late winter for planting out in spring.

Site preparation Loosen the soil and add organic matter; choose a well-drained site.

When Plant divisions from autumn through to early spring.

Spacing Set the divisions 90–120cm (3–4ft) apart.

How much One plant per person.

Temperature alert
Rhubarb needs cold weather before it starts to grow. To force rhubarb, dig the crowns up in November and leave them on the soil, exposed to frosts for several days to help them produce early shoots.

Harvesting

Make sure you don't harvest any rhubarb stalks during the first year of growth. The following year, you can harvest a few stalks from each plant. Beginning the third year, you can harvest for two months, but don't remove more than one-half of the stalks at any one time.

To remove a stem grasp it with your hand and gently twist it, then snap it free at the base. Cut off the leaves and compost them (never eat rhubarb leaves – they contain oxalic acid, a toxin). When most of the emerging stalks are thin, it's time to stop picking for the year.

In the spring rhubarb plants may send up flower stalks. You can cut these off or allow them to bloom, especially if the rhubarb is in a flower bed. Remove the stalks before the seeds dry and fall. Allowing the plants to flower may leave an open spot at the centre of the crown. This allows the remaining buds more space to develop and reduces the need to divide the plants as often.

Storing Rinse the stems with water or wipe them clean with a moist cloth. Store stalks in perforated plastic bags in the refrigerator, where they will last for two weeks. You can also cut rhubarb stems into pieces for freezing.

Quick Tip

Sweet herb
Rhubarb has a tart flavour and normally needs lots of sugar to make it palatable. You can cut down the amount of sugar required by adding some chopped leaves of the herb sweet cicely to the rhubarb while it is cooking.

PROBLEM SOLVER

Sap on stems; stems decay. Rhubarb curculios do not usually cause serious damage, but if the plants are heavily infested, destroy them. Pull any dock plants nearby, because the larvae feed on dock and then pupate in the soil, producing the next generation of adults.

Plants don't leaf out, or they leaf out but then die back. This is a sign of crown rot, which is caused by a fungus. Dig out the plants and destroy them. Replant in a well-drained spot. Be sure to plant disease-free divisions.

For an early crop force dormant rhubarb in the garden by covering it with a large bucket.

Rhubarb grows vigorously and you will need to divide it periodically to avoid overcrowding.

BEST OF THE BUNCH

'Glaskin's Perpetual' Reliable from seeds; good crops of bright red stems.
'Stockbridge Arrow' Good for forcing for an early crop. Long, thick, tender, well-coloured stems of a good flavour.
'Victoria' Green stalks with rosy sheen at base; not stringy.

Glossary

acidic
With a pH value below 7.0.

alkaline
With a pH value above 7.0.

annual
A plant that germinates, flowers, sets seeds and dies within one season.

balanced fertiliser
A fertiliser that contains equal amounts of nitrogen, phosphorus and potassium – the three main plant nutrients.

bare root
A transplant that has been lifted from the open ground instead of grown in a container.

beneficial insects
Insects that pollinate garden crops or prey on or parasitise garden pests.

beneficial nematodes
i) Nematodes that prey on certain garden pests.
ii) Nematodes that help break down organic matter in the soil or compost heaps.

biological control
Using a naturally occuring organism to control a plant pest or disease. For example, red spider mites can be controlled by a predatory mite, *Phytoseiulus persimilis*, which eats the pest.

blanching
i) Growing a crop such as chicory in darkness to avoid bitterness and grow pale, tender shoots.
ii) Heat treatment of vegetables before freezing to prevent deterioration.

bolting
Premature flowering of vegetables such as lettuce usually making them unfit for eating.

brassica
A member of the cabbage family, botanically known as Brassicaceae or Cruciferae.

broadcast
Scattering over the soil in a random fashion; the term applies to seeds and fertilisers.

canker
A dead spot on a plant stem caused by a fungus or bacterium; a disease that is typified by formation of cankers.

cap
A hard crust that forms on the soil surface, usually after rain or watering.

catch crop
A fast-growing crop that can be grown in between two longer-term crops.

check
An interruption in the steady development of a plant, caused by adverse conditions such as cold weather.

clamp
A storage method for vegetables, often roots, which involves covering them with an insulating layer of straw and soil.

cloche
A small, movable row or plant cover used to warm soil or protect plants from cold or wind.

compost
i) The decomposed remains of plants and garden waste, used as a soil conditioner.
ii) A proprietary growing medium for plants in containers. Seed or sowing compost is suitable for raising seeds and cuttings, potting compost for growing on older plants and all-purpose compost for both uses. They contain different levels of fertiliser.

compound fertiliser
A fertiliser with more than one plant nutrient.

corm
A swollen, solid underground stem that resembles a bulb.

cotyledon
A seed leaf of an embryo plant; the first leaf or pair of leaves that develops. Cotyledons are usually a different shape and size to the 'true leaves' that follow.

cover crop
A crop sown to prevent soil erosion, suppress weeds and conserve soil moisture; sometimes synonymous with green manure crop.

crown
The junction of the roots and stems in some perennial plants. Asparagus and rhubarb are two vegetables that sprout from crowns.

curing
Placing harvested crops in specific temperature and humidity conditions for a length of time to prepare them for storage.

cut-and-come-again
A method of harvesting by cutting off plant parts just above the central growing point, so that plants will resprout and produce additional harvestable leaves or stems. This harvest technique is most commonly used with lettuce.

cuttings
Sections of plant stems, leaves or roots that are removed from a plant and induced to sprout roots and grow into a new plant.

damping off
A fungal disease that infects germinating seeds and seedlings, causing them to rot at soil level, topple over and die; it prefers cool, moist conditions. Damping off can rot seeds before they sprout.

deficiency
A lack of one or more of the nutrients essential to a plant's growth, shown by a variety of specific symptoms such as yellowing of the leaves between the veins or browning of leaf tips.

diatomaceous earth
A crystalline mineral product that can be scattered on the soil as a barrier against soft-bodied pests such as slugs and snails. It can also be sprinkled on plants so that the sharp edges of the particles pierce the insect's protective outer coverings, leading to dehydration and death.

dibber
A tool for making planting holes in the soil or planting compost.

divisions
Sections of perennials formed by pulling or cutting one plant apart into several pieces. Many perennial herbs can be separated into divisions, which can be replanted, eventually increasing the supply of the herb.

drip hose
A garden hose or a part of a drip irrigation system that has small holes or openings. When attached to a water source, drip hoses emit water slowly, providing even watering.

dormant
Alive but not actively growing or developing; in a state of suspended animation until the appropriate conditions for growth are present.

draw hoe
A hoe for making drills in the soil for sowing seeds, or for drawing up soil round plants.

drill
A long, shallow depression in the soil in which seeds are sown.

earthing up
Method involving pulling soil up round plants. This may be to stabilise the root system in the soil, so that the plant is less likely to be blown over or to protect the edible parts of the plant from light to improve their eating quality.

F1 hybrid
The first generation of plants resulting from a cross between two known parents.

fluid sowing
Sowing seeds suspended in a gel or similar fluid medium. This helps prevent the seeds and newly germinated seedlings from drying out and also helps space the seeds in the row.

foliar feeding
Applying fertiliser that can be taken up by the leaves of a plant as opposed to its roots. This is a quick way of supplying nutrients and is often used to apply trace elements to plants showing symptoms of a deficiency. The fertiliser must be specifically formulated for foliar feeding; normal fertilisers may scorch the leaves of plants if applied in this way.

forcing
Placing plants in a dark, sometimes warm position so that the resulting growth is pale and tender, without bitterness. Used for plants such as chicory and rhubarb.

frame
An area enclosed by walls and a transparent glass or plastic cover for plant protection; similar to a cloche but in a fixed position.

friable
Soil that is crumbly and worked to a fine, even texture, suitable for seeds or planting.

fungicide
A substance used to kill fungal diseases or prevent disease spores from germinating.

green manure
Plants that are grown to be dug into the soil to improve its fertility and structure. Leguminous plants are often used because of their ability to convert atmospheric nitrogen into a form that can be used by plants.

growing bags
Commercial sacks of compost in which vegetables can be grown from seeds to maturity. They are commonly used for vegetables such as tomatoes, sweet peppers and aubergines. Careful attention must be paid to watering because the small amount of compost in the bag is prone to drying out.

hand-picking
Removing garden pests from plants by hand or using implements such as tweezers or chopsticks. You can kill the pests by physical methods such as crushing them or dumping them into a bucket of soapy water.

harden off
To gradually accustom plants raised under cover (in a greenhouse, frame or indoors) to colder conditions in the open, preventing the change in conditions from checking growth.

heirloom variety
An open-pollinated, cultivated form of a plant that has been in cultivation for a long period of time (generally before 1940).

herbicide
A substance used to kill plant growth.

horticultural fleece
A lightweight synthetic fabric that allows a high proportion of sunlight, air and moisture to penetrate, but that provides protection from cold air temperature and wind; also called floating cloche. If properly sealed a fleece provides a physical barrier against insects.

hose-end dilutor
A hose attachment filled with a concentrated solution of fertiliser or other chemical. The solution is diluted to the correct application rate by the water flowing through the hose.

humus
Decomposed organic matter, which is a valuable addition to soil, improving its structure and capacity to hold water.

inoculant
A powder containing bacteria that interact with the roots of a leguminous plant (such as beans and peas) to enable nitrogen fixation to occur. Commercial inoculants are crop-specific.

insecticidal soap
A commercial formulation of fatty acids that can be diluted with water and sprayed on plants to kill some types of insect pests.

insecticide
A substance used to kill insects.

intensive planting
Setting crops more closely than the standard spacing recommendation for that crop, in order to make the best use of available space; it requires careful crop management and soil enriched with high levels of organic matter for a successful harvest.

larva(e)
Immature stage of an insect – for example, caterpillars are the larvae of moths and butterflies; grubs are the larvae of beetles.

leaf mould
Decomposed leaves from deciduous trees, which should be composted separately from other garden waste because they will take much longer to rot down.

legumes
Plants, such as peas and beans, belonging to the family Fabaceae. These plants have specialised roots that, in association with specific soil-dwelling bacteria, can convert atmospheric nitrogen into nitrate (a form of nitrogen that can be absorbed by the plant roots).

loam
Fertile soil consisting of a mixture of sand, clay, silt and organic matter.

maincrop
A crop that is produced through the main part of the growing season, as opposed to a crop that is produced particularly early or late in the season. Maincrop varieties are those varieties that will produce their crop through this part of the season.

micro-organism
A living organism that can be seen only with the aid of a microscope. In gardens particularly important micro-organisms are those that help to break down organic matter in the soil, and those that cause plant diseases – often fungi, bacteria or viruses.

mulch
A layer of organic or inorganic matter placed over the soil surface to protect it from cold, heat or wind or to retain soil moisture.

nematode
Microscopic, threadlike soil-dwelling animals. Some types cause disease-like symptoms in plants such as stunting and yellowing by parasitising plant roots. Other types are helpful to gardeners because they break down organic matter or are capable of parasitising plant pests.

nitrogen-fixing
The ability to convert atmospheric nitrogen into a useful form for plants. Nitrogen-fixing bacteria live in nodules on the roots of legume plants, which have this ability; they need less fertilising than many other crops.

NPK
An abbreviation for nitrogen, phosphorus and potassium, the major essential plant nutrients. A fertiliser pack that states 'N:P:K 7:7:7' means the fertiliser contains 7 per cent nitrogen, 7 per cent phosphorus and 7 per cent potassium. Generally, only the numbers are provided, but they are always in the order nitrogen, phosphorus and potassium.

open-pollinated
Plants produced from flowers that have been fertilised by those of the same variety in the field, not by hybrids that are a deliberate cross between two different varieties. The plants produced from open-pollinated varieties will be the same as their parents; hybrids produce a new variety, which will not breed true.

organic
i) Deriving from anything that has once been alive; usually applies to manures and composts that consist of decomposed plant or animal remains.
ii) A method or substance thought to do minimal ecological damage such as organic gardening, in which plants are grown without the use of chemical pesticides or fertilisers and in which the presence of beneficial insects and organisms are promoted, while soil fertility is maintained; an 'organic pesticide' is a pesticide of natural origin as opposed to a manufactured chemical.

organic matter
Soil additives and improvers of organic origin such as compost, leaf mould, farmyard manure, seaweed and spent hops.

overwinter
A method to keep tender plants through the winter in a dormant or protected state so that they will last through or survive the winter.

pan
A hard area some distance below the soil surface through which roots will find it difficult to penetrate. It often occurs when soil is cultivated to the same level for a number of years.

perennial
A plant that persists from year to year.

pH
The measure of acidity or alkalinity of soil. A reading of pH 7.0 is neutral: higher than pH 7.0 indicates alkalinity, while a reading lower than pH 7.0 indicates acidity.

photosynthesis
The process in which plants manufacture sugars from sunlight.

plant out
To transplant young plants raised under cover or indoors into a garden bed; also called set out. The plants may need to be hardened off.

plug plants
Commercially available seedlings that have been raised in individual soil blocks, ready for planting out.

pollination
The fertilisation of the female parts of a flower by the male pollen, necessary to form fruits or seeds. Pollination is often carried out by insects or wind, but sometimes it is carried out by gardeners to ensure a good crop.

pot up
To plant rooted cuttings or seedlings in individual pots.

plumule
The tip of the shoot as it emerges from the seed, protected by the cotyledons.

potager
A formal, decorative vegetable garden, usually on a small scale.

pricking out
Transplanting seedlings to a wider spacing shortly after germination, in order to give them room to develop.

propagator
Equipment used for raising seeds or cuttings, allowing you to control the conditions to give seedlings a better start. It usually consists of a tray or trays with plastic covers to maintain high humidity, and it may also provide a method for heating the soil.

radicle
The tip of the root as it emerges from a newly growing seed.

respiration
The process in which plants break down sugars for energy, using oxygen from the air and releasing carbon dioxide.

rhizome
An underground stem that often looks like a root. Weeds with rhizomes are difficult to control because any portion of rhizome left in the soil has the ability to grow new shoots and roots to make new plants.

rose
A plastic or metal fitting for a watering can spout or hose that has small holes to break up the water into droplets. A 'fine' rose has the smallest holes and gives the lightest spray, and you should use one for delicate plants such as young seedlings.

rotation
Moving groups of crops to a new position in the vegetable garden each year to avoid the build-up of specific pests and diseases and to avoid the depletion of specific soil nutrients.

root cellar
An underground or partially underground insulated area that remains consistently cool, designed for storing food crops.

rosette
A cluster of leaves that sprout from a central point and radiate in all directions.

self-sow
To grow from seeds that were distributed naturally in the garden from the seed stalks of plants already growing.

set out
See plant out.

side-dress
To apply fertiliser in a band to the soil surface alongside growing crops.

slow-release fertiliser
A fertiliser that will release its nutrients gradually over a long season instead of all at the same time. The fertiliser is often manufactured in the form of pellets coated with varying thicknesses of a material, which is designed to gradually be broken down by moisture and warmth. Some fertilisers such as bonemeal are naturally slow-release types.

soilless compost
A growing compost that does not contain loam (soil); it is usually based on peat or a peat substitute.

stale seedbed
A technique for reducing the number of weeds that can compete with vegetable seedlings. The seedbed is prepared for sowing; then it is left for a short period to allow the germination of weed seeds that have been brought near the soil surface by cultivation. These weed seedlings are then killed by a method that involves minimum soil disturbance (to avoid bringing up more weed seeds) before the crop is sown.

stolon
A creeping underground stem that produces new shoots and roots.

subsoil
The infertile layer of soil below the more fertile layer of topsoil in which plants grow.

successional sowing
To make a series of small sowings of a crop about 7 to 10 days apart. This technique is useful for ensuring a longer harvest period and avoiding a glut.

taproot
A long, deeply penetrating root that tends to regenerate if the top growth is removed such as on a dandelion.

tender
Describing a plant that is adversely affected by cold weather or frost.

thinning
The process of removing seedlings in a newly germinated row to provide sufficient space for those that remain.

thrips
Tiny, delicate winged insects that feed on plants, causing streaking or browning of leaves and stems as well as distorted growth.

tilth
The condition of a well-worked soil that has been reduced to a fine, crumbly texture. See also friable.

topsoil
The uppermost fertile layer of soil in which a plant's roots grow. See also subsoil.

trace elements
Plant nutrients that are vital but required in only tiny amounts and include such elements as iron, magnesium, copper and boron. A deficiency of these nutrients can produce a range of noticeable symptoms such as yellowing of the leaf between the veins, but it can be corrected by specialised trace element fertilisers.

transpiration
The process in which water is absorbed by the roots, passes through the plant and evaporates through the leaves.

transplanting
To move young plants to a fresh position to give them more space to develop.

tuber
An underground plant storage organ such as a potato.

variety
Horticulturists use this term as a synonym for cultivar (cultivated variety), which is a cultivated form of a plant that results from controlled breeding techniques or selection. In this sense varieties are named forms of a crop such as 'Kentucky Wonder' beans. Botanists use the term to denote a group of plants that vary in some significant way from others in the same species, but that are not distinctly different enough to warrant being classified as a separate species.

Resources guide

Listed below you'll find organisations that provide gardening information, which can be a useful supplement to the material in this book. All these organisations have websites. If you don't have access to a computer at home, you can visit a local library to use one, usually free of charge. Staff will help you if you're not familiar with computers.

Organisations and societies

Royal Horticultural Society

A gardening charity dedicated to advancing horticulture and promoting good gardening. It has extremely active science and educational departments, organises regular London Flower Shows as well as the world-famous Chelsea Flower Show and runs four gardens – Wisley in Surrey, Rosemoor in Devon, Hyde Hall in Essex and Harlow Carr in North Yorkshire. It also owns the Lindley Library, the world's foremost horticultural collection of books, periodicals and drawings, which is open to the general public as a reference library. Members receive free one-to-one gardening advice from the Society's team of experts, and the website contains a wealth of gardening information available to all.
80 Vincent Square
London SW1P 2PE
Tel: (020) 7834 4333
Website: www.rhs.org.uk

National Vegetable Society

The society exists to help any gardener who is interested in growing vegetables. It maintains trial grounds and gardens, gives members advice on the culture of vegetables, organises panels of lecturers and judges for competitions, maintains a library of books and photographs of vegetables and organises visits to places of interest. Membership and contact details are given on the website.
5 Whitelow Road
Heaton Moor, Stockport SK4 4BY
Tel: (0161) 442 7190
Website: www.nvsuk.org.uk

BBC Gardening

Specialist section of the BBC website devoted to gardening, with a plant finder, growing tips, gardening advice, plant profiles, message boards, newsletter, gardening diary and gardening news stories.
Website: www.bbc.co.uk/gardening

Henry Doubleday Research Association

A charity dedicated to researching and promoting organic gardening, farming and food. It has a thriving research and development section working to improve organic growing in Britain, and its information and education section provides advice to its members as well as the media and industry. It has three organic display gardens: Ryton, near Coventry, Warwickshire; Yalding, near Maidstone, Kent; and Audley End near Saffron Walden, Essex. The Heritage Seed Library saves and preserves hundreds of old and unusual vegetable varieties for posterity, also distributing them to members.
Ryton Organic Gardens
Coventry, Warwickshire CV8 3LG
Tel: (024) 7630 3517
Fax: (024) 7663 9229
website: www.hdra.org.uk

Royal Botanic Gardens, Kew

Based in the famous 120-hectare (300-acre) gardens on the banks of the River Thames in Kew, Richmond, and at Wakehurst Place in West Sussex, this organisation has a variety of departments. Its education department aims to increase public knowledge and understanding of the value and vital importance of plants; the Herbarium conducts research on plant resource inventories and plant classification, while the Jodrell Laboratory undertakes pure and applied research on a range of plant sciences.

The Millennium Seed Bank is part of an international project to safeguard plant species from round the globe against extinction, and it has already successfully secured the future of virtually all of Britain's native flowering plants. At Kew Gardens itself, the student vegetable plots and the wildlife and conservation areas will be of particular interest to vegetable gardeners.
Kew
Richmond, Surrey TW9 3AB
Tel: (020) 8332 5000
Fax: (020) 8332 5197
Website: www.rbgkew.org.uk

National Society of Allotment and Leisure Gardeners

The aim of this organisation is to help everyone enjoy the recreation of gardening, particularly by helping people find and maintain allotments. Members can receive advice on getting started on their allotment, tenancy agreements, self-management schemes, rents, organising shows and many other aspects of allotment gardening.
O'Dell House
Hunters Road
Corby, Northants NN17 5JE
Tel: (01536) 266576
Fax (01536) 264509
Website: www.nsalg.org.uk

Allotments: a plot holders' guide

This official website from the Office of the Deputy Prime Minister provides advice on many aspects of obtaining and using an allotment.
Website: www.odpm.gov.uk/stellent/groups/ odpm_urbanpolicy/documents/divisionhome page/036661.hcsp

Crop Protection Association

The website Common Sense Gardening is designed to give practical advice to gardeners on how to create a healthy garden and get rid of pests, diseases and weeds by using Crop Protection Association members' garden products. There is advice on protecting plants and guidelines on the safe and effective use of garden care chemical products, including instructions on how to dispose of chemicals safely, and information on withdrawn products.
4 Lincoln Court
Lincoln Road
Peterborough, Cambridgeshire PE1 2RP
Tel: (01733) 349225
Fax: (01733) 562523
Website: www.garden-care.org.uk

The Herb Society

An educational charity dedicated to encouraging the appreciation and use of herbs, the Herb Society brings together growers and gardeners, botanists and medicinal herbalists, researchers and historians, cooks, crafters, aromatherapists, beauticians and garden designers. It provides information, knowledge and news on all aspects of herbs.
Sulgrave Manor
Sulgrave
Banbury, Oxfordshire OX17 2SD
Tel: (01295) 768899
Website: www.herbsociety.co.uk

Gardening magazines

Amateur Gardening

Editor: Tim Rumball
Wetover House
West Quay Road
Poole, Dorset BH15 1JG
Tel: (01202) 440841
Fax: (01202) 440860
Website: www.amateurgardening.co.uk

BBC Gardeners' World

Editor: Adam Pasco
Woodlands
80 Wood Lane
London W12 0TT
Tel: (08702) 413463
Website: www.gardenersworld.com

Gardening Which?

Editor: Julia Boulton
Castlemead
Gascoyne Way
Hertford, Hertfordshire SG14 1YB
Tel: (08453) 010010
Fax: (01992) 822800
Website: www.gwfreetrial.co.uk

Garden News

Editor: Sarah Page
Bretton Court
Bretton, Peterborough PE3 8DZ
Tel: (01733) 264666
Fax: (01733) 282695

Grow Your Own

Editor: Georgina Wroe
25 Phoenix Court
Hawkins Road
Colchester, Essex CO2 8JY
Tel: (01206) 863495
Fax: (01206) 505945
Website: www.growfruitandveg.co.uk

Kitchen Garden

Editor: Andrew Blackford
12 Orchard Lane
Woodnewton, Peterborough PE8 5EE
Tel: (01780) 470097
Fax: (01780) 470550
Website: www.kitchengarden.co.uk

Organic Gardening

Editor: Gaby Bartai Bevan
Sandvoe
North Roe, Shetland ZE2 9RY
Tel/Fax: (01806) 533319
e-mail: organic.gardening@virgin.net

Suppliers

Listed below are suppliers of seeds and gardening equipment. You can find common seeds and equipment in your local garden centre, but a wider range of seeds and speciality equipment is available through mail-order catalogues and the Internet. All of these companies have websites. If you don't have a computer at home, you can visit a local library and seek the help of staff.

Seed suppliers

D. T. Brown & Co.
Provides a wide range of vegetable seeds.
Bury Road
Kentford
Newmarket, Suffolk CB8 7PR
Tel: (0845) 1662275
Fax: (0845) 1662283
Website: www.dtbrownseeds.co.uk

Samuel Dobie & Son
Long-established seed company with a wide range of vegetables.
Long Road
Paignton, Devon TQ4 7SX
Tel: (0870) 1123623
Fax: (0870) 1123624
Website: www.dobies.co.uk

Mr Fothergill's Seeds Ltd.
Good range of vegetable seeds.
Gazeley Road
Kentford
Newmarket, Suffolk CB8 7QB
Tel: (01638) 751161
Fax: (01638) 554084
Website: www.mr-fothergills.co.uk

S. E. Marshalls & Co.
Long-established seed company with a wide range of vegetables.
Alconbury Hill
Huntingdon, Cambs PE28 4HY
Tel: (01480) 443390
Fax: (01480) 443391
Website: www.marshalls-seeds.co.uk

Nickys Nursery Ltd.
Large selection of vegetable seeds, including organic.
Fairfield Road
Broadstairs, Kent CT10 2JU
Tel/Fax: (01843) 600972
Website: www.nickys-nursery.co.uk

Organic Gardening Catalogue
Wide range of mainly organic varieties. The official catalogue of the Henry Doubleday Research Association.
Riverdene Business Park
Molesey Road
Hersham, Surrey KT12 4 RG
Tel: (0845) 1301304
Fax: (01932) 252707
Website: www.organiccatalog.com

The Real Seed Catalogue
Non-hybrid and heirloom varieties selected for flavour.
Brithdir Mawr Farm
Cligwyn Road
Newport, Pembrokeshire SA42 0QJ
Tel: (01239) 821107
Website: www.realseeds.co.uk

Robinson's Mammoth Vegetable Seeds
Exhibition, heirloom and unusual vegetable varieties – not just onions!

Sunny Bank
Forton, Nr Preston, Lancs PR3 0BN
Tel: (01524) 791210
Fax: (01524) 791933
Website: www.mammothonion.co.uk

Roguelands Heirloom Vegetable Seeds Co.
Rare heirloom and open-pollinated varieties shipped worldwide from the USA.
1475 SunGlo Drive
Grants Pass, OR 97527
USA
Website: www.seedfest.co.uk

Seeds of Italy
A wide range of typically Italian vegetable varieties.
Phoenix Industrial Estate
Rosslyn Crescent
London Borough of Harrow HA1 2SP
Tel: (020) 8427 5020
Fax: (020) 8427 5051
Website: www.seedsofitaly.sagenet.co.uk

Suttons Seeds
Long-established seed company with a wide range of vegetables.
Woodview Road
Paignton, Devon TQ4 7NG
Tel: (0870) 2202899
Fax: (0870) 2202265
Website: www.suttons-seeds.co.uk

Tamar Organics
Good range of mainly organic vegetables.
Tavistock Woodlands Estate
Gulworthy
Tavistock, Devon PL19 8DE
Tel: (01822) 834887
Fax: (01822) 834284
Website: www.tamarorganics.co.uk

Thompson & Morgan (UK) Ltd.
Long-established seed company with a wide
range of vegetables.
Poplar Lane
Ipswich, Suffolk IP8 3BU
Tel: (01473) 688821
Fax: (01473) 680199
Website: www.thompson-morgan.com

Edwin Tucker & Sons Ltd.
Good range of vegetable seeds, including
some organic varieties.
Brewery Meadow
Stonepark
Ashburton, Newton Abbot, Devon TQ13 7DG
Tel: (01364) 652233
Fax: (01364) 654211
Website: www.edwintucker.com

Unwins Seeds
Long-established seed company with a wide
range of vegetables.
Alconbury Hill
Huntingdon, Cambs PE28 4HY
Tel: (01480) 443395
Fax: (01480) 443396
Website: www.unwinsdirect.co.uk

Equipment suppliers

Agralan Ltd.
Biological controls and wide range of garden
products, including horticultural fleece and
plant protection mesh, cloches and
environmentally friendly pest controls.
The Old Brickyard
Ashton Keynes
Swindon, Wilts SN6 6QR
Tel: (01258) 860015
Fax: (01258) 860056
Website: www.agralan.co.uk

Agriframes
Special kitchen garden section featuring
vegetable cages, plant supports, horticultural
fleece, ground cover material, watering
equipment and greenhouse accessories.

79 Place Road
Cowes, Isle of Wight PO31 7AF
Tel: (01983) 209209
Fax: (01983) 282612
Website: www.agriframes.co.uk

Crocus Limited
Very informative site with a vast range of
plants, garden tools and equipment, plus
interesting articles and advice.
Nursery Court
London Road
Windlesham, Surrey GU20 6LQ
Tel: (0870) 787 1413
Website: www.crocus.co.uk

Ferndale Lodge
Wide range of garden products, with a
special 'vegetable garden' section.
Woodview Road
Paignton, Devon TQ4 7NG
Tel: (0870) 444 1342
Fax: (0870) 444 0826
Website: www.ferndale-lodge.co.uk

Green Gardener
Specialises in biological and environmentally
friendly pest-control methods, plus
wormeries, worms for the garden, home
composters and wildlife products.
1 Whitmore Wood
Rendlesham, Suffolk IP12 2US
Tel: (01394) 420087
Fax: (01394) 420064
Website: www.greengardener.co.uk

Just-Green Ltd.
Supplies a wide range of eco-friendly
products designed to promote natural
solutions and bio-diversity in the garden.
Unit 14
Springfield Road
Springfield Industrial Estate
Burnham-on-Crouch, Essex CM0 8AU
Tel: (01621) 785088
Fax: (01621) 783800
Website: www.just-green.com

LBS Garden Warehouse
Company supplying a very wide range of
gardening items, including greenhouse
accessories, watering equipment, netting and
plant supports, composts, fertilisers, tools,
clothing and safety equipment.
Standroyd Mill
Cottontree, Colne, Lancs BB8 7BW
Tel: (01282) 873333
Fax: (01282) 869850
Website: www.lbsgardendirect.co.uk

The Organic Gardening Catalogue
The official catalogue of the Henry Doubleday
Research Association, supplying seeds,
fertilisers, composts, pest and weed controls,
tools and books.
Riverdene Business Park
Molesey Road
Hersham, Surrey KT12 4 RG
Tel: (0845) 1301304
Fax: (01932) 252707
Website: www.organiccatalog.com

Two Wests and Elliott Ltd.
A wide range of gardening products,
particularly for protected cropping –
greenhouse sundries, cloches, tunnels,
propagators, watering equipment and more.
Unit 4
Carrwood Road
Sheepsbridge Industrial Estate
Chesterfield, Derbyshire S41 9RH
Tel: (0870) 4448274
Fax: (01246) 260115
Website: www.twowests.co.uk

Index

Please note that page references for main entries are in **bold** numerals.

Picture credits and acknowledgements

Picture Credits

Abbreviations: T = Top; M = Middle; B = Bottom; L = Left; R = Right

Back Cover: Garden Picture Library Juliette Wade (T); **Bud Cole** (BL); **Mark S. Courtier** (BR).

Agrohaitai Ltd www.agrohaitai.com: 181 (B), 183 (MR). **Anthony Blake Photo Library:** Maximilion Stock Ltd 258 (BR). **Ian Armitage:** 124; 181 (TL); 182 (ML, BR); 274; 275. **T. C. Bird:** 37; 74 (BR); 76 (TL); 103; 162. **David Cavagnaro:** 210 (TR). **Jane Courtier:** 24 (TL); 77; 96; 101 (BL); 149 (BL); 165 (TL, TR); 271 (T). **Flora Graphics Inc:** 231 (ML). **Garden Picture Library:** Lamontagne 17 (B); Juilette Wade 19 (BL); Eric Crichton 20 (B); Ron Sutherland 22 (T); Friedrich Strauss 26 (TR); Mel Watson 28; Gary Rogers 29 (R); Friedrich Strauss 32 (TL); Linda Burgess 35 (B); Christopher Gallagher 42 (TL); Janet Sorrell 44 (BL, BR); Mayer/Le Scanff 47; David Cavagnaro 127; Jacqui Hurst 173; Stephen Hamilton 209 (TL); Mayer/Le Scanff 215; Philippe Bonduel 230 (ML); David Cavagnaro 231 (MR); Philippe Bonduel 232 (B); Lamontagne 233; Mayer/Le Scanff 234 (TL); David Cavagnaro 240; Bob Challinor 245; A. I. Lord 253 (TL); Laslo Puskas 253 (MR); Jerry Pavia 257 (BR); Mayer/Le Scanff 258 (TL); Jerry Pavia 261 (M); Clive Nichols 263; Leigh Clapp 267; Howard Rice 271 (BR). **Gardens Monthly:** Jacqui Dracup 93. **Gardening Which?:** 183 (B). **GardenWorld Images:** 201; 202 (B). **John Glover:** 5; 12; 18 (R); 21 (BL); 27 (T, B). **Jerry Harpur:** Bob Dash 16; Chaumont 22 (TL); Jane Adams 23 (BR); New York Botanics 25 (ML); Maggie Geiger NYC 26 (MR); Dr. John Rivers 29 (TL); Old Rectory, Sudborough 141 (TR); 185. **Marcus Harpur:** Geoff Whiten 23 (TR); Gelmham House 25 (MR). **Harris Seeds** www.harrisseeds.com: 232 (T). **Neil Hepworth:** 63. **Holt Studios:** 98 (L).
JB Illustrations: 17 (T); 41 (TR); 58 (BR); 117 (T). **Johnny's Selected Seeds:** www.johnnyseeds.com 231 (TR). **J. W. Jung Seed Co** Phone: (800) 247-5864 www.jungseed.com; **R. H. Shumway's** Phone: (800) 342-9461 www.rhshumway.com;

Totally Tomatoes Phone: (800) 345-5977 www.totallytomato.com; **Vermont Bean Seed Company** Phone: (800) 349-1071 www.vermontbean.com: 9 (TM); 230 (TR); 169; 179 (B); 199; 229; 230 (TR). **Krivit Photography:** Mike Krivit 2. **Mariquita Farm (USA)** Phone: (831) 761-3226 www.mariquita.com: 137 (T); 175; 160 (TR, BM); 203 (TL); 212; Jeanne Byrne 235; 260 (ML, BR). **Photolibrary.com:** Kathryn Kleinman 239; Schnare & Stief 242 (TR). **Photos Horticultural:** (TR); 13; 40 (TL); 45; 65; 72–73; 128; 140 (BR); 143; 147 (BR); 155 (BR); 161 (BL, MR); 177 (TL, MR); 188 (TL); 191 (ML, BR); 193; 202 (TL); 213; 221; 225; 261 (BR). **Dr. Barrington Rudine:** 236 (B). **Denis Ryan:** 7 (BR); 34 (TL); 38 (TL); 42 (BR); 48 (TL); 54 (TL); 56 (TL); 71; 74 (TL); 75; 80; 82 (TL); 91; 95 (TL, BR); 97; 99; 109; 110; 112 (TL); 120 (TL); 149 (BR); 187; 214 (BR); 223; 242 (BL). **Le Scanff-Mayer:** Le Jardin Plume 6 (B); St Jean-de-Beauregard 10; Le Jardin Plume 15; 'La Hussonniere' 18 (TL); 'Potager Arc-en-Ciel' Chateau de Bosmelet 20 (TL); Les Jardins du Prieure N. D. d'Orsan Maisonnais 24 (BR); Le Jardin Plume 31; 101 (T); 234. **Seminis** Dan Croker www.seminisgarden.com: 44 (TL); 139 (BL); 152 (MR); 211 (B); 236 (T). **Jason Smalley:** 36 (TL); 151 (ML); 157; 243 (BL). **Sygenta Group, ROGERS ®:** Super Sugar Snap 146–47 (M); Cream of the Crop 229; Kentucky Blue 150. **Thompson and Morgan (UK) Ltd** Phone: 01473 688 821www.thompson-morgan.com: 19 (MR); 48 (BM); 130; 131 (MR); 133; 134 (B); 136; 138; 139 (BM); 145; 146 (BL, M); 151 (TL); 152 (BL); 153; 154 (ML, BR); 155 (TL); 156 (TL); 163; 164; 165 (BL, MR); 166; 167; 170; 171; 172; 178; 186 (BR); 188 (BM); 189 (M, BR); 195; 196 (BR); 197; 210 (M, B, R); 211 (T); 216 (TR, MR); 217 (BL, M); 219; 222 (TL); 227; 228; 231 (BM); 232 (M); 254 (BR); 261 (TL); 268; 269; front and back endpapers. **Roy Williams:** 1; 3; 8 (TL, BL, TM, BM, MR); 9 (TL, BL, BM, MR); 30 (TL); 34 (M, BM, BR); 49; 50; 51; 57 (TL); 88; 92 (TL); 100; 116 (TL); 125; 126 (TL); 131 (TL); 132; 134 (TL); 135; 137 (MR); 140 (TL); 142 (TL); 144; 148; 158; 160 (ML); 168 (TL); 174; 176; 179 (TL); 180; 183 (TL, TR); 184 (L); 186 (TL); 188 (TR); 189 (TR); 190; 192; 194; 196 (TL); 198; 200; 203 (BR); 204 (TL); 205; 206; 211 (MR);

214 (TL); 216 (BL); 217 (TR); 218; 220; 222 (L); 224; 226; 230 (BR); 237 (TL, BR); 238 (TL); 244 (TL); 246; 247; 248; 249; 250; 251; 252; 254 (TL); 255; 256; 257 (TL); 259; 262 (TL); 264 (TL); 266; 270; 272; 273; 276; 277; 278; 279. **Mark Winwood:** 6 (TL); 14 (TL); 7 (TM, BL); 32 (TR); 33; 34 (MR); 35; 38 (BM, BR); 39 (BL, BM, BR); 40 (BM, BR); 41 (BL, BR); 43 (TL, M, BL); 46 (TL); 52; 53; 54 (BL, BM); 55; 56 (BM, BR); 57 (BL, BM); 58 (TL); 59; 60; 64; 66; 67; 68; 69; 78; 83; 84 (TL, MR); 86; 87; 90; 92 (BL, BM, BR); 94; 98 (MR); 102; 108 (TL); 111; 112 (BR); 113; 114 (TL, MR); 115; 116 (MR); 117 (BM, BR); 118; 119; 120 (BM, MR, BR); 121; 122; 123; 129; 141 (B); 159; 192 (BM, BR); 207 (BL, BM, BR); 208 (BL, BM); 209 (TM); 264 (BM, BR); 265.

Acknowledgements

Toucan Books would like to thank the following for their assistance in the preparation of this book:

Pat Alburey, Ian Armitage, Nick Armitage, Susan Bosley at ROGERS ® Brand vegetable Seeds, David Cavagnaro, Dan Croker at Seminis, Liz Dobbs, Dolly El Mahdi at Sanders Garden World, Christine Faull at Sygenta International AG, Andrew Griffin at Mariquita Farm, Paivi Jamsen at Kotimaiset Kasvikset, Marylin Keen at Thompson and Morgan (UK) Ltd., Shirun Li at AgroHaitai Ltd., Julia Paul at American Takii Inc., Hugh and Eleanor Paget, Gloria and Barry Rudine, Denis Ryan, Dotti Schultz and Maureen Artco at Jung Seed, Jess Walton, Ashley Warren at Photos Horticultural, Mark Winwood.